D1238636

Software Development

and Management For

Microprocessor-Based

Systems

Tomlinson G. Rauscher
Xerox Corporation
Rochester, New York

Linda M. Ott
Michigan Technological University
Houghton, Michigan

Prentice-Hall, Inc., Englewood Cliffs, New Jersey 07632

Library of Congress Cataloging-in-Publication Data

RAUSCHER, TOMLINSON G.
    Software development and management for
microprocessor-based systems.

    Includes index.
    1. Computer software—Development.
2. Microprocessors—Programming.   I. Ott,
Linda M., 1950-19   II. Title.
QA76.76.D47R38 1987   005.26   86-30477
    ISBN   0-13-822933-3

Cover design: *Photo Plus Art*
Manufacturing buyer: *Gordon Osbourne*

To David, Tasha, April, and Nathan

Printed in the United States of America

10 9 8 7 6 5 4 3 2 1

ISBN   0-13-822933-3   025

PRENTICE-HALL INTERNATIONAL (UK) LIMITED, *London*
PRENTICE-HALL OF AUSTRALIA PTY. LIMITED, *Sydney*
PRENTICE-HALL CANADA INC., *Toronto*
PRENTICE-HALL HISPANOAMERICANA, S.A., *Mexico*
PRENTICE-HALL OF INDIA PRIVATE LIMITED, *New Delhi*
PRENTICE-HALL OF JAPAN, INC., *Tokyo*
PRENTICE-HALL OF SOUTHEAST ASIA PTE. LTD., *Singapore*
EDITORA PRENTICE-HALL DO BRAZIL, LTDA., *Rio de Janeiro*

CONTENTS

PREFACE

The purpose of our book is to describe a set of techniques for developing software for large microprocessor-based systems, and for managing such development activities. The book is practical in its orientation; it describes a particular set of techniques that have demonstrably improved the effectiveness of microprocessor development and management.

The topics of microprocessor software development and management have grown in interest for several reasons:

o   Microprocessors are being used in a large and increasing number of applications to provide greater functionality at a lower cost: consumer products, appliances, automobiles, industrial control, personal computers, office equipment, and so forth.

o   The software systems for microprocessors in such applications are increasing in size, complexity, and sophistication, thus creating a demand for more effective software development and management.

o   Many software developers of microprocessor systems have little training in developing the large software systems that typify modern microprocessor-based products.

o   Many managers of microprocessor-based system products have little knowledge or experience in managing large software projects.

o   The software development cost for microprocessor-based systems is large (often tens or hundreds of man-years), typically larger than the cost of developing the electronic hardware on which the software runs, and almost always larger than it should be.

Our book is intended for two principal audiences:

o   Students at the upper class or graduate level who study microprocessor software in electrical engineering, computer engineering, computer science, or related programs of study. Such students seldom have the opportunity to work on large projects, and thus lack the knowledge of a practical development environment to which many of them will graduate.

o   Industrial practitioners who want to develop and manage significant microprocessor software activities. These professionals may have experience writing small programs on microprocessors or writing programs for large data processing systems. This basis coupled with the information presented in our book provides strong capabilities for developing and managing microprocessor-based systems.

We have used material in this book with hundreds of people in these two groups, effecting substantial improvements in personal and corporate capabilities.

We approach the subject of microprocessor software development assuming that the reader has some knowledge of microprocessors and programming. Readers should have a working knowledge of microprocessors, have written small assembler language programs for a particular microprocessor, and have done small programming projects with a higher level language to understand the fundamentals of programming concepts. There are a number of books that address such topics; our book is a second book addressing advanced topics for large microprocessor-based systems. Using introductory knowledge as a starting point, we describe in Chapters 1 through 10 specific techniques for engineering significant microprocessor software systems. The techniques cover the phases of software engineering — requirements specification, design specification, coding and debugging, testing, and maintenance — concentrating on microprocessor applications with emphasis on real-time aspects. To illustrate techniques, the examples used are short and address typical microprocessor applications, so that they can be grasped quickly. The book describes specific techniques that address the entire software development life cycle for microprocessor applications, in contrast to surveying a large number of techniques concentrating on one phase of software development, or orienting the techniques toward business data processing applications.

In a similar manner, we approach the subject of microprocessor software management assuming that the reader has some knowledge of management activities such as general project planning, PERT methods, task assignments, and delegation of authority. In the second part of the book, Chapters 11 through 19, we address software management for microprocessor-based systems by extending relevant aspects of traditional managerial concepts such as planning, staffing, organizing, and reviewing to facilitate developing software for microprocessor-based products. Facilities required for developing microprocessor software are described. The special problems of managing embedded microprocessor software are examined in detail. Recommendations are given for developing software technology from both the practical aspects of architecture, tools, and techniques, and the personal aspects of professionals who constitute a staff. The book concludes with software management lessons that address problems typically encountered when microprocessors play a significant role in the product development repertoire in a company. The software development of a real microprocessor-based product in a large company is reviewed and critiqued.

In writing the book we have incorporated several concepts to increase its utility to students and professionals. The book uses a practical technique orientation to software development and management for microprocessors, based on real product development experiences; it is not a survey of theoretical concepts. The book concentrates on microprocessor examples; it is not a general data processing book. It addresses life cycle aspects of software development and management, not just the details of a methodology to support one phase of product development. It describes techniques that are integrated with one another throughout the development process; it is not a collection of independent articles addressing specific issues within the development process. The book is organized to present material in the order engineers and managers will be comfortable reading, building on coding and debugging knowledge and using this as motivation for design, requirements, testing, and maintenance. As the coding and debugging phase of software development is the phase with which engineers and managers are the most familiar, we present it first, even though it is neither the first phase nor the most important phase in microprocessor software development. With a thorough understanding of coding and debugging, readers will better understand the need for the design specification phase and the requirements specification phase, the most important phase in software development. The book also includes a chapter that summarizes techniques for microprocessor development in chronological order (Chapter 10) and a chapter that summarizes specific management directions (Chapter 19).

Many people assisted us in the preparation of the book. Steve Palumbo, Dan Auman, and John Kemp of Xerox Corporation helped with the preparation of several figures on software design. William Stumbo of Xerox assisted in the preparation of the index. Andrea and Roger Hopkins of Publishease prepared many of the figures. Jeanne Paige of Xerox Corporation typed several drafts of the book over an extended period; her patient competence made preparation of the manuscript enjoyable. Marie Vasapolli and Nancy Taylor of Xerox made noteworthy contributions as well. Finally we would like to thank our colleagues at Xerox Corporation and Michigan Technological University for their encouragement and support during this work. Their reviews and comments improved not only the presentation but the substance of the book as well. Michael Nekora of Xerox made several insightful comments, which we hope we have conveyed to the reader.

1

INTRODUCTION TO

MICROPROCESSOR SOFTWARE

SYSTEMS DEVELOPMENT

1.1 The Role of Software in the Microprocessor Revolution

The decade of the seventies will surely be remembered for witnessing the commercial introduction and utilization of microprocessors. Not only did their deployment revolutionize the use of electronics in a multitude of applications, but their continued improvement demonstrated incredible technological maturation. From the simple characteristics of the first four-bit microprocessors to the sophisticated features of modern sixteen-bit and thirty-two-bit microcomputers, the capabilities provided by these microelectronic marvels have increased dramatically. While capabilities have increased, the cost of employing these "computers-on-a-chip" has, surprisingly, decreased when examined on a cost-per-function basis. The increasing availability of capable, inexpensive microprocessors has facilitated the development of increasingly sophisticated systems, ranging from simple calculators to real-time systems that simultaneously support several activities and input/output devices.

The ability of microprocessors to support complex applications has been made possible not only by improved hardware capabilities such as greater functionality of instructions, larger on-chip memories, and faster instruction execution times, but also by larger, more powerful software systems. Whereas the size of early microprocessor programs ranged only up to a few thousand bytes, modern systems frequently reach fifty thousand bytes and more. The effort involved in developing software systems of such capabilities requires technological knowledge, engineering discipline, and management direction. The development of these capabilities often proceeds at a slower rate than that of the microprocessor hardware technology. When this is coupled with the realization that developing large software systems for microprocessors is exponentially more complex than developing small systems (with which people typically experience some success in initial attempts), it is easy to see why software development has been criticized for products that are expensive, late, and unreliable.

Microprocessor software systems development need not deserve this reputation. With the appropriate application of engineering and management tools and techniques, microprocessor software systems development can be a rewarding and successful enterprise. The purpose of this book is to assist in the accomplishment of this goal.

It is appropriate to examine the historical background which has led to the poor opinion in which software is often held today. Early microprocessor software development activities tended to emphasize the differences from traditional software development, citing justifications such as

o   Close functional relationship to hardware being replaced

o   Small program sizes

o   Use of low-level languages, particularly machine and assembler languages

The current trend in microprocessor systems deviates from these viewpoints:

o   Microprocessors are being used where flexibility and expandability are required; specially designed VLSI chips and "programmable logic arrays" are now being used to replace hardware of moderate complexity where microprocessors were formerly used.

o   As mentioned earlier, large programs are as much the rule as the exception.

o   Higher level languages can, should, and are being used in most microprocessor applications.

It is useful to note, however, that microprocessor software often exhibits differences from the typical data processing programs, which constitute a significant portion of traditional software systems. These differences include the following:

o   Microprocessor software frequently represents only a small part of a system composed of several electrical, mechanical, and other components. The end user need not (and often is not) aware that a microprocessor is integrated in the system.

o   Microprocessor manufacturers seldom supply extensive support system software (although this trend is changing), and, as a result, developers frequently must design and implement all the microprocessor software for their system. This ranges from low-level operating system tasks such as interrupt and I/O handling to high-level application specific tasks.

o   Microprocessors often support real-time systems, wherein immediate response to asynchronous external events characterize normal requirements.

o   The principal memory for program storage in many microprocessor systems is read-only memory (ROM), due to its cost savings over other memory types, such as electrically programmable ROM (EPROM) and read/write random access memory (RAM). The cost per system aspect is especially important when considering that microprocessor products often have sales or usage volumes in the tens and hundreds of thousands (such as calculators, automobiles, cash registers, and games).

o   Another aspect of products with imbedded microprocessors is that companies often produce product families in which microprocessor use may vary in only minor ways among products in the same family.

These variations on traditional software systems result in the use of tools and techniques that are peculiar to microprocessor software development. Much of the development activity for microprocessor software, however, adapts techniques used in traditional software development.

It has been interesting to follow the technology for developing software for microprocessor systems because history has, to a large extent, repeated itself. The use of machine language, assemblers, macroassemblers, compilers, and debuggers bears a strong resemblance to their development for larger computers two decades earlier. The reasons for this are technological and organizational:

o   The first developers of microprocessors were technologists whose principal expertise was in microelectronics, not software.

o   The first developers of microprocessor-based systems were engineers
      whose principal expertise was in control systems, not software.

This situation, combined with the recognition of cost, schedule, and
reliability problems in microprocessor software products, motivates the
study of advanced software system development for microprocessor
products.

In describing advanced software system development for
microprocessors, we build on the fundamental knowledge of microprocessor
capabilities, instruction sets, assemblers, and so on, with which the reader
is assumed to be familiar. In this book we focus on

o   The software engineering development cycle for microprocessor-based
      systems

o   Management of microprocessor software development projects,
      ranging from small one-man projects to large team projects

The remaining sections of this chapter introduce these concepts and
motivate further examination. To provide a foundation for microprocessor
software systems, the methods and tools described in detail in subsequent
chapters are based on experience with large computer systems, yet they
have been refined and extended to address the special characteristics and
requirements of microprocessor systems. These methods and tools can
significantly improve the development and end product of microprocessor
software activities.

1.2 The Software Development Life Cycle

In one common view of microprocessor system development an engineer
carefully develops the design of an electronic system, builds a breadboard
version, tests the hardware using oscilloscopes or other equipment, and
then writes a few lines of assembler language to load into the
microprocessor to make the system work. This simplistic perspective on the
combination of hardware and software relegates software development to
the role of a technician in the traditional engineering development cycle.
Software development for modern microprocessor systems involves much
more than merely writing simple machine or assembler language routines
to direct the microprocessor to perform simple functions. Software
development must be recognized as an engineering discipline based on
common engineering tenets and extended through experience to include the
total development cycle.

The phases in the software development cycle for microprocessor systems are the following (see Figure 1-1):

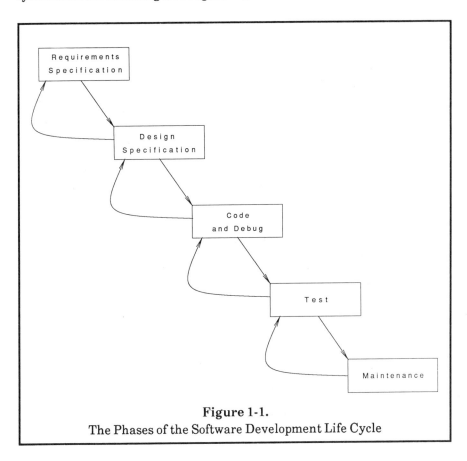

Figure 1-1.
The Phases of the Software Development Life Cycle

o   **Requirements specification,** the result of which is a requirements specification document that describes *what* the software must do. This includes factors such as
   - functions to be performed
   - performance to be achieved
   - resource constraints to be met during development, production, and maintenance

o   **Design specification,** the result of which is
   - A high level design specification document that describes *how* the software will be structured to solve the problems identified

in the requirements specification. This structural description describes the partitioning and decomposition of the software into major functional components that constitute a system to solve the specified problem.

-   A detailed design specification document which can readily be transformed into implementable components in a computer programming language. This design document comprises detailed descriptions of the logic and data that constitute each of the many components in a system.

o   **Code and debug,** in which an engineer transforms the design document on a component-by-component basis into a programming language and removes the syntactic and semantic errors introduced at this stage.

o   **Test,** which comprises at least two parts:

-   Unit testing demonstrates that individual program components perform the actions described in the detailed design specification document.

-   Integration testing, in which successively larger groups of program components are combined and tested within the microprocessor-based product system, until it can be shown that criteria described in the requirements specification document are satisfied. Following this system test, the software is released.

o   **Maintenance,** which consists of correcting software errors that were not detected during testing, and upgrading the software to perform new or different functions.

The following aspects of this phased plan are fundamental to proper development of software systems:

o   The output of each phase is a specification document that describes, in varying degrees of detail, the problem or its solution. Each specification document is input to subsequent phases for further refinement.

o   The output of each phase is reviewed and approved to ensure proper problem identification and solution through the transformations in each of the phases.

o   The information developed in each phase is fed back into the results of the previous phase so that improvements or changes suggested by the new information can be incorporated into the development process.

When considering the phases in the software development life cycle it is important to reflect on the proportion of time allocated to the different phases. A commonly held view, especially in microcomputer systems, is that the code and debug phase is the most important, and therefore it should consume the most time, see Figure 1-2(a). When the philosophy of devoting most of the time to code and debug is applied in microprocessor software development, it is often the case that so many problems arise that development cost and schedule expand enormously, and most of the life cycle is devoted to maintenance as shown in Figure 1-2(b). A principle of modern software engineering is that proper requirements specification, design specification, coding and debugging, and testing can both improve software quality and decrease resources devoted to software development. Thus it should be the case that coding constitutes only a very small portion of development time and resources, and that requirements and design specification receive considerable attention, as indicated in Figure 1-2(c).

One reason for the variety of views illustrated in Figure 1-2 is the variety of people who interact with or participate in the software development process. As microprocessor systems grow in number and functional richness, more and more people become associated with software development. The list includes

o   Engineers, who once performed all of the development tasks but who now may specialize in coding, testing, and maintenance

o   Analysts, who prepare the requirements and design specifications

o   Customers, who may review and approve requirements specifications and other documents

o   The management team, which seeks to satisfy customer requirements (both specified and perceived) and to minimize resource utilization through allocation and control activities

The people in each of these groups employ a wide variety of tools and techniques to perform their jobs. Techniques such as structured design and structured programming, coupled with hardware/software tools such as interactive editing and high level language compilers, not only improve the capabilities of engineers and analysts, but they also have a positive impact

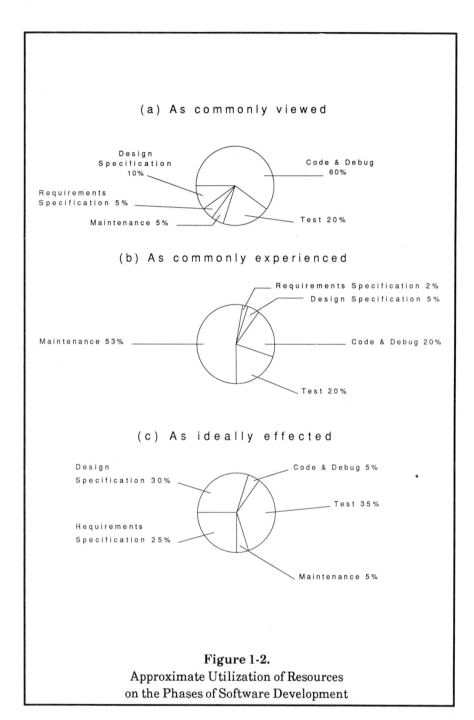

Figure 1-2.
Approximate Utilization of Resources
on the Phases of Software Development

on activities of customers and managers. Later chapters will describe tools and their utilization for microprocessor software system development.

1.3 Microprocessor Software System Management

The management of microprocessor software system development is a microcosm of general management activity, and thus applies the following functions[1] to achieve the objective of delivering a microprocessor software system:

(1) Planning – formulation of proposed activities that achieve the desired objective

(2) Organizing – the building of a staff and establishment of effective working teams to perform planned activities within a working environment for the purpose of achieving an objective

(3) Actuating – the directing and influencing of group members to achieve not only individual objectives but group objectives as well

(4) Controlling – evaluating group performance against plans, and developing and implementing alternative plans if required

The straightforward application of these principles does not ensure that microprocessor software development projects will be successful. There are several reasons for this:

o   It is too often the case that microprocessor software managers do not have the proper training or experience in microprocessor technology or software technology. This is due to the fast development of microprocessor technology and the perceived lesser importance of software technology.

o   Microprocessor technology is a relatively new technology in many organizations, and thus is far less mature than other technologies such as other aspects of electronic and mechanical technology. Where microprocessor technology is relatively new, software technology is usually newer.

[1]After George R. Terry, <u>Principles of Management</u> (Homewood, Illinois: Richard D. Irwin, Inc., 1972).

o   Planning for microprocessor software development projects is often based on poor assumptions; project duration, for example, is computed based on coding productivity (lines of code produced per week) without realizing that coding accounts for only a small percentage of project activity.

o   Organizing competent work teams is difficult due to the shortage of trained software engineers; the demand exceeds the supply.

o   Actuating may be difficult because
    -    managers, lacking experience in microprocessors and software technologies, cannot understand the engineering problems, and
    -    engineers in the contemporary marketplace have different criteria for self-actualization from the criteria traditionally perceived

o   Controlling may be difficult for a number of reasons. Principal among these are
    -    The lack of tools for supporting microprocessor development. This lack often results in excessive expenditure of personnel time, usually the most valuable resource in a project.
    -    The unintentional triggering of Brooks's Law: "Adding manpower to a late software project makes it later."[2]

An important aspect in the solution of these problems is better understanding of software technology; a detailed discussion of solutions is deferred to the latter part of the book.

1.4 Anatomy of Software Systems for Microprocessors

The process of software development and management for microprocessor systems described in the previous sections is a means to an end, namely, the microprocessor software system product. Among such products are some basic structural concepts that are fundamental to the design of the majority of microprocessor systems. The tradeoff analysis which leads to variations in the basic structure also merits consideration.

---

[2]Frederick P. Brooks, Jr., The Mythical Man-Month — Essays on Software Engineering (Reading, Massachusetts: Addison-Wesley, 1975), p. 25.

The software in microprocessor system products may be classified into three components:

o   Operating system software

o   Applications software

o   Diagnostics software

Operating system software extends the basic capabilities of the host microprocessor system to provide services such as handling interrupts, performing special input/output procedures (like filtering), managing timers, performing multiple independent tasks concurrently, and coordinating intertask communication. In extending the basic system capabilities, the operating system may be viewed as presenting a "virtual machine" interface to the applications and diagnostics software (see Figure 1-3). The applications and diagnostics programs use not just the bare hardware facilities but a system whose capabilities have been extended by the operating system functions. Applications software uses the virtual machine capabilities to perform the functions described in the requirements specification document. Thus, the applications software provides a virtual machine interface to the users, who do not have to be aware that the system employs a microprocessor. Diagnostics software checks the operation of the host microprocessor system to determine if it is operating correctly. Diagnostics have become increasingly important in microprocessor systems due to the number of products placed, the high use of these products, and the desire to isolate failures quickly.

All three software components directly affect the ability of a microprocessor system to meet the requirements described in a specification. The applications software performs specific functions desired, the operating system software in providing services to applications software has a major effect in system performance, and diagnostics software is a determining factor in serviceability criteria such as mean time to repair. From the functional, performance, and serviceability aspects of a requirements specification, the three software components should be introduced into the design documentation. While implementation (coding and debugging) of the components may follow different routes (perhaps using different languages), the three converge in integration testing where their interdependent aspects in both function and performance must be confirmed.

Although microprocessor software systems typically demonstrate the applications, operating system, and diagnostics construction, a wide variation exists in the capabilities of these components among

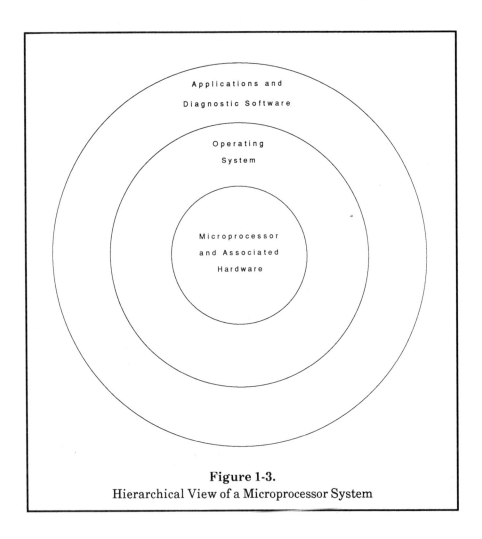

Figure 1-3.
Hierarchical View of a Microprocessor System

microprocessor-based products. This variation is due to the differences in functional complexity and performance requirements among products. Products that support multiple users and multiple I/O devices, such as word processing systems, may require a powerful operating system and a sophisticated diagnostic package. On the other hand, products with relatively simple functions, such as hand-held calculators, may require only an elementary operating system and no diagnostic software. It may be cheaper, for example, to throw away a hand-held calculator than to repair it.

In a larger context, a similar tradeoff analysis should be performed in specifying functions to be implemented in hardware and functions to be implemented in software. The selection of hardware or software for an implementation medium depends on performance, cost, and flexibility. Hardware implementation generally

o   Improves performance because special circuits can perform faster than general programmable devices

o   Costs more because the special circuits cost more than memory for microprocessor software instructions

o   Provides less flexibility because special circuits cannot be changed as easily as microprocessor software

Such analysis carries down to microprocessor software design decisions as well. Execution time to perform a function can often be traded for memory size to perform the same function. As another example, the cost of a certain memory type (RAM, ROM, and so forth) can be traded against the flexibility in making changes or updates to the software resident in that memory.

The important point is that design decisions typically affect many aspects of the system, and thus have implications on many parts of the requirements specification. The multitude of design decisions in microprocessor systems must be coordinated so that not only are the requirements satisfied, but also that conceptual integrity is assured. "It is better to have a system omit certain anomalous features and improvements, but to reflect one set of design ideas, than to have one that contains many good but independent and uncoordinated ideas."[3] It is important, therefore, to separate clearly the requirements specification from the design — the *what* from the *how* — and to review the implications of the design decisions on the requirements specification, when deciding the functions to be allocated to software (or hardware) components.

[3]Frederick P. Brooks, Jr., The Mythical Man-Month — Essays on Software Engineering (Reading, Massachusetts: Addison-Wesley, 1975), p. 42.

1.5 Introducing the Rest of the Book

Software development for microprocessor systems is playing an increasingly important role in many organizations, and thus warrants a more detailed study than has usually been afforded in the past. The subject merits study not only by engineers and their managers, but also by others who interface with microprocessor product development. The remainder of this book describes detailed recommendations for developing and managing microprocessor software. It presents tools and techniques that can make microprocessor software projects successful; it is not a survey of techniques, rather, it is a selection that addresses the problems identified in this chapter.

2

CODING

MICROPROCESSOR SOFTWARE

2.1 Introduction

It is appropriate to begin a detailed examination of the phases in the microprocessor software development cycle with coding discussed in this chapter, and debugging discussed in Chapter 3. Even though it is neither the first phase nor the most important phase, coding and debugging is nevertheless the phase with which engineers and managers are the most familiar. In spite of this familiarity, the performance of most engineers in coding can be improved significantly.

The purpose of the coding and debugging phase (sometimes called the implementation phase) is to transform the detailed design specification into a syntactically correct computer program and to ensure that the translation (compilation or assembly of the program into microprocessor machine language) keeps the same semantics (meaning) intended by the programmer. Of fundamental importance in the coding and debugging phase is the recognition that the program produced will be read and interpreted not only by computers but also by engineers, including the time when the original programmer is unavailable for questioning. Thus, engineers must code their programs so that other engineers, with only a modicum of previous knowledge, can understand their code and modify it.

2.2 Selecting a Programming Language

One of the most hotly debated topics in microprocessor software development is the selection of a programming language. The two general alternatives are assembler languages (perhaps augmented by macros) and higher level languages.

Before examining the arguments for the two sides, consider the trends in microprocessor systems development:

o   Since microprocessor systems are frequently produced in large quantities, it is important to minimize the cost per unit. The size of the program memory is an important factor in cost determination.

o   Since microprocessor systems are frequently used in real-time control systems, program execution efficiency is important.

o   Microprocessors are used where flexibility and expandability are required.

o   Microprocessors are used in systems to perform very complex functions.

The case for assembler languages emphasizes the control that an engineer has over the hardware. Because engineers using an assembler language employ straightforward representations of microprocessor machine language instructions, they can determine exactly how much memory space and execution time will be required by their programs.

The case for higher level languages is based on the following points:

o   The productivity of engineers in coding a program is greatly increased by higher level languages due to their procedural orientation (which mirrors the design specification) and due to their obviating the need for knowing the details of the microprocessor being used. Studies have shown that programming productivity, measured in *lines of code* produced in a specified unit of time, is independent of the language being used (although it does depend on the application and other factors). Since each line of higher level language code performs the same function as several assembler language statements, the productivity advantage of higher level languages is significant.

o   Testing and reviewing code written in a higher level language is much simpler than with assembler language.

o   The understandability of a higher level language is most important in the maintenance phase, especially when an engineer making changes is not the original implementor. The use of a higher level language can decrease resources required for maintenance by more than half in most cases (much more than half if an engineer used assembler language tricks in his code).

o   Software components written in a higher level language can often be used in subsequent development or reengineering projects, even if the system uses a different microprocessor. As many manufacturers produce families of related products, this "code capture" offers significant savings in a multisystem development environment.

o   The number of higher level languages that can be used in microprocessor programming continues to increase, making it possible to program almost every microprocessor in some higher level language.

o   Microprocessor manufacturers are giving more support to higher level languages, and the efficiency of the code produced is improving. In addition, microprocessor manufacturers are beginning to provide support for popular languages such as Pascal.

Because microprocessor software programs require increasing size, flexibility, and expandability, the case for selecting a higher level language is compelling. In addition to these points, a close examination of higher level languages reveals that their disadvantages are not significant:

o   The size of code for a program produced by optimizing compilers for higher level languages closely approaches that produced by assembler language programmers. In fact, compilers often do better global optimization than assembler language programmers. It is usually not cost effective to try to squeeze code into a certain size memory, as illustrated by Figure 2-1. In addition, most microprocessor software products should leave some memory unused to accommodate future extensions such as changes and enhancements. Therefore, any memory that might be saved by using an assembler language is usually not worth the extra cost incurred in coding in assembler language.

o   The portion of code that constrains real-time computation or critical response times is usually only a small part of an entire microprocessor program. This portion of code can often be improved by algorithmic or data structure changes.

Given the aspects of microprocessor systems and development constraints, a higher level language is the clear choice in all but a very few microprocessor software development projects. As microprocessor systems mature in complexity, grow in size, and increase in usage, the preference for higher level languages will become more pronounced due to improved productivity

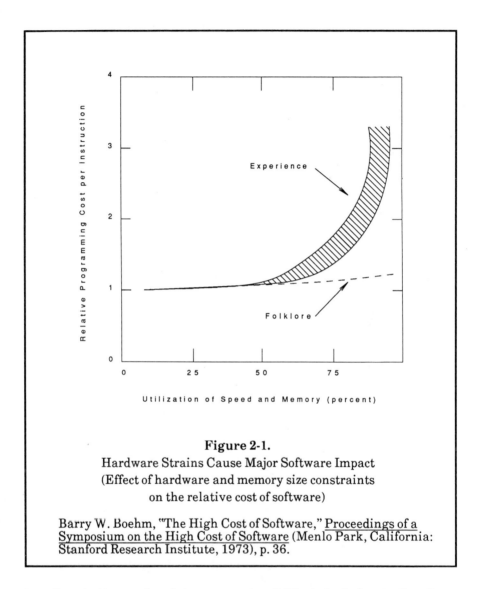

Figure 2-1.
Hardware Strains Cause Major Software Impact
(Effect of hardware and memory size constraints
on the relative cost of software)

Barry W. Boehm, "The High Cost of Software," Proceedings of a
Symposium on the High Cost of Software (Menlo Park, California:
Stanford Research Institute, 1973), p. 36.

in coding, testing, and maintenance; extensibility to include new functions
and adapt for new products; increased availability; and improved
performance. In rare cases assembler language may be justified for real-
time considerations, but even then it will generally be isolated to a few
software components in a microprocessor system.

2.3 Coding Techniques — Introduction

"Programming is, among other things, a kind of writing."[1] It is a kind of writing that is read not only by machines but by humans. With a significant part of the program development cycle devoted to activities which require program reading (such as debugging, reviewing, and maintenance), writing can be seen to be of fundamental importance. As with other kinds of writing, there are good writing styles and poor writing styles. The writing suggestions described in this chapter provide the basics of a style which makes programs easy to read. This section does not describe programming techniques such as designing algorithms and data structures; rather, its purpose is to demonstrate the way such techniques can best be communicated to readers of a program.

There are two aspects in communicating programs:

o   The implementation of algorithms and data structures in the programming language, e.g., the translation of the algorithm expressed in the design language to an algorithm expressed in the higher level programming language.

o   The presentation of the algorithms and data structures to the reader of the program.

Of the two aspects, algorithm presentation is the simpler to comprehend, yet it is seldom realized with complete effectiveness. For this reason we address it first.

2.4 Coding Techniques — Presentation

The two fundamental tenets of good programming presentation style are

Make the program self-documenting.[2]

Specify explicitly; unspecified assumptions will be misinterpreted.

[1]Gerald M. Weinberg, The Psychology of Computer Programming (New York: Van Nostrand Reinhold, 1971), p. 5.

[2]After Frederick P. Brooks, Jr., The Mythical Man-Month — Essays on Software Engineering (Reading, Massachusetts: Addison-Wesley, 1975), Chapter 15.

By incorporating a program's documentation with its source code, the code is more readable and hence more valuable. In addition, the documentation is readily accessible so that it is easy to maintain concurrence between the program and its documentation. Self-documenting does not mean that a program guide is written as comments in the language being used and prefixed to the source program in one big file. It does mean that the program and its documentation form an integrated package for a reader (perhaps the original programmer himself) to use.

When writing a program, an engineer typically assumes many factors about the environment in which the program will run. Unless these assumptions are specified explicitly in the program documentation, misunderstandings that lead to program bugs will arise. Some of these factors and examples of typical problems appear in Table 2-1.

Table 2-1.
Some Factors Often Assumed in Programming
with Examples of Assumptions that Lead to Program Bugs

Factor	Assumption	Problem
Microprocessor architecture	Eight-bit word length	When a program is moved to a 16-bit microprocessor, masks, addresses, and some variables may be treated differently.
Operating system	Timer resolution is one microsecond	A new release of the operating system may change the resolution to five microseconds and thus affect critical real-time response.
Programming language	All variables are global	A new release of the compiler makes local variables the default, thus changing values of variables with the same name in different program components.
Environment of the program component	Variables passed to the component are nonnegative	A negative variable results in the program component terminating abnormally due to execution of an illegal instruction.

Most coding presentation techniques are special cases of the two fundamental tenets. The first technique is

Use the general form shown in Figure 2-2
for each component in a self-documenting program.

Component Header

Prologue

Declarations with Comments

Initializations with Comments

Paragraph 1 Documentation
Paragraph 1 Code

Paragraph 2 Documentation
Paragraph 2 Code

.

.

.

Paragraph n Documentation
Paragraph n Code

Component Terminator

Figure 2-2.
General Form for a Component in a Self-Documenting Program

Several guidelines should be used in writing a program in this form. The first guideline addresses the component header, which is usually a statement that names the component and identifies the component as a program, procedure, or function. For example:

PROGRAM COMPARE_INPUT_AGAINST_NORM (INPUT, OUTPUT);

The guideline is

Make the name in the component header descriptive.

The descriptive name should summarize the purpose of the component, be it a large program component or a small procedure. A version number should be used in the name of the entire program to differentiate versions from previous compilations or debug runs. Examples of such names are

SCAN_KEYBOARD

CONVERT_BCD_TO_DECIMAL

SINE

If the programming language used restricts the number of characters in names, so that it is difficult to make names descriptive, make the name in the component header mnemonic.

    The second guideline addresses the prologue which is descriptive documentation about the program component:

Use the format in Figure 2-3
for the prologue of a program component.

In describing the purpose of a component, a prologue should summarize the function performed by the component, for example, by describing the transformation performed. If required, the prologue should refer to the standard literature to simplify the task of a reader in understanding the program. Listing the input and output parameters for a component describes the interface to calling procedures and clarifies the effects of the program component on the environment. Listing the procedures that the component calls identifies the component's role in the system structure. The prologue should also identify the original author, each programmer who modifies the original version, and the reasons for modifications so that the history of program changes can be tracked.

    In declaring the variables used in a program component, use the following guidelines:

Declare all variables.

Use descriptive names for variables.

Group logically related variables together,
e.g., loop variables, temporary variables.

Comment each variable to describe its purpose.

Purpose:
Input Parameters:
     Parameter 1:
     Parameter 2:

     .

     .

     .

     Parameter m:
Output Parameters:
     Parameter l:
     Parameter 2:

     .

     .

     .

     Parameter n:
Procedures Called:
     Procedure l:
     Procedure 2:

     .

     .

     .

     Procedure p:
Original Author:
Date Code Completed and Debugged:
Modifications:
     (l) Modifying Programmer:
        Date of Modification:
        Reason for Modification:
     (2) .

      .

      .

      .

Figure 2-3.
Format for the Prologue of a Program Component

Declaring all variables serves as a reference point for data items and reduces assumptions about variable usage. Do not be too brief in developing descriptive names for variables. Fortran's original limitation of six characters per variable name has had a severe effect on good programming style. Use underscores, dashes, or other punctuation marks to separate words in a variable name, e.g., TOTAL_KEY.

Using descriptive names will clarify intent in the program code. When declaring variables, list all common attributes (length, dimension, representation, etc.) even if the compiler assumes some attributes as defaults. This is an example of the explicit specification maxim. By commenting each variable, the declaration part of the program will become a complete legend for ready reference in program writing and debugging.

Following the declarations, the initialization of variables should appear.

Set the initialization apart
from surrounding portions of code.

Comment initializations that are not obvious.

Commenting is especially important for those variables involving number conversions. For example:

```
UPPER_MASK: = 240; {SET THE HIGH ORDER BYTE OF AN EIGHT BIT
                    WORD TO ALL ONES.  DECIMAL '240' = BINARY
                    '11110000' }
```

A useful coding technique, which combines the concepts of data declaration and initialization, is the defined constant.

Use defined constants to replace
common numeric specifications.

Defined constants are commonly used values referenced by specific names in programs; they are used like constants but are named as variables. Defined constants are especially useful in referring to the numbers that reference system parameters, such as the assignments of names to I/O line numbers.

Much as in normal writing,

Set off paragraphs of code
by liberal use of white space (blank lines).

The documentation at the beginning of each code paragraph should be a program comment that describes the subfunction to be performed by the next several lines of code. Typical paragraph sizes are 2-5 documentation lines and 4-10 code lines. With the goal of fewer than 8 paragraphs per component, the size of each component can be kept to the desired 1-3 pages of printed output. A very useful technique in writing paragraph documentation is to

Extract paragraph documentation
from the design document.

Thus, the design document may be considered a skeleton for the program, a skeleton which is completed by filling in the code that implements the design. As a general rule, code within a paragraph need not be commented, as such code should be self-explanatory and comments would be redundant. Programmers all too frequently interpret the direction to comment their programs by writing unnecessary comments such as the following:

I := I + 1; { INCREMENT I BY 1 }

Such comments are superfluous and are no substitute for documentation of function at the beginning of a paragraph.

The guideline for additional comments is

Within paragraphs, comment only
code whose meaning is not obvious.

Such comments are especially applicable when "tricks" (higher level language statements that achieve a desired result by using an artifact of the language or compiler for a purpose that differs from the design intent) are used to achieve efficiency.

The understandability of the code in a paragraph can be enhanced by applying the following guidelines:

Group statements logically.

Indent statements within
loop and selection blocks.

Put multiple statements on one line
when they constitute a simple concept.

Following these guidelines.will result in programs that are easy to read; this readability should facilitate code understanding, the subject of the next section.

2.5 Coding Techniques — Algorithm Implementation

The actions a program component performs will be understandable only if its meaning can be determined from the implementation of its algorithm in a higher level language. Fundamental to the meaningful implementation of an algorithm is the concept of structured programming. In a broad sense structured programming encompasses all the "good" programming techniques described in this chapter. Rather than define an all-inclusive "structured programming," we examine structured programming in a narrow sense and discuss other techniques whose implementation in programming makes the meaning of algorithms readily discernible.

In implementing algorithms
use structured programming.

Structured programming is a style of programming that limits the flow of control constructs to three basic structures (see Figure 2-4):

o   Sequential execution

o   Selection

o   Repetition

These three control constructs are sufficient to perform any program control construction desired. The implication is very important: *go to* statements (unconditional transfers of control from one program point to another) are not required in programs. While structured programming in the strict sense limits control structures to these three constructs and prohibits *go to* statements, in a more general sense one may use other constructs so long as the following guideline is observed:

Limit control flow constructs to those
which have a single entry point and a single exit point.

The use of such control flow constructs allows code components to be read from top to bottom, which makes them easier to understand and hence to debug and modify. The basic constructs of Figure 2-4 may thus be augmented with constructs of Figure 2-5.

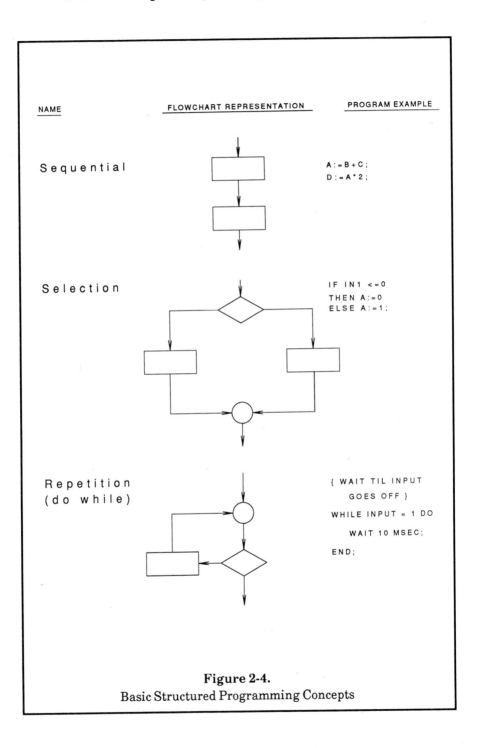

Figure 2-4.
Basic Structured Programming Concepts

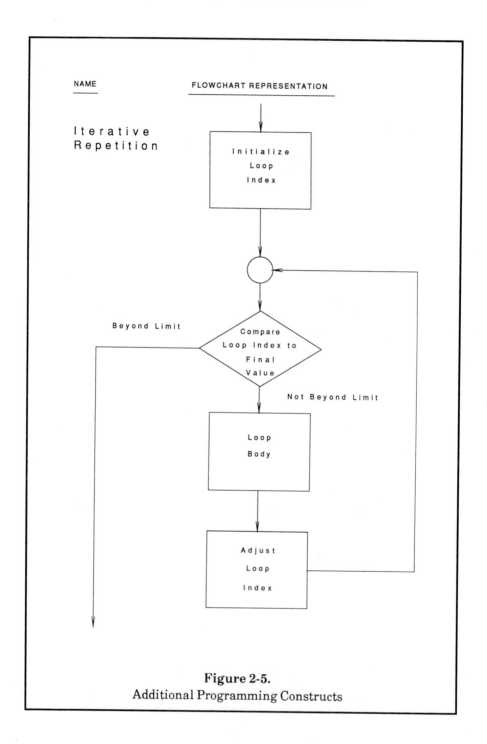

Figure 2-5.
Additional Programming Constructs

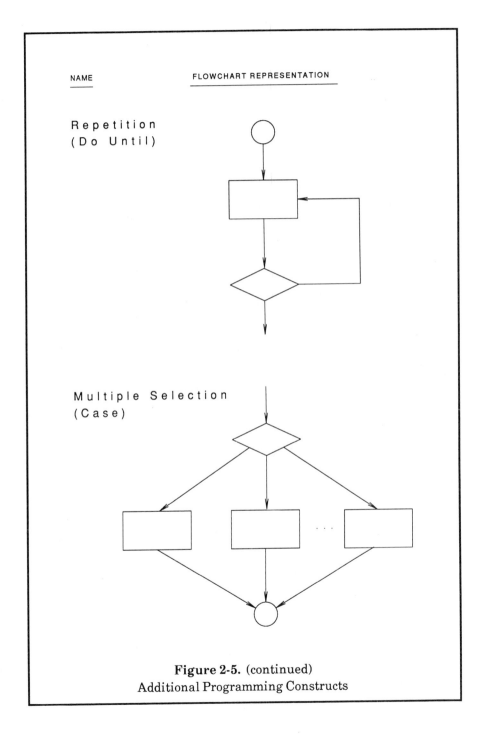

Figure 2-5. (continued)
Additional Programming Constructs

Two additional constructs which are supported in some languages are

o   Loop exit, which transfers control to the end of the repetitive loop being performed, and

o   Next index, which transfers control to the loop index adjustment in an iterative repetition loop

These constructs, shown in Figure 2-6, should be used with care as they may violate the single entry point, single exit point guideline when used in nested loops. An example of such a violation appears in Figure 2-7.

Just as the loop exit and next index constructs can be misused, the other constructs can be used in ways that obfuscate the algorithm being implemented. Thus, the use of structured programming constructs should be restricted according to the following guidelines.

Avoid nesting repetitive loops too deeply.

Loops nested five or more deep are difficult to follow and make the code harder to debug and modify.

Avoid THEN-IF and null ELSE constructs.[3]

As illustrated in Figure 2-8, which shows the pseudocode for a program segment, using an IF statement in the THEN clause of another IF statement can make the algorithmic logic difficult to follow. Such use also leads to the dangling ELSE problem, i.e., the difficulty of determining with which IF statement each ELSE clause is associated. THEN-IF constructs can sometimes be avoided by using compound conditions in the first IF statement; when this is not feasible, clarify the intention by using indentation and white space. To summarize these two guidelines a general goal is

Minimize the number of control paths
through program components.[4]

---

[3]From Brian W. Kernighan and P. J. Plauger, The Elements of Programming Style (New York: McGraw-Hill, 1978).

[4]From Anthony I. Wasserman, Software Engineering — The Key to Quality Systems, 1979.

NAME   FLOWCHART REPRESENTATION

Loop Exit

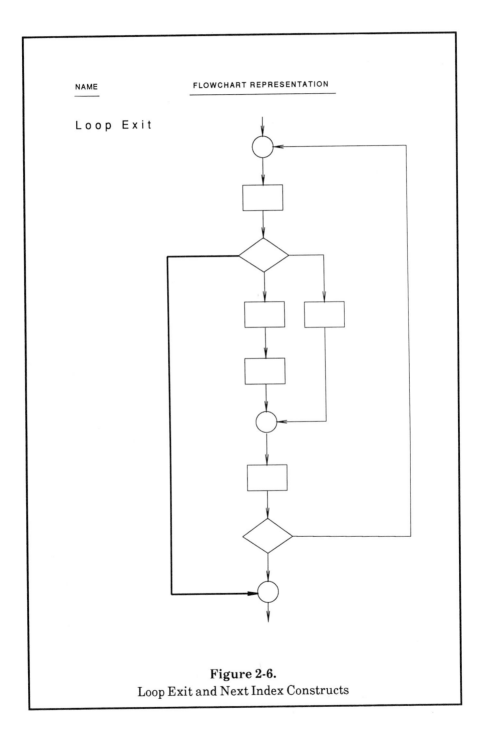

Figure 2-6.
Loop Exit and Next Index Constructs

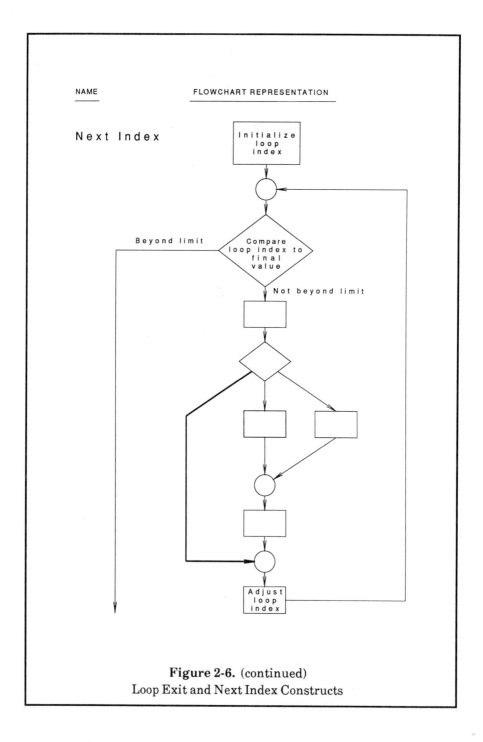

Figure 2-6. (continued)
Loop Exit and Next Index Constructs

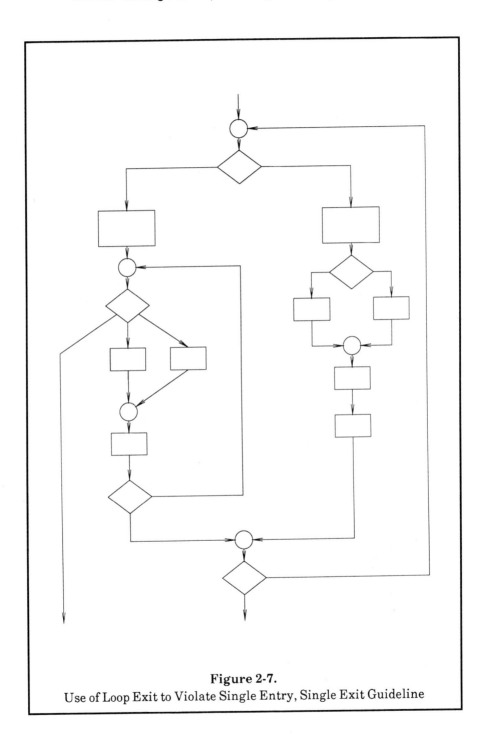

Figure 2-7.
Use of Loop Exit to Violate Single Entry, Single Exit Guideline

```
IF IN1 = 1
THEN IF IN2 = 0 OR IN3 = 0
THEN IF IN4 = 1
THEN OUT1 = 1
ELSE
ELSE OUT1 = 0
ELSE OUT2 = 1
```

Figure 2-8.
Pseudocode for a Program Segment
Showing Confusing Use of THEN-IF Construct

Another general guideline is

Avoid programming tricks.[5]

Programming tricks usually employ some aspect of the programming environment: the microprocessor, the operating system, the programming language, and so forth. The following discussion addresses the usage of programming tricks:

Avoid side effects.

Side effects are changes to a program, like changing a variable's value, that are unintended or nonobvious. Two particular examples where side effects can be troublesome lead to the following guidelines:

Avoid global data.

Avoid aliases.

[5]From Anthony I. Wasserman, Software Engineering — The Key to Quality Systems, 1979.

Global data should be avoided because one program component can change the value of a global data item without the knowledge of other components. This complicates debugging and program extension. Aliases are multiple names for program entities such as data structures; their use should be avoided for the same reason as avoiding global data.

Eliminate or isolate system dependencies.

System dependencies are particular implementation aspects of the microprocessor, the operating system, or the programming language. As discussed earlier, assumptions about these environmental aspects should be clearly documented. In addition, while tricks are often employed for "efficiency" reasons, these dependencies should be avoided. Everybody has a bag of tricks, but the tricks of one engineer can be confusion to another.

Figure 2-9 illustrates many of the maxims discussed. The reader is encouraged to read the program carefully and judge the extent to which the guidelines have been followed.

```
Procedure Compare_Input_Against_Norm (Norm, Average_Input: Integer;
                                      Var Difference: Integer);

{ Purpose
     This process is part of a process control system in which
     temperature is the controlling variable (see Figure 4-1).
     This process computes the difference between the input variables
     Average_Input and Norm.
  Input Parameters
     Norm - an integer that represents the nominal temperature.
            Its value should be between 90 and 110 inclusive.
     Average_Input - an integer that represents the average of the
            last five input temperatures.  Its value should be
            between 85 and 115 inclusive.
  Output Parameters
     Difference - an integer that has the value Average_Input - Norm.
  Procedures Called - None                                                }

{Local variable definitions and initializations}
   Const Min_Norm = 90;  {The minimum allowable value of the input Norm}
         Max_Norm = 110; {The maximum allowable value of the input Norm}
         Min_Avg_Input = 85;  {Minimum allowable value of input Average_Input}
         Max_Avg_Input = 115; {Maximum allowable value of input Average_Input}

Begin

   {Check that input variables lie within proper range}
      If (Norm < Min_Norm) or (Norm > Max_Norm)
        then writeln ('Norm of', Norm, ' is outside of range.');
      If (Average_Input < Min_Avg_Input) or (Average_Input > Max_Avg_Input)
        then Writeln ('Average_Input of', Average_Input, ' is outside of range.')

   {Compute the difference to return to the calling process}
      Difference := Norm - Average_Input;

End;
```

Figure 2-9.
A Simple Pascal Procedure
Illustrating Concepts Described in This Chapter

3

DEBUGGING

MICROPROCESSOR SOFTWARE

3.1 Introduction

Debugging is the initial procedure of executing a program component or set of program components to determine if it is operating as expected. If an engineer finds errors in the program, i.e., bugs[1], the engineer isolates and corrects the errors by making changes to the program. The more complete and formal exercising of a program takes place in the testing phase of the software life cycle, which is described in Chapter 8. Debugging is an activity which actually starts in earlier phases of the software life cycle and requires interaction with a software/hardware system. The first section in this chapter describes the impact of debugging on implementation techniques; the second section discusses hardware and software tools for coding and debugging.

[1]According to computer science lore, the term "bug" was coined in the 1940s when the Harvard Mark I computer failed to operate properly because one of its relays would not close completely, thus prohibiting contact and the resulting circuit completion. Upon inspection, the relay problem was found to be caused by a dead moth which had become lodged in the relay mechanism. When the dead moth was removed from the machine (i.e., it was de-"bugged"), proper operation was restored.

3.2 Debugging Techniques

3.2.1 Instrumentation

To aid engineers in locating errors in program components, it is helpful for a program component itself to assist in the process. Instrumentation is the addition of code to a program component to provide information about program status. The term "instrumentation" has evolved from the old practice of attaching hardware instruments to microprocessor systems to obtain information. The instrumentation code does not contribute to the functionality of the program. The information is provided by outputting to one or more devices in the debug environment: CRT, printer, and so on.

Instrument program components
before starting the debugging process.

Instrumentation is sometimes called "antibugging" because it emphasizes preventative rather than reactive error isolation. There are several common instrumentation techniques which should be used in most microprocessor applications:

Provide information on control flow
in all program components.

Information on control flow should be provided at several locations in each program component:

o   At the entry point. Code that outputs a message saying the component has been entered should be the first executable code in a component.

o   At the exit point. Program components like other program structures should have a single entry point and a single exit point.

o   Before and after references to other program components.

o   At other key points, such as before and after larger loops or selection statements.

Another key idea in instrumenting is

Check data passed to a program component
for validity and reasonability.

A data item may be invalid because it is of the wrong type; for example, a number was expected but a character was received. A data item may be unreasonable because its value is outside the expected range; for example, a positive number was expected but a zero was received. In such cases an error message should be reported, and an assumption should be made so as to continue execution. If no such assumption is realistic, program execution should be terminated. An extension of this practice is

Provide information about the values of important variables at certain points in program components.

This can be done simply by outputting the values or by comparing actual values to expected values and outputting information only if the actual values differ from the expected values. Other information such as execution time can be useful in instrumentation. Program locations at which to provide such information should correspond to locations mentioned earlier in following control flow.

While the information provided in instrumentation code should be displayed to the programmer, it is useful to output the information to a computer file for later analysis. In addition to the general techniques described, it is useful to develop specific instrumentation techniques for particular microprocessor applications, for example, outputting certain information for special input conditions. To illustrate the difference between an instrumented and uninstrumented program component, refer to Figure 3-1 which shows the program component of Figure 2-9 with instrumentation added.

3.2.2 The Debugging Process

In implementing a program component or set of program components, the following steps should be performed:

(1) Code. Write the higher level language instructions that effect the algorithms of the design specification.

(2) Compile. Transform the higher level language instructions that constitute a component into an executable form.

(3) Link. Combine the compiled components to form a software system.

(4) Load. Place the linked software system into the memory of the microprocessor system.

```
Procedure Compare_Input_Against_Norm (Norm, Average_Input: Integer;
                                      Var Difference: Integer);

{ Purpose
     This process is part of a process control system in which
     temperature is the controlling variable (see Figure 4-1).
     This process computes the difference between the input variables
     Average_Input and Norm.
  Input Parameters
     Norm - an integer that represents the nominal temperature.
            Its value should be between 90 and 110 inclusive.
     Average_Input - an integer that represents the average of the
            last five input temperatures.  Its value should be
            between 85 and 115 inclusive.
  Output Parameters
     Difference - an integer that has the value Average_Input - Norm.
  Procedures Called - None                                            }


{Local variable definitions and initializations}
     Const Min_Norm = 90;  {The minimum allowable value of the input Norm}
           Max_Norm = 110; {The maximum allowable value of the input Norm}
           Min_Avg_Input = 85;  {Minimum allowable value of input Average_Input}
           Max_Avg_Input = 115; {Maximum allowable value of input Average_Input}

Begin

     {***Record Procedure entry***}
        Writeln ('*** Entered Compare_Input_Against_Norm');

     {Check that input variables lie within proper range}
        If (Norm < Min_Norm) or (Norm > Max_Norm)
           then writeln ('Norm of', Norm, ' is outside of range.');
        If (Average_Input < Min_Avg_Input) or (Average_Input > Max_Avg_Input)
           then Writeln ('Average_Input of', Average_Input, ' is outside of range.');

     {Compute the difference to return to the calling process}
        Difference := Norm - Average_Input;

     {***Check the value of Difference for reasonability***}
        If (Difference > 10) or (Difference < -10)
           then Writeln ('*** Difference of',Difference,' may lead to problems ***');

     {***Record Procedure exit***}
        Writeln ('*** Exited Compare_Input_Against_Norm')

End;
```

Figure 3-1.

The Procedure of Figure 2-9 with Instrumentation Added

(5)   Test.   Determine   the   results   of   running   the   software   on   the
      microprocessor system.

If the test results do not match the expected results, then the steps have to
be repeated, i.e., the debugging process must be undertaken. The following
paragraphs describe each of these activities, though the debugging process
is based on a simple procedure:

(1)   Use the data provided by instrumentation to make observations about program behavior.

(2)   Based on these observations, make a hypothesis about the cause of the problem. Change the code to correct the problem, or if the cause is not known exactly, change the code to provide more instrumentation.

(3)   Repeat the five steps: code, compile, link, load, test.

If the change does not confirm the hypothesis, then remove the incorrect fixes and repeat the process using the additional instrumentation information.

In the coding phase of the debugging process,

Comment the code added for instrumentation.

Comment the code changes which are intended to fix problems.

The comments should include the programmer's name, the date, and the reason for the change. These code changes should not become permanent parts of the program component file until debugging has been completed. This means two versions of a program should be maintained during debugging.

A useful technique in debugging, available with some higher level language compilers, is the "compilable comment." A compilable comment is a higher level language statement that is normally treated as a comment, i.e., the compiler generates no code for it. When the compile comments option is enabled, however, the compiler treats the statement as if it were not a comment, i.e., it generates code for the statement. It is often advantageous to make instrumentation code compilable comments, for then the instrumentation code can be treated as statements when debugging the component and as comments afterward in order to reduce the volume of output and save real time during program execution.

In order to debug the program component under consideration, it is usually necessary to link it with other components it references or which reference it. As a general rule:

Proceed in a top-down manner in coding and debugging.

This concept of top-down implementation reflects top-down design discussed in Chapters 4 and 5, where a more detailed description is presented. Basically, this means that program components that perform major functions are implemented before the components implementing the subfunctions referenced by the major functions. With top-down implementation, linking must be performed in a certain way to enable component debugging.

Use stubs and drivers to link
a program component for debugging.

A stub is a program component that replaces a component called by the one being debugged. A stub consists of

o   The component header

o   Comments that describe its use as a stub (following the prologue guidelines presented earlier)

o   Commented instrumentation code to record component entry

o   Commented code that checks data passed to it, performs simple checking or transformation functions, and returns data to the calling component

o   The component terminator

Similarly, a driver is a program component that references (calls) the component being debugged. Stubs and drivers are critical in debugging component interfaces and enabling components to run in an environment that approximates the real one. Figure 3-2 shows the roles of stubs and drivers in debugging a component. Figure 3-3 shows a sample program stub.

Following the linking of the program components to be tested and their loading into the microprocessor system, program execution is initiated. For debugging to be a successful and efficient operation, the selection of test data must be given consideration.

Generate sets of test data to exercise
not only the normal cases
but the boundary conditions
and special cases as well.

The results of the execution should be recorded on a CRT, a printer, or in special cases some real-time data collection recorder such as magnetic tape. The results of the program execution should then be compared, either manually or automatically, to the expected results. If the actual results match the expected results, then the remaining test data should be used in additional executions until all program executions yield expected results. If

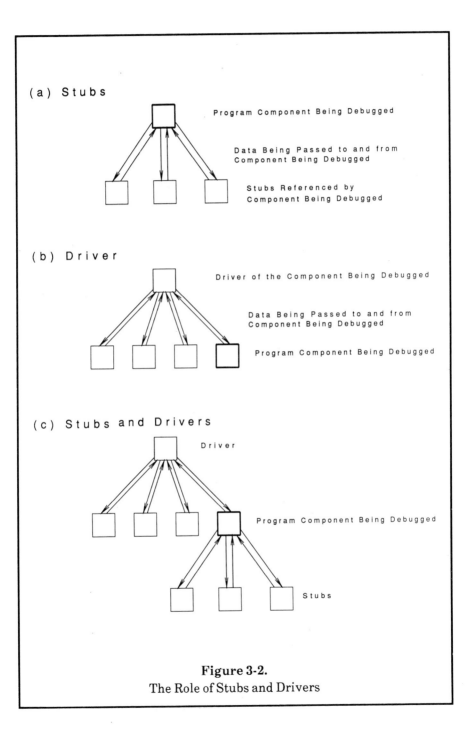

Figure 3-2.
The Role of Stubs and Drivers

```
Procedure Compare_Input_Against_Norm (Norm, Average_Input: Integer;
                                Var Difference: Integer);

{ *** THIS IS A STUB ***}

{ Purpose
     This process is part of a process control system in which
     temperature is the controlling variable (see Figure 4-1).
     This process computes the difference between the input variables
     Average_Input and Norm.
  Input Parameters
     Norm - an integer that represents the nominal temperature.
            Its value should be between 90 and 110 inclusive.
     Average_Input - an integer that represents the average of the
            last five input temperatures.  Its value should be
            between 85 and 115 inclusive.
  Output Parameters
     Difference - an integer that has the value Average_Input - Norm.
  Procedures Called - None                                          }


{Local variable definitions and initializations}
     Const Min_Norm = 90;  {The minimum allowable value of the input Norm}
           Max_Norm = 110; {The maximum allowable value of the input Norm}
           Min_Avg_Input = 85;  {Minimum allowable value of input Average_Input}
           Max_Avg_Input = 115; {Maximum allowable value of input Average_Input}

Begin

     {***Record Procedure entry***}
        Writeln ('*** Entered Compare_Input_Against_Norm');

     {Check that input variables lie within proper range}
        If (Norm < Min_Norm) or (Norm > Max_Norm)
        then writeln ('Norm of', Norm, ' is outside of range.');
        If (Average_Input < Min_Avg_Input) or (Average_Input > Max_Avg_Input)
        then Writeln ('Average_Input of', Average_Input, ' is outside of range.');

     {Compute the difference to return to the calling process}
     {*** Return typical value from stub ***}
        Difference := 6;

     {***Record Procedure exit***}
        Writeln ('*** Exited Compare_Input_Against_Norm')

End;
```

Figure 3-3.

A Stub for the Procedure of Figure 3-1

the actual results do not match the expected results, then the steps
mentioned previously — observe, hypothesize, change, test — should be
performed. Two techniques can be most useful in executing programs to
which changes have been made:

o   Use the interactive aspects of microprocessor support systems to make code changes, link, load, and initiate execution in a short period of time.

o   Use a compile time switch or set a data item in the test data, so that instrumentation code in the program is executed.

During program execution on an interactive system, special execution modes may be used to provide additional information:

o   Single step mode, in which execution is temporarily halted following the execution of each instruction (machine language or higher level language).

o   Breakpoint mode, in which execution is temporarily halted at selected time intervals or selected instructions.

o   Trace mode, in which machine and program status is output at selected time intervals or selected instructions.

The single step and breakpoint modes allow several actions to be performed during program suspensions: querying machine and program status, changing machine and program status, changing the program execution mode, and so forth.

Having observed program execution results in order to make hypotheses about the causes of problems in the code, there are several common coding mistakes for which programs should be inspected:

Check that variables have been properly initialized.

Check that variable values are not affected
by references to other program components (side effects).

Check that single data elements
in a data structure with multiple elements
are referenced properly, e.g., valid subscripts in arrays.

Check for off-by-one errors,
e.g., performing loops one time too few or one time too many.

Isolating the cause of program errors may be compounded by the interrelationships of multiple bugs or real-time problems (such as "logic lockup" in which the microprocessor instruction counter is changed inexplicably) caused by other parts of the microprocessor system. These types of problems may require careful instrumentation to diagnose.

3.2.3 Debugging Perspectives

As the mechanics of the debugging process can have a major impact on the efficiency of finding and correcting program errors, the following guidelines should be used:

Plan your debug sessions:
prepare sets of test data and
develop objectives each set is to test,
before starting a debug session.

Use system debug time wisely;
avoid spending all your time on one problem,
get the proper instrumentation data,
and proceed to other problems.
If you are trying to solve one problem,
have a plan for isolating it.

Keep a log book, recording what was tested and changed,
where in the program changes were made,
who made them, when they were made,
and why they were made.

While the microprocessor system should be used to aid in program isolation, it should not be used carelessly.

Do not substitute instrumentation
and other techniques for proper problem analysis.

One traditional practice in debugging is machine language patching. This almost always leads to more problems than it fixes, therefore,

Machine language patching
should almost never be performed.

Only when other techniques take hours to perform should patching be considered, and then only as a last resort.

3.3 Coding and Debugging Tools

While coding and debugging should constitute only a small fraction of system development time, these activities can consume inordinate amounts of time if appropriate tools are not available. The hardware and software tools for microprocessor coding and debugging may be much more expensive than the microprocessor system of the final product, and this is sometimes viewed as not being cost effective. Since the human engineers working on a product are the most valuable of all project resources, the deployment of suitable tools to assist software engineers yields a high return in productivity, project time, product quality, and personnel morale. In addition, the cost of a good microprocessor support system can often be spread across many development projects, even when the microprocessor changes from one product to another.

Coding and debugging tools may be broadly classified as hardware or software tools, and as offline or host tools. Offline tools employ computers or microprocessors separate from the microprocessor in a product configuration, whereas host tools interact with or make use of the actual microprocessor in a product configuration.

The principal hardware tools used in coding and debugging are

o   Minicomputer and large computer systems

o   Microprocessor development systems

o   Product simulators

Minicomputer and large computer systems provide powerful features, usually unavailable on microprocessor-based systems, to facilitate program preparation and storage. These features include

o   A variety of input/output terminals for interacting with the system at high speeds

o   Large memories and fast CPUs that facilitate compiling and linking of large programs

o   Large on-line file capabilities for storing all the versions of program components and documentation

o   Output devices for printing documentation and listings of software tool runs

These systems support the usual offline software development tools (editors, compilers, linkers, etc.) and additionally may provide a library system for file management control.

Use a library system for controlling versions
and configurations of components, test data, and documentation.

Whether the library system is manual, semiautomatic, or completely automatic, it is vital to track components through versions which may differ as a result of debugging changes or as a result of minor changes to environmental requirements. This is especially critical as program components are grouped into subsystems for testing. After programs are linked on minicomputer or large computer systems, they are typically stored on floppy disks for loading into the microprocessor debug system, or else are directly downloaded via a communication link to the microprocessor debug system.

Modern microprocessor development systems usually have the following components:

o   A CRT terminal for user interaction.

o   A floppy disk drive for reading and writing programs.

o   A microprocessor-based hardware system that not only executes the microprocessor program created by the engineer, but also monitors its execution to provide interactive debugging facilities. When the microprocessor executing the product program resides on one of the product boards, this debugging feature is called in-circuit emulation.

These systems usually supply the basic software development tools plus an interactive debugger, however, tool execution may be slow compared to large systems. There are a number of microprocessor development systems with a variety of levels of sophistication available on the market. Although their initial cost may seem large for microprocessor products, they should be considered as minimal configurations for microprocessor software development.

An important aspect of microprocessor system products is the embedding of microprocessors in large, real-time systems. In developing such a product,

> "One needs a logical simulator for it. This gives a debugging
> vehicle long before the real target exists. Equally important, it
> gives access to a dependable debugging vehicle even after one

has a target machine available. Dependable is not the same as accurate. So a dependable simulator on a well-aged vehicle retains it usefulness far longer than one would expect."[2]

The moral for microprocessor-based systems is clear:

> *For sophisticated microprocessor-based products,*
> *debug the software on a simulator*
> *controlled by the product microprocessor.*

Although a simulator, in its product orientation, is special purpose, it should be usable for several products in a family. Advanced simulators provide the capability of being reconfigurable under software command.

The principal software tools used in coding and debugging are

o   Editors

o   Compilers (and assemblers)

o   Linkers

o   Loaders

o   Debuggers

An editor is a program that allows one to manipulate text on the computer support system. Typical operations are file creation, storage, retrieval, and modification (additions, deletions, changes, copies, and so forth). The file may contain a program component, test data, documentation, or other information. An editor should be used in an interactive mode, however, it must be used properly. Some software engineers can use interactive editors effectively in creating programs. Others feel that the entering and editing of programs on a computer system is a clerical task, and is most efficiently performed by clerical personnel.

Higher level language compilers translate the program (entered into the system via the editor) into the microprocessor machine language, or some representation thereof. A compiler also provides information that is useful in program debugging and modification.

---

[2]Frederick P. Brooks, Jr., The Mythical Man-Month — Essays on Software Engineering (Reading, Massachusetts: Addison-Wesley, 1975), p. 132.

o   A listing of the program showing separation of program components, the statement number for each statement, and a list of errors. There may be additional information such as the nesting depth of each statement.

o   A list of identifiers (variable names, procedure names, and so forth) and the numbers of statements in which they are referenced.

This information should be used in the initial stages of debugging. For example, identifiers that are referenced in only one statement may be misspelled versions of other identifiers. Other software tools that may be associated with a compiler are preprocessors and macroprocessors. These tools extend the language being used to provide facilities such as

o   Structured programming constructs

o   Inclusion of other information, for example, common data declarations

Yet another tool is a "pretty printer" which prints program statements in a format that facilitates reading, for example, indentation of the statements nested in selection or loop constructs.

The linker or linkage editor resolves references among program components and produces a load module, ready for storing into the microprocessor memory. In addition to listing errors in intercomponent references, the linker should produce a memory map showing the correspondence between microprocessor memory locations and the program statements and data items. This information is essential in case machine level debug is required.

Loaders take two forms. In one form, a loader takes the load module produced by the linker, and loads it into the microprocessor memory or the simulated microprocessor memory. Since many microprocessor systems use PROM or ROM memory, another type of loader is the "PROM programmer," which takes a load module and burns it into PROM chips for insertion into the microprocessor system.

The final category of software tool is the debugger or simulator. This may be a stand-alone tool (a pure software simulator, for example) or a tool that interacts with a hardware debug/simulator system. The debugger should be an interactive tool that provides the ability to

o   Initiate program execution

o   Interrupt and suspend program execution

o   Inspect and change code at the higher level language level (which may require recompilation and relinking) and at the machine language level (although this feature should be needed only rarely)

o   Inspect and change data items at the higher level language level and at the machine language level

o   Select trace and breakpoints

Additional features, such as saving the status of a debug run for later resumption and recording status in real time, can greatly enhance one's debugging capabilities.

4

DESIGN PRESENTATION

FOR MICROPROCESSOR SOFTWARE

4.1 Introduction

In developing software for microprocessor systems, the design phase activities are seldom given the amount of attention they deserve, and as a consequence the resulting implementations seldom meet the quality standards that are desired or achievable. Because the design process builds a foundation on which the implementation (i.e., coding) will succeed or fail, significant time should be devoted to the design activity as described in Chapter 1 (see Figure 1-2). There is almost always a strong impetus to begin coding as soon as possible on a project so there will be some visible results early in the project life cycle. Supposed justification for this early implementation may be attributed to the enabling of a prototype, but such an early implementation may become "cast in concrete" and serve as a poor basis for a complete system. The tendency to start coding as soon as possible should be resisted because the production of a good design is much more important to the overall success of a project.

4.2 The Role of the Design Phase

The purpose of the design phase of software development is to transform the requirements specification into a design specification from which the implementation can proceed in a straightforward manner. The quality of a design is measured by the ease of its implementation and the characteristics of the resulting implementation: efficiency, reliability, maintainability, and so forth. The following design characteristics have been shown to be useful in developing quality implementations and thus, should be goals for design specifications

o   Hierarchical — A hierarchical design describes how a system is to be implemented in terms of multiple levels of detail. Indeed, the design synthesis activity is a two-stage process — high level design and detailed design. These stages may be broken into several successive stages where each new stage adds additional detail to the hierarchy. The highest level of a design specification simply summarizes the functions of the system; successively lower levels expand this information so that the lowest level of design specification corresponds to the code that implements the system. The value of a hierarchical design is its presentation of the necessary information at each level and the suppression of unnecessary details to lower levels, so that comprehension of the design is enhanced by limiting the scope of what needs to be understood at one time.

o   Modular — A modular design describes how a system is to be implemented in terms of discrete components. The components in a good design are highly independent, so that the development and understanding of one component does not depend upon the design of another component. The internal aspects of a component in a good design are cohesive, so that a module does not deal with multiple functions or information items. The value of a modular design, when coupled with a hierarchical design, is its presentation of the necessary information in pieces that can be studied independently yet can be easily understood.

o   Consistent — A consistent design is one in which the levels of hierarchy and the components that constitute the design specification demonstrate similarities in presentation, i.e., there is not a significant disparity among related modules at any level in the hierarchy in terms of size, amount of detail, and interface to other modules. Consistent application of design guidelines result in a consistent design, which makes reading, reviewing, modifying, and implementing straightforward.

Design specifications with these characteristics can be developed by applying the guidelines of structured analysis, top-down design, hierarchical decomposition, structured design, and modularization which are described in the later sections of this chapter and the next chapter.

A good design avoids errors in several ways:[1]

o   The partitioning of modules avoids system bugs.

o   The suppression of detail makes flaws in the structure more apparent.

o   The small size of the components permits comprehension by single individuals.

o   The design can be reviewed at each of its refinement steps, so errors can be found earlier in the development process.

4.3 Phases of Software Design

The process of designing a software system consists of two phases: analysis and synthesis. In the analysis phase, the requirements specification input to the design phase is studied and transformed into a description that summarizes the operation of the system. In the synthesis phase, the structure of the microprocessor software system is developed, first in the form of a simple hierarchical graph structure and then in a detailed textual description.

In the analysis phase of designing a software system, one examines the information in the requirements document and then classifies the information into two fundamental categories: data and processes. The data are then further classified as data input to the system, data output from the system, and intermediate data used internally by the system. The overall system transformation process is partitioned into smaller processes that use the system input data and intermediate data and produce system output data or intermediate data. The processes, when partitioned properly, correspond to well-defined activities, so the flow of data among processes corresponds to a logical representation of the operation of the system. After data and processes are positioned, some additional information completes the model. This information shows interfaces to the external environment, such as the sources and destinations of data, and data storage facilities to introduce a time factor into the system operation. To summarize, the fundamental concept of analysis is to present in a clear way a logical model of how a system operates.

---

[1]Frederick P. Brooks, Jr., The Mythical Man-Month — Essays on Software Engineering (Reading, Massachusetts: Addison-Wesley, 1975), p. 143.

The synthesis phase of designing a software system starts with the specification of the system function (the overall process transformation) as the topmost component in a downward branching tree, as shown in Figure 4-1. Each successive design step describes the function of a component in more detail by breaking it into several subcomponents and describing the subcomponents and the interfaces between the subcomponents ("children" components) and the original component ("parent" component). The children components describe the parent component functions in more detail and may be illustrated in a tree as shown in Figure 4-1. While design synthesis proceeds in a top-down manner until the lowest level specifies the detail required to initiate coding, the design specification must be constantly reviewed to ensure that the constraints described in the requirements specification can be satisfied: development time, manpower, real time, memory size, and so forth. In fact, as several design alternatives are considered and found to be lacking, it may be necessary to change the requirements specification document. Thus, design synthesis is not strictly a top-down process but rather one that is fundamentally top-down with feedback loops to consider implementation constraints and refine previous design decisions. It has been observed that "most software design is still done bottom-up, by developing software components before addressing interface and integration issues."[2] This approach can lead to designs that are found to be invalid late in the development process; such late discoveries are expensive and time consuming to fix properly.

The design synthesis activity should be divided into two major phases: high level design and detailed design. In the high level design activity, one specifies the function of the software (as described in the design analysis and requirements document) in the topmost component, the root of the tree. Next, the subfunctions (from the analysis and requirements documents) are described and allocated to the principal architectural components of the system, such as the applications software, the diagnostics software, and the operating system. These functions are then decomposed into lower level components, and this process continues to the point where each component is manageable by one person. A manageable component is one that can be readily comprehended by one person and can be implemented within the time and resource constraints.

In the detailed design phase the logical structure resulting from high level design is transformed and further decomposed into a procedural

[2]Barry W. Boehm, "Software Engineering," IEEE Transactions on Computers, vol. C-25, no. 12 (December 1976).

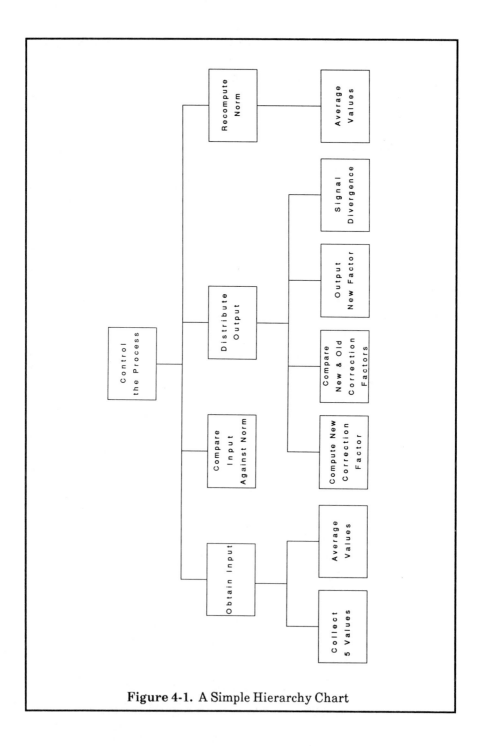

Figure 4-1. A Simple Hierarchy Chart

decomposition. The final result of the hierarchical decomposition is a set of procedures which when implemented constitute the final software product. The high level and detailed design activities are thus distinct but interdependent. The high level design phase takes the requirements specification and produces a logical design. The detailed design phase takes the logical structure and produces a physical structure.

4.4 Design Phase Output

The output of the design activity is a design document which, as described in Chapter 2 on coding techniques, should serve as a skeleton for the program to be implemented. Thus, the final program consists of the design document paragraphs serving as comments and the programming language statements that effect the design. Preliminary versions of design documentation, particularly the documentation of the high level design, serve as intermediate status points of significant value in a project. These checkpoint versions are important because the design activity constitutes such a large portion of total project time. These versions are not only read by the designer, they may also be read by

o   The programmer, who may be someone other than the designer

o   The members of review teams, who read the document for design quality, functional accuracy, and resource utilization

o   The project managers who are monitoring project progress

o   The customer who may be interested in seeing tangible results, especially since there should not be a strong thrust to implement code early

With such a large number of people reading design documentation it is important to examine the development of readable designs. This chapter will address the presentation of the design to the reader of the design specification, while the next chapter describes the technique for developing a design specification from a requirements specification for microprocessor-based systems. Because design presentation is simpler to comprehend yet is seldom realized with great effectiveness, it will be addressed first.

4.5 A Note on Terminology

Before discussing design presentation, it is appropriate to review some terminology to clarify the following discussion. To this point, we have generally used the term "component" to refer to a chunk of code or a piece of design. "Component" is a generic term that refers to a logical or physical entity (in a design specification or program) which deals with some complete concept. Examples of components are program subroutines, program procedures, programs themselves, and nodes in design trees. An example of an entity that is usually not a component is a program segment formed from the arbitrary division of a program into two parts. The term "module" usually refers to a particular kind of component such as a program subroutine, procedure, or function. One typical definition of the term "module" follows:

> "A module is any collection of executable program statements meeting all of the following criteria: (1) it is a closed subroutine, (2) it can be called from any other module in the program, and (3) it has the potential of being independently compiled."[3]

While this definition may help narrow the notion of "module," the term "modular" applies to designs as well as programs. Many authors use the term "module" and other terms such as "segment," "routine," or "subprogram" to refer to particular types or sizes of components. But we will use the term "module" in a general sense to apply more broadly than just programs:

> "A module is a lexically contiguous sequence of statements, bounded by boundary elements, having an aggregate identifier."[4]

This definition means that

o   The statements in a module follow one another from a logical (and usually physical) viewpoint.

o   There are distinct initial and terminal points in a module representation (the boundary elements).

[3]Glenford J. Myers, Composite/Structured Design (New York: Van Nostrand Reinhold Company, 1978), p. 11.

[4]Adapted from Edward Yourdon and Larry L. Constantine, Structured Design: Fundamentals of a Discipline of Computer Program and Systems Design (Englewood Cliffs, New Jersey: Prentice-Hall, 1979), p. 37.

o   A module can be referenced by a specific identifier.

o   A module may contain or reference other modules.

Another term that is used with a variety of meanings is "specification," which generally means a description of details. Since this term can actually be applied to all phases of software development, we will use the term in the context of a particular phase, as in "design specification," meaning "design documentation."

4.6 Design Presentation Overview

There are two techniques for presenting design information to the various readers of the design documentation: graphical and textual. The graphical or pictorial presentation illustrates the operation of the system or the structure of the design so that its fundamental aspects can be readily discerned. A simple example of a graphical presentation is the tree diagram shown in Figure 4-1. The textual presentation describes the details of the design, e.g., the descriptions of the functions of each component, the interfaces between modules, the data items used by each component, and the algorithms that effect the function of a component. Figure 4-2 shows an excerpt from a textual design document.

4.7 Graphical Displays

There are two types of graphical displays that should be used in developing a design specification for a microprocessor software system:

o   System flow diagrams

o   System structure diagrams

4.7.1 System Flow Diagrams

System flow diagrams present the logical operation of the system; one can determine system behavior by following the various paths in a system flow diagram. The two types of system flow diagrams are

o   Data flow diagrams

o   Finite state machine diagrams

```
          COMPARE INPUT AGAINST NORM (NORM,AVERAGE_INPUT) RETURNS (DIFFERENCE)

  REF
  PAGE  ****************************************************************************************************
        *                                                                                                *
  31     *  1   .. PURPOSE                                                                                 *
  32     *  2   ..... THIS PROCESS IS PART OF A PROCESS CONTROL SYSTEM IN WHICH                            *
  33     *  3   ..... TEMPERATURE IS THE CONTROLLING VARIABLE (SEE FIGURE 4-1).                            *
  34     *  4   ..... THIS PROCESS COMPUTES THE DIFFERENCE BETWEEN THE INPUT VARIABLES                     *
  35     *  5   ..... AVERAGE_INPUT AND NORM.                                                              *
  36     *  6   .. INPUT PARAMETERS                                                                        *
  37     *  7   ..... NORM - AN INTEGER THAT REPRESENTS THE NOMINAL TEMPERATURE.                           *
  38     *  8   ............ ITS VALUE SHOULD BE BETWEEN 90 AND 110 INCLUSIVE.                             *
  39     *  9   ..... AVERAGE_INPUT - AN INTEGER THAT REPRESENTS THE AVERAGE OF THE                        *
  40     * 10   ............ LAST FIVE INPUT TEMPERATURES. ITS VALUE SHOULD BE                             *
  41     * 11   ............ BETWEEN 85 AND 115 INCLUSIVE.                                                 *
  42     * 12   .. OUTPUT                                                                                  *
  43     * 13   ..... DIFFERENCE - AN INTEGER THAT HAS THE VALUE AVERAGE_INPUT - NORM.                     *
  44     * 14   .. PROCEDURES CALLED - NONE                                                                *
  45     * 15   ..                                                                                         *
  46     * 16   CHECK THAT THE INPUT VARIABLES LIE WITHIN THE PROPER RANGE                                 *
  47     * 17   ..                                                                                         *
  48     * 18   COMPUTE THE DIFFERENCE TO RETURN TO THE CALLING PROCEDURE                                  *
  49     * 19   ..                                                                                         *
  50     * 20   CHECK THE VALUE OF DIFFERENCE FOR REASONABILITY                                            *
        *                                                                                                *
        ****************************************************************************************************
```

Figure 4-2.
An Excerpt from a Textual Design Document
Describing a Module in Figure 4-1

4.7.1.1 Data Flow Diagrams

A data flow diagram (also known as a bubble chart or a data flow graph) shows the flow of data in a system, not the flow of control. A data flow diagram (DFD) consists of four basic elements (see Figure 4-3):

o   Data flows, represented by named arrows showing the direction of flow

o   Processes, represented by named circles (bubbles)

o   Sources and destinations of data, represented by named squares

o   Data stores, represented by named rectangles

These aspects of DFDs can be explained with references to the DFD in Figure 4-4, which shows a DFD for the operation of a simple calculator.

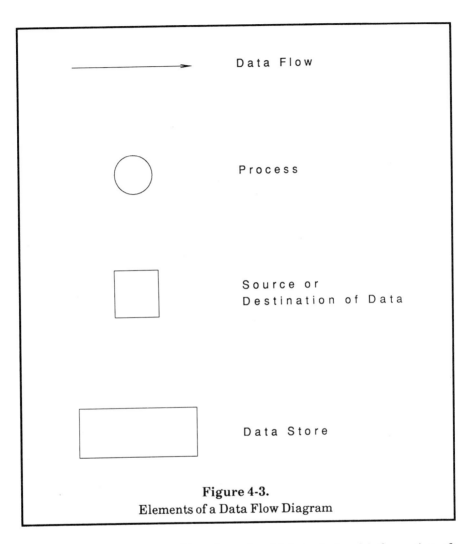

Figure 4-3.
Elements of a Data Flow Diagram

"A data flow is a pipeline through which packets of information of known composition flow."[5] In Figure 4-4, the keystrokes of a user constitute a data flow. In microprocessor software systems data flows are system inputs, system outputs, or software data structures. The system inputs and

---

[5]Definitions in this section are from Tom DeMarco, <u>Structured Analysis and System Specification</u> (Englewood Cliffs, New Jersey: Prentice-Hall, 1979).

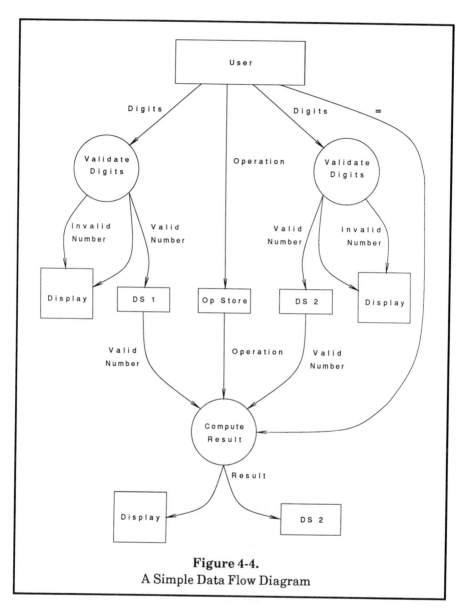

Figure 4-4.
A Simple Data Flow Diagram

outputs are frequently hardware derived; for example, the group of digits in the calculator example arise from the electrical signals generated by the depression of keys on the calculator. Another input example is the data obtained from a sensor in a process control system. An output example is a signal generated to initiate some physical activity such as turning on a furnace or an alarm. The software data structures in microprocessor software systems are usually simple because real-time systems seldom use complex structures and complex structures take longer to manipulate. Complex structures such as the multibyte records used in business data processing computer systems are traditionally handled in large computer systems. This does not imply that microprocessors are incapable of handling complex structures; it is simply that microprocessors are more widely used in applications where simple data structures are required. Where microprocessors process more complex data structures, the more traditional software development approaches apply.

"A process is a transformation of incoming data flow(s) into outgoing data flow(s)." Examples of processes in Figure 4-4 are the bubbles with the labels "Validate Digits" and "Compute Result." The "Validate Digits" process would perform such operations as checking for multiple decimal points or for too many digits for the calculator to handle.

A data store is a temporary repository of data. Examples of data stores in microprocessor systems are registers and floppy disk files. The calculator data flow shown in Figure 4-4 uses registers for storing operand and operator data. In larger computer systems and semiautomatic systems, examples of data stores are tape files and card files.

A source or destination of data in a microprocessor software system is any entity, lying outside the context of the software system, that is an originator or receiver of data. The external entity may be a person or an output device; examples in Figure 4-4 are the user who generates inputs and the display which receives data.

In reviewing Figure 4-4, note that there is no flow of control implied, yet the example is intended to handle the following sequence of user operations: enter digits, enter operation, enter digits, enter equal sign. When the flow of control in a system is complex, it may be more appropriate to use a finite state machine (see next section) to model the behavior of a system.

Data flow diagrams should present the operation of the microprocessor software system in a manner that is easy to understand. In a system of any significant size or complexity, a DFD as defined to this point would be so big that it would be unwieldy and difficult to understand. To avoid this problem, one should use hierarchical data flow diagrams. These are just DFDs in which processes represent more detailed DFDs rather than simple operations. When developed in this way, each DFD can be readily understood, and comprehension of the operation of the entire microprocessor software system is improved.

Data flow diagrams for microprocessor software systems are special cases of the DFDs used in traditional computer system analysis.[6] The differences include the use of control information as another type of data in DFDs; control information is very common in microprocessor systems. Another difference used here is that DFDs will deal only with the microprocessor software system; we will not address the larger semiautomatic system (which includes manual operations) in which the microprocessor resides.

4.7.1.2 Finite State Machines

Another model for describing the operation of a microprocessor system is the finite state machine (FSM). In this context an FSM consists of

o   A set of states with a designated initial state

o   A set of transitions among states

A transition occurs when control passes from one state to another, that is, when external events (i.e., inputs) stimulate the system. An action or output is associated with each transition. The action may be null. Figure 4-5 shows an FSM that corresponds to the DFD in Figure 4-4.

Each of the arrows representing transitions between states corresponds to an input into the system. The label above each transition arrow describes the input that causes the transition and the resulting action. Thus, Figure 4-5 shows that a transition from the Initial State occurs when a digit is input to the system. The action associated with the receipt of the input digit is to display the digit on the calculator. The next state (Collect Digits 1) collects digits and displays them until an operation (the add, subtract, multiply, or divide key) is input; the operation causes a transition to the state Collect Operation and resets the display on the calculator (so the next digit entered will first clear the display). From the state Collect Operation a digit received causes the digit to be displayed and a transition to Collect Digits 2, which collects digits until an "equal sign" input is received. This causes a transition to the Final State and the output of the result.

---

[6]See DeMarco, op. cit., and Chris Gane and Trish Sarson, Structured Systems Analysis: Tools and Techniques (Englewood Cliffs, New Jersey: Prentice-Hall), 1979.

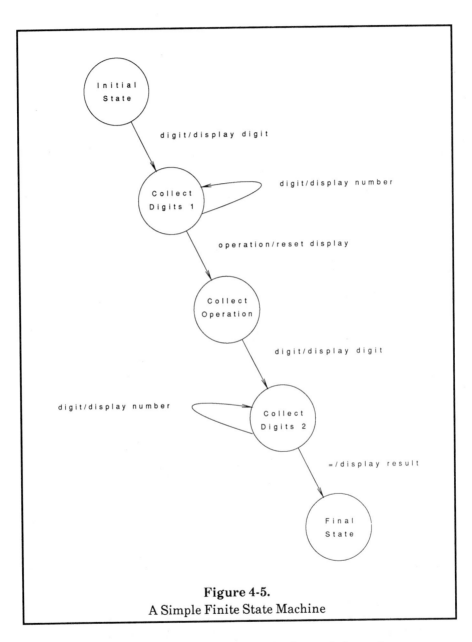

Figure 4-5.
A Simple Finite State Machine

The FSM model is especially appropriate for real time microprocessor software systems because it shows what happens when any input arrives, regardless of the state of the system. Thus, an FSM model can help avoid the common type of error which arises from the occurrence of an unexpected input at a certain point in time. It is easy to see that the FSM shown in Figure 4-5 is incomplete because it does not specify transitions for all combinations of states and inputs. For example, what happens if an "equal" operator is input while in the state "Collect Digits 1"? Another advantage of FSMs is that they can easily be represented in a tabular form as shown in Figure 4-6. The table in Figure 4-6 shows the next state for each combination of states and inputs, i.e., the table entries show the transition for each pair of states and inputs. Another table could show the specific actions to be performed for each transition. This tabular form facilitates further analysis, such as finding unspecified transitions.

4.7.2 System Structure Diagrams

There are two types of system structure diagrams:

o   Hierarchy charts

o   Structure charts

Whereas the data flow diagram and finite state machine present the operation of the system, the hierarchy chart and structure chart present the structure of the software that effects the system. Indeed, the lower levels of both the hierarchy and structure chart show the physical packaging of software into distinct modules.

4.7.2.1 Hierarchy Charts

The hierarchy chart is the simpler of the two graphical presentations used in design and so will be considered first. A hierarchy chart is a tree structure in which the nodes represent system functions (in a general sense, not the program sense) or modules, and the connecting edges represent subfunction inclusion or module reference. Figure 4-1, for example, shows a simple hierarchy chart for a microprocessor-based process control system. This example, which is intended to illustrate concepts of hierarchy charts and is not necessarily intended to exemplify good design, should be interpreted as follows:

(1)   The function of the software system is to "Control the Process" of some automatic closed loop process control system, for example, controlling the temperature in an industrial furnace.

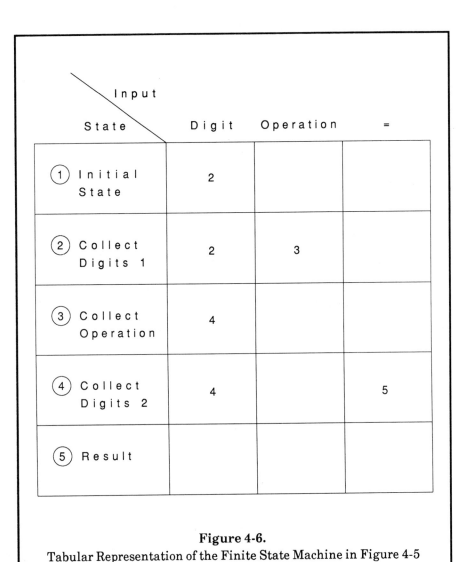

Figure 4-6.
Tabular Representation of the Finite State Machine in Figure 4-5

(2) The principal function "Control the Process" is composed of the four subfunctions:

    (a) "Obtain Input," which determines the present status of the closed loop system, e.g., the present temperature of the furnace.

    (b) "Compare Input Against Norm," which compares the present status to the desired status.

(c) "Distribute Output," which outputs the correction factor for controlling the closed loop process or signals divergence of the process, e.g., to shut down the furnace when the algorithm says to keep increasing the temperature yet the sensing thermometer has broken and always indicates a temperature of zero.

(d) "Recompute Norm," which changes the desired nominal value due to the expected degradation of the sensing thermometer over time.

(3) The function "Obtain Input" is in turn composed of two subfunctions: "Collect 5 Values" and "Average Values," so that the input used in later calculations will filter the noisy variations of the sensing thermometer.

(4) The function "Distribute Output" is in turn composed of four subfunctions: "Compute New Correction Factor," "Compare New and Old Correction Factors," "Output New Factor," and "Signal Divergence." These close the loop in the process control system and indicate an unstable process.

(5) The function "Recompute Norm" uses the "Average Values" subfunction in computing the new nominal value.

The hierarchy chart gives a simple graphical representation of the structure of the microprocessor software system. Detailed descriptions of the design of the software are left to the textual representations described later in this chapter. Furthermore, a hierarchy chart does not differentiate logical and physical structures, nor does it show interfaces among modules (i.e., data and control flow among modules). For example, a program following the design of Figure 4-1 could be implemented in several ways:

o   One program module corresponding to "Control the Process" calls four subroutines sequentially and passes data to and receives data from each subroutine.

o   Four program modules, corresponding to the four design modules at the middle level of the tree run concurrently, but under control of the top-most module. This scheme would be useful if the time required to "Recompute Norm" necessitates temporary suspension of the execution of the other modules.

o   Four program modules, corresponding to the four design modules at the middle level of the tree, operate sequentially with each passing data and control to the next module (and the last module to the first).

o   Four program modules, corresponding to the four design modules at the middle of the tree, operate concurrently in parallel. Each of the first three modules passes data to the next module and in so doing "wakes it up" to perform a function.

Structural details such as these can be specified in the more specific form of graphical design presentation: the structure chart.

4.7.2.2 Structure Charts

A structure chart is a tree-like graphical representation of the structure of a program that shows

o   The modules in the program

o   The relationships between the modules

o   The flow of data and control information between modules

The notation for structure chart components appears in Figure 4-7.
      A structure chart differs from a hierarchy chart in the following ways:

o   It shows the data and control information passed between modules.

o   It shows asynchronous invocations that indicate parallel execution of program modules.

o   It shows each module only once; thus, a structure chart is not strictly speaking a tree structure.

To illustrate these concepts, Figure 4-8 shows the program represented by the hierarchy chart of Figure 4-1 designed to perform the second implementation described on the previous page. Because the structure chart contains more information than the hierarchy chart it usually plays a more important role in the implementation of a software system.
      To review the discussion to this point on design presentation, we have described four different graphical aids used in microprocessor software design:

o   Data flow diagrams (DFDs) and finite state machine diagrams (FSMs) are system flow diagrams that present the logical operation of the system.

o   Hierarchy charts and structure charts are system structure diagrams that present the design of the software system.

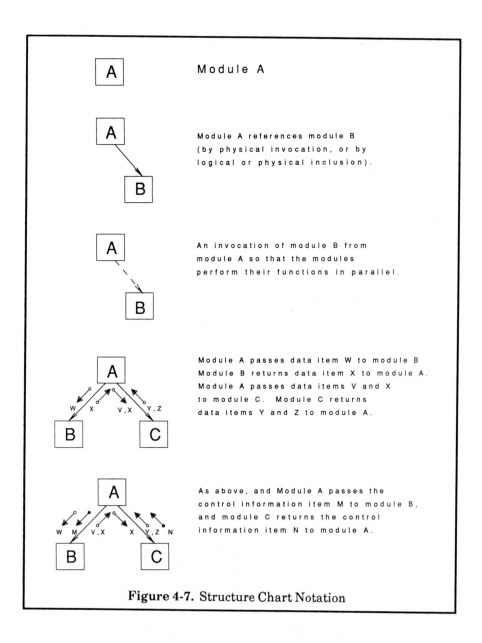

Figure 4-7. Structure Chart Notation

Flow charts have been explicitly excluded from this discussion; indeed, flow charts should not be used. The four diagrams already introduced present high level design information better than flowcharts. Program design

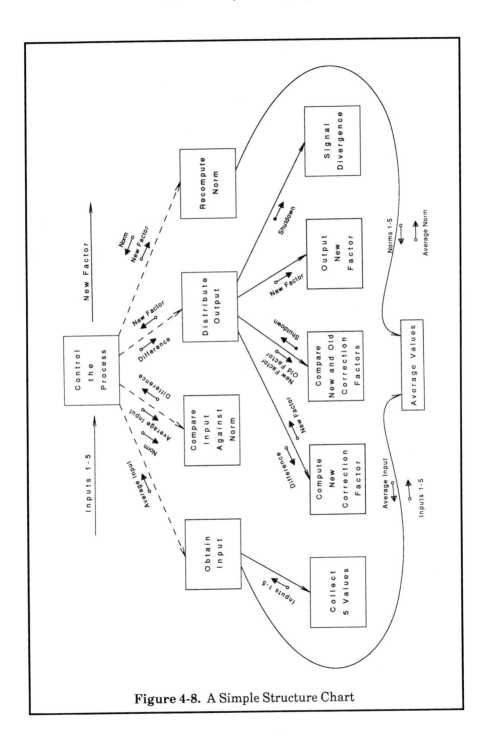

Figure 4-8. A Simple Structure Chart

languages, to be discussed subsequently, present detailed design information better than flow charts and are easier to manipulate.

4.8 Textual Documentation of Design

The graphical aids discussed previously provide important information about the operation and structure of a software system. Their value lies in their ability to communicate concepts readily; recall the old adage that a picture is worth a thousand words. To convey design details to the implementor, it is necessary to complement a graphical presentation with a textual presentation. The purpose of textual documentation is therefore to communicate to the implementor the details of design, namely :

o   Descriptions of the functions that each component in the software system performs

o   Specifications of the interfaces between components (both data and control interfaces)

o   Specifications of algorithms to implement functions

o   Specifications of data items used

With this information, the implementor can produce code to effect the system.

There are usually several other people involved in the software development process who will use the textual design documentation:

o   A review team will examine the design for correctness and completeness, to ensure that the design realizes the features specified in the requirements document.

o   A manager or project leader may allocate resources (such as ROM program memory, RAM data memory, and real time) to modules in the design.

o   A software tester should use the design document to ensure that each code module performs the functions allocated to it.

o   A software engineer who performs maintenance will refer to the design document before making significant changes to the code.

Thus, the textual design documentation serves many purposes, and should contain information such as resource allocations in addition to the information required to implement the design.

The textual design documentation closely corresponds to that of the hierarchy and structure charts, i.e., most modules identified in a hierarchy or structure chart will be described in detail in the textual design documentation. Thus, the textual descriptions must describe program components at a variety of levels of detail — from the general functional descriptions corresponding to modules high in the structure chart to the detailed algorithm specifications for modules at the bottom of the structure chart.

4.8.1 Program Design Languages

To provide such a variety of information, a program design language should be used to document the design. A program design language has two complementary aspects:

o   A set of explicit design constructs, patterned after the syntax of procedure-oriented higher level languages. The constructs may be structural (e.g., module header or terminator), functional (assignment, arithmetic operation, logical operation), control (selection or repetition), or data declaration.

o   A set of informal data manipulation capabilities, which are expressed in English.

Because program design languages use the vocabulary of a natural language (English) to describe specifics of the particular application in free form and use the syntax of an artificial language (a procedure-oriented higher level language) to structure the design descriptions, they are often referred to as "pidgin languages" or "structured English."

4.8.2 The PDL Language and Processor

While a simple text processor available on many microcomputer systems can serve as a tool for transcribing a design written in a program design language, the PDL language and processor produced by Caine, Farber and Gordon, Inc. is useful for expressing the design of a microprocessor software system.[7] PDL will be used as an example in subsequent discussions because

[7]Stephen H. Caine and E. Kent Gordon, "PDL — A Tool for Software Design," 1975 NCC Proceedings (Montvale, New Jersey: AFIPS, 1975).

it has a set of useful features in addition to the minimal syntactic elements of a program design language.

A design specification document consists of a set of modules; each module description specifies the design details mentioned earlier: functional description, interface specification, algorithm specification, and data specification. Generally, there is a module in the design specification for each module in the structure chart. In PDL, these modules are called "flow segments" and are specified by writing:

%SEGMENT segment-name

Note that PDL uses the percent sign to distinguish certain keywords. PDL provides special facilities for presenting certain types of information in a design document:

o   A text segment contains comments to the reader of the design document and is specified by writing

%TEXT segment-name

o   A data segment explicitly defines data items and is specified by writing

%DATA segment-name

o   A title for the design document may be specified by writing

%TITLE title-of-design-document

Using these features, Figure 4-9 shows the PDL statements that represent the structure of the design shown in Figure 4-8. Note in Figure 4-9

o   There is a flow segment for each module in the design.

o   Parent flow segments reference child flow segments, i.e., the modules they call.

o   Flow segments describe their interfaces by listing input variables in parentheses after the segment name and output variables in parentheses after the "RETURNS" key word.

o   A statement with a period for its first non-blank character is a comment.

Detailed specification of the algorithm for a module in a PDL design document is written in free-form English following the "%SEGMENT" header with the following special statements and constructs:

```
%TITLE FIGURE 4-9.  SAMPLE PDL DOCUMENT
%TEXT DESIGN PURPOSE
THIS PDL DESIGN REPRESENTS THE STRUCTURE OF THE DESIGN
SHOWN IN FIGURE 4-8 FOR A MICROPROCESSOR-BASED PROCESS
CONTROL SYSTEM.  THIS PROCESS CONTROL SYSTEM READS FIVE
VALUES AND OUTPUTS A CORRECTION FACTOR.  IT SENDS A
SHUTDOWN SIGNAL IF THE INPUTS HAVE DIVERGED SIGNIFICANTLY
FROM THE NORM.
%DATA SYSTEM INPUT AND OUTPUT VARIABLES
.. DATA VARIABLES - ALL 16 BIT INTEGERS
     INPUT_1
     INPUT_2
     INPUT_3     .. 5 SAMPLED INPUT TEMPERATURES
     INPUT_4
     INPUT_5
     NEW_FACTOR  .. THE ADJUSTMENT FACTOR THE SYSTEM OUTPUTS
%SEGMENT CONTROL THE PROCESS
OBTAIN INPUT ( ) RETURNS ( AVERAGE_INPUT )
COMPARE INPUT AGAINST NORM ( NORM,AVERAGE_INPUT ) RETURNS ( DIFFERENCE )
DISTRIBUTE OUTPUT ( DIFFERENCE ) RETURNS ( NEW_FACTOR )
RECOMPUTE NORM ( NEW_FACTOR ) RETURNS ( NORM )
%SEGMENT OBTAIN INPUT ( ) RETURNS ( AVERAGE_INPUT )
COLLECT 5 VALUES ( ) RETURN ( INPUT_1,...,INPUT_5 )
AVERAGE VALUES ( INPUT_1,...,INPUT_5 ) RETURNS ( AVERAGE_INPUT )
%S COMPARE INPUT AGAINST NORM ( NORM,AVERAGE_INPUT ) RETURNS ( DIFFERENCE )
%SEGMENT DISTRIBUTE OUTPUT ( DIFFERENCE ) RETURNS ( NEW_FACTOR )
COMPUTE NEW CORRECTION FACTOR ( DIFFERENCE ) RETURNS ( NEW_FACTOR )
COMPARE NEW & OLD CORRECTION FACTORS ( NEW_FACTOR,OLD_FACTOR ) RETURNS( SHUTDOWN )
OUTPUT NEW FACTOR ( NEW_FACTOR )
SIGNAL DIVERGENCE ( SHUTDOWN )
%SEGMENT RECOMPUTE NORM ( NEW_FACTOR ) RETURNS ( NORM )
AVERAGE VALUES ( NORM_1,...,NORM_5 ) RETURNS ( AVERAGE_NORM )
%SEGMENT COLLECT 5 VALUES ( ) RETURNS ( INPUT_1,...,INPUT_5 )
%SEGMENT COMPUTE NEW CORRECTION FACTOR ( DIFFFERENCE ) RETURNS ( NEW_FACTOR )
%S COMPARE NEW & OLD CORRECTION FACTORS( NEW_FACTOR,OLD_FACTOR ) RETURNS( SHUTDOWN )
%SEGMENT OUTPUT NEW FACTOR ( NEW_FACTOR )
%SEGMENT SIGNAL DIVERGENCE ( SHUTDOWN )
%SEGMENT AVERAGE VALUES ( IN_1,...,IN_5 ) RETURNS ( AVG )
%END
```

Figure 4-9.

PDL Statements Representing the Structure

Of the Design Shown in Figure 4-8

o   There are several control flow keywords in PDL to facilitate use of structured programming constructs. These fall into three groups — IF, DO, and RETURN — and are illustrated in Figure 4-10.

o   A label on a statement is an identifier followed by a colon.

o   A comment is any statement whose first non-blank character is a left parenthesis or a period.

Figure 4-11 uses these special PDL statements and constructs to add more detail to the PDL statements in Figure 4-9. Thus Figure 4-11 shows the PDL statements that represent a more detailed design of the structure chart in Figure 4-8. Note the liberal use of English to specify the algorithms, the passing of parameters through lists following module names, and the data dictionary in a separate component.

The PDL processor takes the design specification expressed in the PDL language and prints a design specification document. The format of the document facilitates reading and cross-referencing, which simplifies

```
        IF condition $_1$
                statement $_{11}$
                statement $_{12}$

                        .
                        .
                        .
                statement $_{1n_1}$
        ELSEIF condition $_2$
                statement $_{21}$
                statement $_{22}$

                        .
                        .
                statement $_{2n_2}$

                .
                .
                .
        ELSE
                statement $_{m1}$
                statement $_{m2}$

                        .
                        .
                statement $_{mn_m}$
        ENDIF


        DO  selection or repetition criteria
                statement $_1$
                statement $_2$

                        .
                        .
                statement $_n$
        ENDO
                Notes: The keyword CYCLE in a DO group means
                        terminate the current iterative execution of
                        a DO loop and test to determine if another
                        iteration is to be performed.
                        The keyword UNDO terminates the
                        execution of a DO group, and transfers
                        control to the next statement after the
                        ENDO statement.

        RETURN  optional return values
```

Figure 4-10.
Control Flow Keywords in PDL
(PDL keywords are capitalized)

```
%TITLE FIGURE 4-11. SAMPLE PDL DOCUMENT
%TEXT DESIGN PURPOSE
THIS PDL DESIGN REPRESENTS A MORE DETAILED SPECIFICATION OF THE DESIGN
SHOWN IN FIGURE 4-8 FOR A MICROPROCESSOR-BASED PROCESS
CONTROL SYSTEM.  THIS PROCESS CONTROL SYSTEM READS FIVE
VALUES AND OUTPUTS A CORRECTION FACTOR.  IT SENDS A
SHUTDOWN SIGNAL IF THE INPUTS HAVE DIVERGED SIGNIFICANTLY
FROM THE NORM.
%DATA SYSTEM INPUT AND OUTPUT VARIABLES
.. DATA VARIABLES - ALL 16 BIT INTEGERS
     INPUT_1
     INPUT_2
     INPUT_3      .. 5 SAMPLED INPUT TEMPERATURES
     INPUT_4
     INPUT_5
     NEW_FACTOR  ..  THE ADJUSTMENT FACTOR THE SYSTEM OUTPUTS
%SEGMENT CONTROL THE PROCESS
NORM <- INITIAL_VALUE  .. INITIALIZE THE NOMINAL TEMPERATURE
DO THE FOLLOWING PROCESSES CONCURRENTLY AND REPEATEDLY
.. THE COMPLETION OF ONE PROCESS SIGNALS THE START OF THE NEXT
OBTAIN INPUT () RETURNS (AVERAGE_INPUT)
COMPARE INPUT AGAINST NORM (NORM,AVERAGE_INPUT) RETURNS (DIFFERENCE)
DISTRIBUTE OUTPUT (DIFFERENCE) RETURNS (NEW_FACTOR)
RECOMPUTE NORM (NEW_FACTOR) RETURNS (NORM)
ENDDO
%SEGMENT OBTAIN INPUT () RETURNS (AVERAGE_INPUT)
COLLECT 5 VALUES () RETURNS (INPUT_1,...,INPUT_5)
AVERAGE VALUES (INPUT_1,...,INPUT_5) RETURNS (AVERAGE_INPUT)
RETURN AVERAGE_INPUT
%S COMPARE INPUT AGAINST NORM (NORM,AVERAGE_INPUT) RETURNS (DIFFERENCE)
DIFFERENCE <- AVERAGE_INPUT - NORM
RETURN DIFFERENCE
%SEGMENT DISTRIBUTE OUTPUT (DIFFERENCE) RETURNS (NEW_FACTOR)
COMPUTE NEW CORRECTION FACTOR (DIFFERENCE) RETURNS (NEW_FACTOR)
IF THIS IS THE FIRST TIME THIS PROCESS IS CALLED
INITIALIZE OLD_FACTOR TO BE THE SAME AS NEW_FACTOR
ENDIF
COMPARE NEW & OLD CORRECTION FACTORS (NEW_FACTOR,OLD_FACTOR) RETURNS(SHUTDOWN)
IF NOT SHUTDOWN
OUTPUT NEW FACTOR (NEW_FACTOR)
OLD_FACTOR <- NEW_FACTOR
RETURN NEW_FACTOR
ELSE
SIGNAL DIVERGENCE (SHUTDOWN)
ENDIF

%SEGMENT RECOMPUTE NORM (NEW_FACTOR) RETURNS (NORM)
IF THIS PROCESS HAS NOT BEEN INVOKED 5 TIMES
STORE NEW_FACTOR IN THE NEXT NORM_# VARIABLE
ELSE
ADD NEW_FACTOR TO THE LIST OF NORM_# VARIABLES & DELETE OLDEST NORM_#
AVERAGE VALUES (NORM_1,...,NORM_5) RETURNS (AVERAGE_NORM)
NORM <- AVERAGE_NORM
RETURN NORM
ENDIF
%SEGMENT COLLECT 5 VALUES () RETURNS (INPUT_1,...,INPUT_5)
DO 5 TIMES
READ INPUT TEMPERATURE INTO NEXT INPUT_# VARIABLE
ENDDO
RETURN INPUT_1,...,INPUT_5
%SEGMENT COMPUTE NEW CORRECTION FACTOR (DIFFFERENCE) RETURNS (NEW_FACTOR)
NEW_FACTOR <- DIFFERENCE / 5
RETURN NEW_FACTOR
%S COMPARE NEW & OLD CORRECTION FACTORS(NEW_FACTOR,OLD_FACTOR) RETURNS(SHUTDOWN)
IF NEW_FACTOR/OLD_FACTOR IS > 1.2  OR  < .8
RETURN YES  .. THAT IS, SHUTDOWN BECAUSE THE PROCESS IS OUT OF CONTROL
ELSE
RETURN NO
ENDIF
%SEGMENT OUTPUT NEW FACTOR (NEW_FACTOR)
SEND NEW_FACTOR TO PROCESS CONTROLLER
RETURN
%SEGMENT SIGNAL DIVERGENCE (SHUTDOWN)
IF SHUTDOWN
SEND STOP SIGNAL TO PROCESS CONTROLLER
STOP
ELSE
RETURN
ENDIF
%SEGMENT AVERAGE VALUES (IN_1,...,IN_5) RETURNS (AVG)
AVG <- (IN_1 + ... + IN_5) / 5
RETURN AVG
%END
```

Figure 4-11.
PDL Statements Representing a More Detailed Specification
of the Design Shown in Figure 4-8

subsequent software development activities. Figure 4-12 shows the design specification document produced by the PDL processor for the PDL statements shown in Figure 4-11. Note that for brevity, Figures 4-11 and 4-12 omit much of the information described in Figures 2-2 and 2-3; for example, a more detailed design would replace page 6 in Figure 4-12 with Figure 4-2. As illustrated in Figure 4-12, the PDL document comprises several parts:

(1)   A cover page that provides titles and identification.

(2)   A table of contents that lists each segment title and the page on which the segment starts.

(3)   The body of the design, which consists of the flow segments, text segments, data segments, and external segments that constitute the design. Note that the PDL processor underlines keywords and indents the bodies of IF and DO blocks to facilitate reading. In addition, lines that refer to other flow segments list the page numbers on which the referenced segments appear. This facilitates cross-referencing in hierarchical design documents.

(4)   A list of segment reference trees, i.e., a list of segment names indented to show the hierarchical tree structure of the design. The tree described by this list should correspond to the structure chart for the software system being developed.

(5)   A data index that lists all data items in alphabetical order. For each data item, the PDL processor lists the page and line number of its definition (if it was explicitly defined), its type, the segments that reference the data item and the page number of those segments, and, for each referencing segment, the numbers of the lines that reference the data item.

(6)   A flow segment index that lists all flow segments and external segments in alphabetical order. As it does for data items, the PDL processor lists for each flow segment and external segment the location of its definition, its type, the segments that reference it, and their location.

While PDL is not a panacea and does not guarantee the development of high quality designs, it is a useful tool for documenting a design. In addition to presenting a design properly, a good microprocessor software engineer should employ sound design techniques in developing a design specification document.

```
                    PROGRAM DESIGN LANGUAGE PROCESSOR
                              6 OCT 86
                             PDL  04.00
```

```
THIS PDL PROCESSOR IS LEASED FROM CAINE, FARBER, AND GORDON, INC.
USE OF THIS PROGRAM BY UNAUTHORIZED PERSONS IS PROHIBITED.
```

Figure 4-12.
PDL Listing for the PDL Statements in Figure 4-11

```
XEROX CORP                              INPUT LISTING
PDL 04.00


 1   %TITLE FIGURE 4-12. SAMPLE PDL DOCUMENT

 2   %TEXT DESIGN PURPOSE
 3   THIS PDL DESIGN REPRESENTS A MORE DETAILED SPECIFICATION OF THE DESIGN
 4   SHOWN IN FIGURE 4-8 FOR A MICROPROCESSOR-BASED PROCESS
 5   CONTROL SYSTEM.  THIS PROCESS CONTROL SYSTEM READS FIVE
 6   VALUES AND OUTPUTS A CORRECTION FACTOR.  IT SENDS A
 7   SHUTDOWN SIGNAL IF THE INPUTS HAVE DIVERGED SIGNIFICANTLY
 8   FROM THE NORM.

 9   %DATA SYSTEM INPUT AND OUTPUT VARIABLES
10   .. DATA VARIABLES - ALL 16 BIT INTEGERS
11       INPUT_1
12       INPUT_2
13       INPUT_3      ..  5 SAMPLED INPUT TEMPERATURES
14       INPUT_4
15       INPUT_5
16       NEW_FACTOR  ..  THE ADJUSTMENT FACTOR THE SYSTEM OUTPUTS

17   %SEGMENT CONTROL THE PROCESS
18   NORM <- INITIAL_VALUE  ..  INITIALIZE THE NOMINAL TEMPERATURE
19   DO THE FOLLOWING PROCESSES CONCURRENTLY AND REPEATEDLY
20   .. THE COMPLETION OF ONE PROCESS SIGNALS THE START OF THE NEXT
21   OBTAIN INPUT ( ) RETURNS (AVERAGE_INPUT)
22   COMPARE INPUT AGAINST NORM (NORM,AVERAGE_INPUT) RETURNS (DIFFERENCE)
23   DISTRIBUTE OUTPUT (DIFFERENCE) RETURNS (NEW_FACTOR)
24   RECOMPUTE NORM (NEW_FACTOR) RETURNS (NORM)
25   ENDDO

26   %SEGMENT OBTAIN INPUT ( ) RETURNS (AVERAGE_INPUT)
27   COLLECT 5 VALUES ( ) RETURNS (INPUT_1,...,INPUT_5)
28   AVERAGE VALUES (INPUT_1,...,INPUT_5) RETURNS (AVERAGE_INPUT)
29   RETURN AVERAGE_INPUT

30   %S COMPARE INPUT AGAINST NORM (NORM,AVERAGE_INPUT) RETURNS (DIFFERENCE)
31   DIFFERENCE <- AVERAGE_INPUT - NORM
32   RETURN DIFFERENCE

33   %SEGMENT DISTRIBUTE OUTPUT (DIFFERENCE) RETURNS (NEW_FACTOR)
34   COMPUTE NEW CORRECTION FACTOR (DIFFERENCE) RETURNS (NEW_FACTOR)
35   IF THIS IS THE FIRST TIME THIS PROCESS IS CALLED
36   INITIALIZE OLD_FACTOR TO BE THE SAME AS NEW_FACTOR
37   ENDIF
38   COMPARE NEW & OLD CORRECTION FACTORS (NEW_FACTOR,OLD_FACTOR) RETURNS(SHUTDOWN)
39   IF NOT SHUTDOWN
40   OUTPUT NEW FACTOR (NEW_FACTOR)
41   OLD_FACTOR <- NEW_FACTOR
42   RETURN NEW_FACTOR
43   ELSE
44   SIGNAL DIVERGENCE (SHUTDOWN)
45   ENDIF
46   %SEGMENT RECOMPUTE NORM (NEW_FACTOR) RETURNS (NORM)
47   IF THIS PROCESS HAS NOT BEEN INVOKED 5 TIMES
48   STORE NEW_FACTOR IN THE NEXT NORM_# VARIABLE
49   ELSE
50   ADD NEW_FACTOR TO THE LIST OF NORM_# VARIABLES & DELETE OLDEST NORM_#
51   AVERAGE VALUES (NORM_1,...,NORM_5) RETURNS (AVERAGE_NORM)
52   NORM <- AVERAGE_NORM
53   RETURN NORM
54   ENDIF

55   %SEGMENT COLLECT 5 VALUES ( ) RETURNS (INPUT_1,...,INPUT_5)
56   DO 5 TIMES
57   READ INPUT TEMPERATURE INTO NEXT INPUT_# VARIABLE
58   ENDDO
59   RETURN INPUT_1,...,INPUT_5

60   %SEGMENT COMPUTE NEW CORRECTION FACTOR (DIFFFERENCE) RETURNS (NEW_FACTOR)
61   NEW_FACTOR <- DIFFERENCE / 5
62   RETURN NEW_FACTOR

63   %S COMPARE NEW & OLD CORRECTION FACTORS(NEW_FACTOR,OLD_FACTOR) RETURNS(SHUTDOWN)
64   IF NEW_FACTOR/OLD_FACTOR IS > 1.2  OR  < .8
65   RETURN YES  .. THAT IS, SHUTDOWN BECAUSE THE PROCESS IS OUT OF CONTROL
66   ELSE
67   RETURN NO
68   ENDIF

69   %SEGMENT OUTPUT NEW FACTOR (NEW_FACTOR)
70   SEND NEW_FACTOR TO PROCESS CONTROLLER
71   RETURN

72   %SEGMENT SIGNAL DIVERGENCE (SHUTDOWN)
73   IF SHUTDOWN
74   SEND STOP SIGNAL TO PROCESS CONTROLLER
75   STOP
76   ELSE
77   RETURN
78   ENDIF

79   %SEGMENT AVERAGE VALUES (IN_1,...,IN_5) RETURNS (AVG)
80   AVG <- (IN_1 + ... + IN_5) / 5
81   RETURN AVG

82   %END

NO ERRORS DETECTED
```

Listing of PDL statements input to PDL Processor

PDL Processor generates these numbers

Figure 4-12. (continued)
PDL Listing for the PDL Statements in Figure 4-11

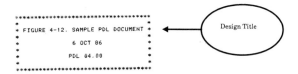

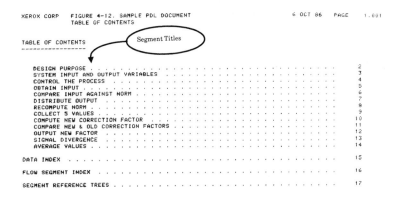

Figure 4-12. (continued)
PDL Listing for the PDL Statements in Figure 4-11

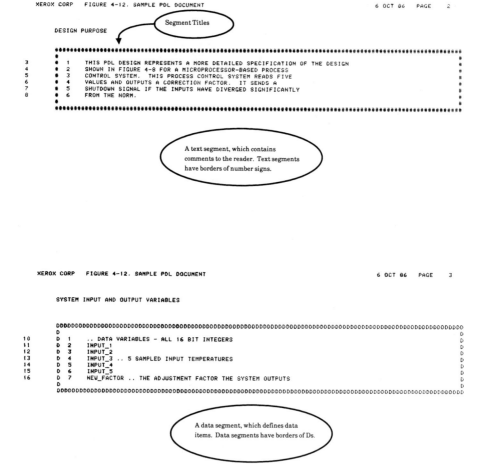

XEROX CORP   FIGURE 4-12. SAMPLE PDL DOCUMENT   6 OCT 86   PAGE   2

DESIGN PURPOSE   Segment Titles

```
•••••••••••••••••••••••••••••••••••••••••••••••••••••••••••••••••••••••••••••••••••••••••••••••••••••••••••••
3        •   1    THIS PDL DESIGN REPRESENTS A MORE DETAILED SPECIFICATION OF THE DESIGN           #
4        •   2    SHOWN IN FIGURE 4-8 FOR A MICROPROCESSOR-BASED PROCESS                            #
5        •   3    CONTROL SYSTEM.  THIS PROCESS CONTROL SYSTEM READS FIVE                           #
6        •   4    VALUES AND OUTPUTS A CORRECTION FACTOR.  IT SENDS A                               #
7        •   5    SHUTDOWN SIGNAL IF THE INPUTS HAVE DIVERGED SIGNIFICANTLY                         #
8        •   6    FROM THE NORM.                                                                    #
         •                                                                                         #
•••••••••••••••••••••••••••••••••••••••••••••••••••••••••••••••••••••••••••••••••••••••••••••••••••••••••••••
```

A text segment, which contains
comments to the reader. Text segments
have borders of number signs.

XEROX CORP   FIGURE 4-12. SAMPLE PDL DOCUMENT   6 OCT 86   PAGE   3

SYSTEM INPUT AND OUTPUT VARIABLES

```
DDDDDDDDDDDDDDDDDDDDDDDDDDDDDDDDDDDDDDDDDDDDDDDDDDDDDDDDDDDDDDDDDDDDDDDDDDDDDDDDDDDDDDDDDDDDDDDDDDDDDDDDD
         D                                                                                          D
10       D   1    .. DATA VARIABLES - ALL 16 BIT INTEGERS                                            D
11       D   2    INPUT_1                                                                            D
12       D   3    INPUT_2                                                                            D
13       D   4    INPUT_3 .. 5 SAMPLED INPUT TEMPERATURES                                            D
14       D   5    INPUT_4                                                                            D
15       D   6    INPUT_5                                                                            D
16       D   7    NEW_FACTOR .. THE ADJUSTMENT FACTOR THE SYSTEM OUTPUTS                             D
         D                                                                                          D
DDDDDDDDDDDDDDDDDDDDDDDDDDDDDDDDDDDDDDDDDDDDDDDDDDDDDDDDDDDDDDDDDDDDDDDDDDDDDDDDDDDDDDDDDDDDDDDDDDDDDDDDD
```

A data segment, which defines data
items. Data segments have borders of Ds.

Figure 4-12. (continued)
PDL Listing for the PDL Statements in Figure 4-11

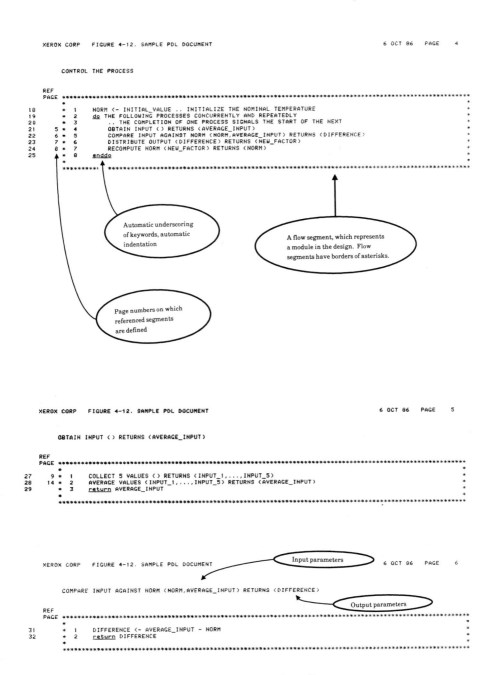

```
XEROX CORP    FIGURE 4-12. SAMPLE PDL DOCUMENT                          6 OCT 86    PAGE    4


        CONTROL THE PROCESS

     REF
     PAGE ***********************************************************************************************
          *                                                                                          *
18        *  1    NORM <- INITIAL_VALUE .. INITIALIZE THE NOMINAL TEMPERATURE                         *
19        *  2    do THE FOLLOWING PROCESSES CONCURRENTLY AND REPEATEDLY                              *
20        *  3       .. THE COMPLETION OF ONE PROCESS SIGNALS THE START OF THE NEXT                   *
21    5   *  4       OBTAIN INPUT ( ) RETURNS (AVERAGE_INPUT)                                         *
22    6   *  5       COMPARE INPUT AGAINST NORM (NORM,AVERAGE_INPUT) RETURNS (DIFFERENCE)             *
23    7   *  6       DISTRIBUTE OUTPUT (DIFFERENCE) RETURNS (NEW_FACTOR)                              *
24    8   *  7       RECOMPUTE NORM (NEW_FACTOR) RETURNS (NORM)                                       *
25        *  8    enddo                                                                              *
          *                                                                                          *
          **********************  ********************************************************************
```

Automatic underscoring
of keywords, automatic
indentation

A flow segment, which represents
a module in the design. Flow
segments have borders of asterisks.

Page numbers on which
referenced segments
are defined

```
XEROX CORP    FIGURE 4-12. SAMPLE PDL DOCUMENT                          6 OCT 86    PAGE    5


        OBTAIN INPUT ( ) RETURNS (AVERAGE_INPUT)

     REF
     PAGE ***********************************************************************************************
          *                                                                                          *
27    9   *  1    COLLECT 5 VALUES ( ) RETURNS (INPUT_1,...,INPUT_5)                                  *
28   14   *  2    AVERAGE VALUES (INPUT_1,...,INPUT_5) RETURNS (AVERAGE_INPUT)                        *
29        *  3    return AVERAGE_INPUT                                                               *
          *                                                                                          *
          ***********************************************************************************************
```

Input parameters

```
XEROX CORP    FIGURE 4-12. SAMPLE PDL DOCUMENT                          6 OCT 86    PAGE    6

        COMPARE INPUT AGAINST NORM (NORM,AVERAGE_INPUT) RETURNS (DIFFERENCE)
```

Output parameters

```
     REF
     PAGE ***********************************************************************************************
          *                                                                                          *
31        *  1    DIFFERENCE <- AVERAGE_INPUT - NORM                                                 *
32        *  2    return DIFFERENCE                                                                  *
          *                                                                                          *
          ***********************************************************************************************
```

Figure 4-12. (continued)
PDL Listing for the PDL Statements in Figure 4-11

```
XEROX CORP    FIGURE 4-12. SAMPLE PDL DOCUMENT                          6 OCT 86   PAGE   7


        DISTRIBUTE OUTPUT (DIFFERENCE) RETURNS (NEW_FACTOR)


     REF
     PAGE *********************************************************************************************
            *                                                                                        *
  34   10 *  1    COMPUTE NEW CORRECTION FACTOR (DIFFERENCE) RETURNS (NEW_FACTOR)                     *
  35      *  2    if THIS IS THE FIRST TIME THIS PROCESS IS CALLED                                    *
  36      *  3        INITIALIZE OLD_FACTOR TO BE THE SAME AS NEW_FACTOR                              *
  37      *  4    endif                                                                               *
  38   11 *  5    COMPARE NEW & OLD CORRECTION FACTORS (NEW_FACTOR,OLD_FACTOR) RETURNS(SHUTDOWN)      *
  39      *  6    if NOT SHUTDOWN                                                                      *
  40   12 *  7        OUTPUT NEW FACTOR (NEW_FACTOR)                                                  *
  41      *  8        OLD_FACTOR <- NEW_FACTOR                                                        *
  42      *  9        return NEW_FACTOR                                                               *
  43      * 10    else                                                                                *
  44   13 * 11        SIGNAL DIVERGENCE (SHUTDOWN)                                                    *
  45      * 12    endif                                                                               *
            *                                                                                        *
            *********************************************************************************************
```

```
XEROX CORP    FIGURE 4-12. SAMPLE PDL DOCUMENT                          6 OCT 86   PAGE   8


        RECOMPUTE NORM (NEW_FACTOR) RETURNS (NORM)


     REF
     PAGE *********************************************************************************************
            *                                                                                        *
  47      *  1    if THIS PROCESS HAS NOT BEEN INVOKED 5 TIMES                                        *
  48      *  2        STORE NEW_FACTOR IN THE NEXT NORM_# VARIABLE                                    *
  49      *  3    else                                                                                *
  50      *  4        ADD NEW_FACTOR TO THE LIST OF NORM_# VARIABLES & DELETE OLDEST NORM_#           *
  51   14 *  5    AVERAGE VALUES (NORM_1,...,NORM_5) RETURNS (AVERAGE_NORM)                           *
  52      *  6    NORM <- AVERAGE_NORM                                                                *
  53      *  7        return NORM                                                                     *
  54      *  8    endif                                                                               *
            *                                                                                        *
            *********************************************************************************************
```

```
XEROX CORP    FIGURE 4-12. SAMPLE PDL DOCUMENT                          6 OCT 86   PAGE   9


        COLLECT 5 VALUES ( ) RETURNS (INPUT_1,...,INPUT_5)


     REF
     PAGE *********************************************************************************************
            *                                                                                        *
  56      *  1    do 5 TIMES                                                                          *
  57      *  2        READ INPUT TEMPERATURE INTO NEXT INPUT_# VARIABLE                              *
  58      *  3    enddo                                                                               *
  59      *  4    return INPUT_1,...,INPUT_5                                                          *
            *                                                                                        *
            *********************************************************************************************
```

```
XEROX CORP    FIGURE 4-12. SAMPLE PDL DOCUMENT                          6 OCT 86   PAGE   10


        COMPUTE NEW CORRECTION FACTOR (DIFFFERENCE) RETURNS (NEW_FACTOR)


     REF
     PAGE *********************************************************************************************
            *                                                                                        *
  61      *  1    NEW_FACTOR <- DIFFERENCE / 5                                                        *
  62      *  2    return NEW_FACTOR                                                                   *
            *                                                                                        *
            *********************************************************************************************
```

Figure 4-12. (continued)
PDL Listing for the PDL Statements in Figure 4-11

```
XEROX CORP    FIGURE 4-12. SAMPLE PDL DOCUMENT                            6 OCT 86    PAGE   11


       COMPARE NEW & OLD CORRECTION FACTORS(NEW_FACTOR,OLD_FACTOR) RETURNS(SHUTDOWN)


   REF
   PAGE  **********************************************************************************************
         *                                                                                          *
64       *   1    if NEW_FACTOR/OLD_FACTOR IS > 1.2 OR < .8                                          *
65       *   2        return YES .. THAT IS, SHUTDOWN BECAUSE THE PROCESS IS OUT OF CONTROL          *
66       *   3    else                                                                               *
67       *   4        return NO                                                                      *
68       *   5    endif                                                                              *
         *                                                                                          *
         **********************************************************************************************
```

```
XEROX CORP    FIGURE 4-12. SAMPLE PDL DOCUMENT                            6 OCT 86    PAGE   12


       OUTPUT NEW FACTOR (NEW_FACTOR)


   REF
   PAGE  **********************************************************************************************
         *                                                                                          *
70       *   1    SEND NEW_FACTOR TO PROCESS CONTROLLER                                              *
71       *   2    return                                                                            *
         *                                                                                          *
         **********************************************************************************************
```

```
XEROX CORP    FIGURE 4-12. SAMPLE PDL DOCUMENT                            6 OCT 86    PAGE   13


       SIGNAL DIVERGENCE (SHUTDOWN)


   REF
   PAGE  **********************************************************************************************
         *                                                                                          *
73       *   1    if SHUTDOWN                                                                        *
74       *   2        SEND STOP SIGNAL TO PROCESS CONTROLLER                                         *
75       *   3        STOP                                                                           *
76       *   4    else                                                                               *
77       *   5        return                                                                        *
78       *   6    endif                                                                              *
         *                                                                                          *
         **********************************************************************************************
```

```
XEROX CORP    FIGURE 4-12. SAMPLE PDL DOCUMENT                            6 OCT 86    PAGE   14


       AVERAGE VALUES (IN_1,...,IN_5) RETURNS (AVG)


   REF
   PAGE  **********************************************************************************************
         *                                                                                          *
80       *   1    AVG <- (IN_1 + ... + IN_5) / 5                                                     *
81       *   2    return AVG                                                                         *
         *                                                                                          *
         **********************************************************************************************
```

Figure 4-12. (continued)
PDL Listing for the PDL Statements in Figure 4-11

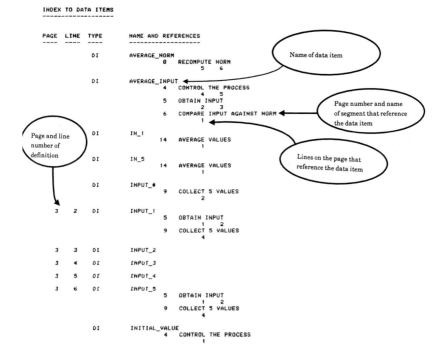

Figure 4-12. (continued)
PDL Listing for the PDL Statements in Figure 4-11

```
XEROX CORP    FIGURE 4-12. SAMPLE PDL DOCUMENT                              6 OCT 86    PAGE   15.002
              INDEX TO DATA ITEMS


INDEX TO DATA ITEMS
-------------------


PAGE  LINE  TYPE     NAME AND REFERENCES
----  ----  ----     -------------------

            DI       NORM_0
                          8    RECOMPUTE NORM
                                    2    4    4
            DI       NORM_1
                          8    RECOMPUTE NORM
                                    5
            DI       NORM_5
                          8    RECOMPUTE NORM
                                    5
  3    7    DI       NEW_FACTOR
                          4    CONTROL THE PROCESS
                                    6    7
                          7    DISTRIBUTE OUTPUT
                                    1    3    5    7    8    9
                          8    RECOMPUTE NORM
                                    2    4
                         10    COMPUTE NEW CORRECTION FACTOR
                                    1    2
                         11    COMPARE NEW & OLD CORRECTION FACTORS
                                    1
                         12    OUTPUT NEW FACTOR
                                    1

            DI       OLD_FACTOR
                          7    DISTRIBUTE OUTPUT
                                    3    5    8
                         11    COMPARE NEW & OLD CORRECTION FACTORS
                                    1
```

Figure 4-12. (continued)
PDL Listing for the PDL Statements in Figure 4-11

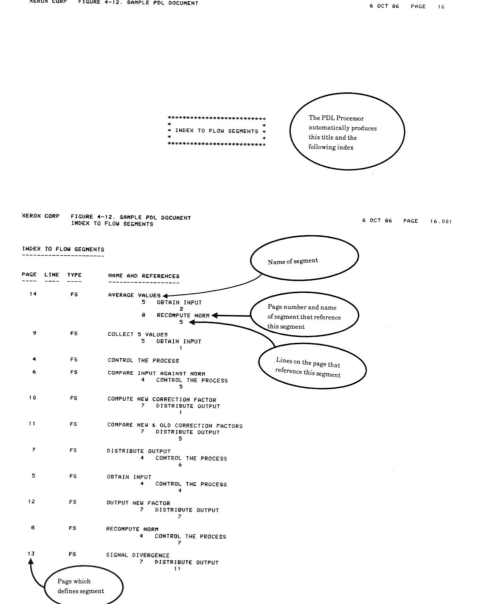

Figure 4-12. (continued)
PDL Listing for the PDL Statements in Figure 4-11

XEROX CORP   FIGURE 4-12. SAMPLE PDL DOCUMENT   6 OCT 86   PAGE   17

```
****************************
*                          *
*  SEGMENT REFERENCE TREES  *
*                          *
****************************
```

The PDL Processor automatically produces this title and the following reference tree

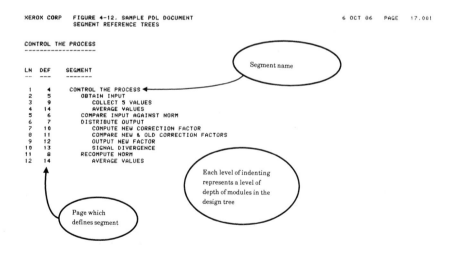

XEROX CORP   FIGURE 4-12. SAMPLE PDL DOCUMENT   6 OCT 86   PAGE   17.001
             SEGMENT REFERENCE TREES

CONTROL THE PROCESS

```
LN  DEF   SEGMENT
--  ---   -------
 1   4    CONTROL THE PROCESS
 2   5      OBTAIN INPUT
 3   9        COLLECT 5 VALUES
 4  14        AVERAGE VALUES
 5   6      COMPARE INPUT AGAINST NORM
 6   7      DISTRIBUTE OUTPUT
 7  10        COMPUTE NEW CORRECTION FACTOR
 8  11        COMPARE NEW & OLD CORRECTION FACTORS
 9  12        OUTPUT NEW FACTOR
10  13        SIGNAL DIVERGENCE
11   8      RECOMPUTE NORM
12  14        AVERAGE VALUES
```

Segment name

Each level of indenting represents a level of depth of modules in the design tree

Page which defines segment

Figure 4-12. (continued)
PDL Listing for the PDL Statements in Figure 4-11

```
*******************************
*                             *
*  END OF DESIGN DOCUMENT  *
*                             *
*******************************
```

```
PDL RUN TIME STATISTICS:
     82 INPUT CARDS PROCESSED
     11 FLOW SEGMENTS
   9102 WORDS OF STORAGE IN  70 PAGES AVAILABLE,  12.57 PERCENT USED
   7958 WORDS UNUSED
      0 PAGE I/O'S;         0 PAGE FAULTS IN     1491 PAGER ACCESS REQUESTS
```

Figure 4-12. (continued)
PDL Listing for the PDL Statements in Figure 4-11

5

DESIGN TECHNIQUES
FOR MICROPROCESSOR SOFTWARE

5.1 Introduction

In recent years, several people have developed techniques for guiding one through the design process to result in the production of design documentation from which coding can be done. While the techniques vary in applicability, most are oriented toward data processing environments, and there has been little analytical pursuit of theories applicable to microprocessor-based systems, especially real-time microprocessor-based systems. Accordingly, the approach we use in developing the design for a microprocessor software system adapts and extends the traditional design approaches.

To introduce the techniques to use in producing a design document, consider the two basic steps that constitute the design process:

(1) Design analysis. From studying the requirements of the microprocessor system, one produces a model of the system behavior and documents it with a data flow diagram (DFD) or finite state machine (FSM).

(2) Design synthesis. In the first phase of design synthesis, called the high level design phase, one transforms the DFD or FSM model of the system into the structure chart or hierarchy chart which represents the logical structure of how the software will work. This transformation is accomplished by a partitioning of function and information using techniques that are the key fundamentals in the design activity. In the second phase of design synthesis, called

detailed design, one transforms the logical structure produced earlier into the physical structure of the final program and documents it using PDL.

Recall that the goal of the design activity is a clear document which describes the structure of a software system (i.e., what its component modules are), the interfaces between modules, the data items used in modules, the functions of modules, and the algorithms that implement functions.

5.2 Design Analysis

The first step in the design process is

Analyze the system behavior by modeling it
with a data flow diagram or a finite state machine.

As a general guideline, the finite state machine model is more applicable to real-time microprocessor systems, and the data flow diagram is more applicable to nonreal-time systems that resemble traditional data processing systems. The reason for these associations is that the finite state machine easily represents the stimulus/response characteristics of real-time systems involving simple data items (such as the signals described in the furnace example in Chapter 4), while the data flow diagram easily represents the more complex data flows of traditional data processing systems.

5.2.1 Analysis Using the Finite State Machine

A finite state machine consists of a set of states with a designated initial state and a set of transitions among states. A transition occurs when control passes from one state to another. A transition is triggered by an input; a transition may also generate an output.

To develop an FSM model of a system:
(1)   List all the possible system inputs.
(2)   List all the system outputs.
(3)   Determine the sequence of inputs that
       generate each output.
(4)   From the sequence determine states.

Although steps 1 and 2 of the process seem trivial, they are the most important steps in the process. The lack of a complete and well-defined list of system inputs and outputs is the most common reason for redoing design and implementation in microprocessor-based software systems. "Complete" means that all the possible inputs and outputs are known. "Well defined" means that the structure and values of each input and output are known and show consistency as a group. For the FSM in Figure 4-4 the inputs are digits, arithmetic operations, and the equal sign. These might be represented by some assignment of four-bit numbers. The outputs are digit displays represented as seven segment displays where each segment may be on or off.

In step 3 one considers all possible sequences of inputs and outputs that occur as a result of these sequences. The set of all sequences of inputs (which may be infinite) can usually be broken down into a small number of cases. For example, in Figure 4-4, the ten digits and four arithmetic operations have been grouped into two classes to reduce the number of possible sequences. It is important to consider all sequences; failure to handle a particular input sequence is a common design error. Having considered all inputs, one should check to see that all outputs are generated by at least one input sequence. The situation where an output that was previously listed does not occur as a result of some input sequence indicates an inconsistency in the requirements specification. This situation should be immediately remedied, and the design progress to the current point reviewed for possible implications of the changes. One should also handle special cases that may occur in microprocessor systems, for example, the simultaneous occurrence of two inputs. In our calculator example assume that two inputs cannot occur simultaneously, that the hardware busses a single valid four-bit value to a data register.

In step 4 one determines the states along with the transitions to produce a diagram like Figure 4-4. On the first pass one should ignore trivial errors so as not to divert attention to the principal function. A trivial error (in the sense that its occurrence is corrected by a simple system abort) in this calculator example would be a display overflow.

5.2.2 Analysis Using the Data Flow Diagram

A data flow diagram consists of the four basic elements shown in Figure 4-3: data flows, processes, sources and destinations of data, and data stores.

> *To develop a DFD model of a system:*
> (1) *List all the possible system inputs. These are the input data flows.*
> (2) *List all the system outputs. These are the output data flows.*
> (3) *Fill in the DFD body — adding processes, sources and destinations of data, data stores, and internal data flows — by working from inputs to outputs, or from outputs to inputs.*
> (4) *Label the process bubbles in terms of inputs and outputs.*

Steps 1 and 2 in drawing a DFD are like steps 1 and 2 in drawing an FSM; however, on the first cut in drawing a DFD it may not be necessary to specify the sources of the inputs or the destinations of the outputs. In drawing a DFD it is frequently the case that the data are structures; in this case make sure that the structures are completely defined.

The key step in drawing a DFD is step 3 — filling in the DFD body. One way to proceed is to work from inputs to outputs, that is, to determine what inputs are needed to generate each output. The generation of each output may require several steps, where the first step takes one or more inputs and transforms (or processes) them into an internal data flow or an output data flow. Subsequent steps take one or more inputs and internal data flows and transform them into other internal data flows or output data flows. By proceeding from input data flows at the left side of the diagram through several transformations, output data flows will be reached at the right side of the DFD. Figure 5-1 illustrates this process.

Another way to proceed in filling in the DFD body is to work backward from the output data flows to the input data flows. This is similar to the forward process but is guided by the knowledge of the inputs required for each process bubble to produce the output of the process bubble.

In filling in the body of a DFD one should also indicate data sources and destinations and data stores. Typical data destinations are microprocessor memory locations indicated by variable names, as shown in the example of Figure 4-4.

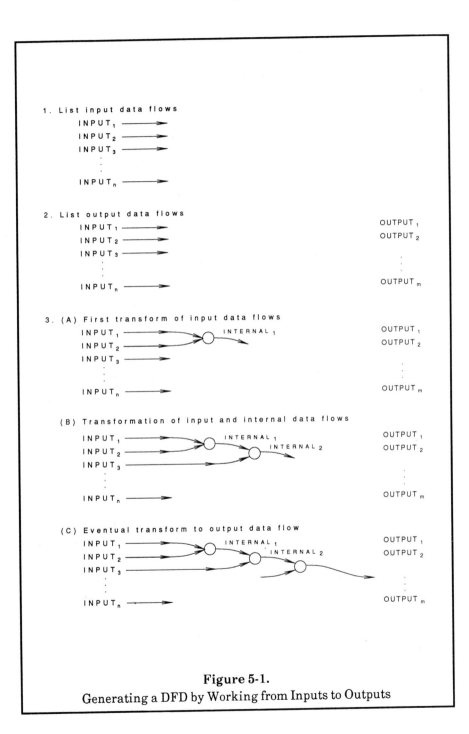

Figure 5-1.
Generating a DFD by Working from Inputs to Outputs

The final step is the labeling of the process bubbles. The general guideline is that process names consist of two words:

(1)   The first word is an imperative transitive verb.

(2)   The second word is the direct object of the verb.

For example, the process names in Figure 4-4 are "Validate Digits" and "Compute Result." An additional guideline to follow in naming processes is to avoid nebulous words such as "process" and "handle." The temptation to use such words usually indicates a process that is not well defined because there are too many inputs and outputs. In this case, break the process up into a set of transformations.

5.2.3 Analysis in Perspective

The purpose of the first version of an FSM or DFD is to describe in rough form the basic operation of the microprocessor system. With this in mind the initial development of an FSM or DFD can be simplified by deferring certain details. The first of these is the initiation and termination of the microprocessor programming system, which should be deferred when they have little or no effect on the steady state system. The temperature monitoring process control system cited earlier exemplifies this situation. Another type of detail which should be deferred is the processing of trivial errors. Trivial errors are those whose occurrence does not have a major impact on system operation. An example of a trivial error is the entering of an invalid character which the system is to ignore; an example of a nontrivial error is a process going out of control which requires a total system shutdown.

When a system is large it is desirable to develop a hierarchical DFD. The top level in a hierarchical DFD is a single diagram called the Context Diagram, which consists of the input data flows, a single process bubble, and the system output data flows. The next diagram, called Diagram 0, shows the same input and output data flows but partitions the process of the Context Diagram into several processes (bubbles) and the internal data flows among them, as shown in Figure 5-2. This partitioning and drawing of new diagrams should continue until each process performs a primitive function that can be easily understood. Note from Figure 5-2 that

o   Partitioned processes have the same input data flows and output data flows as the process they constitute.

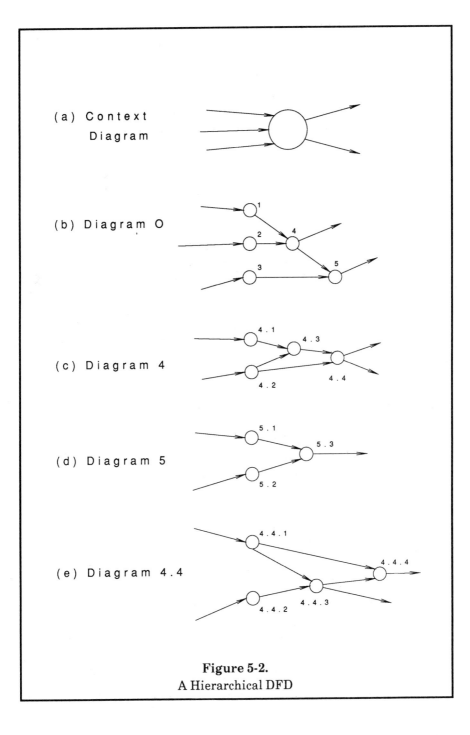

(a) C o n t e x t
      D i a g r a m

(b) D i a g r a m O

(c) D i a g r a m 4

(d) D i a g r a m 5

(e) D i a g r a m 4 . 4

Figure 5-2.
A Hierarchical DFD

o   The numbering of processes proceeds as follows:

(1) Number the process bubbles in Diagram 0 sequentially starting with number one.

(2) Number each subsequent diagram with the number of the process it partitions at the next higher level.

(3) Number each process in these new diagrams with the diagram number, followed by a period, followed by the number of the process bubble in that diagram.

With this convention, the level number of a diagram is one more than the number of periods in the numbers assigned to its process bubbles. Figure 5-2 illustrates these concepts.

While the first version of the FSM or DFD describes the basic operation of the microprocessor system in rough form, the final version must describe the operation of the system exactly. Before proceeding to design synthesis, then, it is necessary to ensure the correspondence between the FSM or DFD and the requirements specification.

5.3 Design Synthesis − High Level Design

5.3.1 The High Level Design Process

The second step in the design process is

> *Transform the DFD or FSM model of the system behavior*
> *into a structure chart or hierarchy chart*
> *which represents the logical structure*
> *of how the software will work.*

To transform a DFD or FSM into a hierarchy chart or structure chart one partitions its information and expands it in a hierarchical way. The first step in drawing a structure chart is

> *Draw a single box (process module)*
> o *whose inputs are the input data flows of the DFD*
>   *or FSM*
> o *whose outputs are the output data flows of the DFD*
>   *or FSM, and*
> o *whose name is a verb-object pair that describes the*
>   *function of the microprocessor software system*

Successive steps in drawing a structure chart follow this procedure:

(1) *Partition the process described in a box into subprocesses, so that each subprocess performs a subset of the functions performed by the parent process in the DFD or FSM.*

(2) *Draw a box for each subprocess on a horizontal line below the parent box and give it a verb-object name.*

(3) *Assign each of the inputs and outputs from the parent process to the appropriate subprocesses, and create intermediate input/output data items as required, using the notation of Figure 4-7.*

(4) *For each subprocess, expand the information about the processing function or data specification if required before proceeding to the next step.*

This process of hierarchical decomposition of function, top down expansion, and stepwise refinement should be continued until

o The functions of the modules in the structure chart effect all the requirements described in the requirements document.

o The implementation of each module in the structure chart can be described succinctly, e.g., in one to two pages of PDL.

In this process of developing a structure chart, one should decompose not only the functions but also the data. Thus, at each step the data structures that serve as input to or output from a module may be decomposed and assigned to particular sub-modules. This decomposition and allocation will later be recorded in PDL and cross-referenced in the PDL listing to form part of a data dictionary. The collection of information that forms a data dictionary will be referenced frequently during the design process:

o The structure of the data

o The representation in the microprocessor system (bit, byte, etc.)

o The range of legal values for the data items

o The modules that reference the data items

In many microprocessor systems, especially real-time systems, the data have an elementary structure that correspond directly to input/output signals so that they need not be decomposed.

The key step in the high level design process is the partitioning of a process into subprocesses. The technique used in performing the partitioning is the key factor in determining the quality of the final design. While partitioning may follow the ad hoc partitioning used to create a hierarchical DFD, there are two well-known strategies for performing the partitioning in the design process.

Use transform analysis (or transform centered design) and transaction analysis (or transaction centered design) in partitioning.

5.3.2 Transform Analysis

The fundamental concepts in transform analysis are the identification of a central transform (process) and the use of the central transform in building a structure chart. "The central transform is the portion of the DFD that contains the essential functions of the system and is independent of the particular implementation of the input and output."[1] A useful technique in finding the central transform is to identify the fundamental process in the DFD by pruning off its input- and output-related data flows. This may be accomplished by following three steps:

(1)   Follow each input data flow from its origin toward the middle of the DFD. The data flows may be modified in minor ways by various process bubbles, but continue to follow them to the point where they are significantly transformed by a process. Mark the data flow inputs where the significant transformation occurs.

(2)   Follow each output data flow inward from its exit point in the DFD toward the middle of the DFD. The data flows may be modified in minor ways by various process bubbles, but continue to follow them to the point where they first appear as recognizable data flows related to the ultimate output data flows. Mark these points on the data flow where the ultimate output has just been produced, but not yet formatted.

(3)   Join the marks on the data flows together by drawing a line connecting them. This will result in a curve enclosing some part of the DFD. The enclosed part is the prime candidate for the central transform.

[1]Meilir Page-Jones, The Practical Guide to Structured Systems Design (New York: Yourdon Press, 1980), p. 183.

For example, it is easy to identify the central transform in the DFD in Figure 4-4 using these three steps. Having identified the central transform, partition the processes into a hierarchy with one superior process (or function) and several subordinate processes (or functions). The relationship between the levels may be considered to be one of the boss and the workers. The superior process is one that performs all the functions of the subordinate processes, but accomplishes this through delegation to subordinates. The subordinates fall into three groups:

o   The processes of the central transform

o   The processes providing input to the central transform

o   The processes that transform output from the central transform

The latter two groups can often be factored into manageable processes by considering as a group those processes which result in a data flow entering or leaving the central transform. Figure 5-3 shows a DFD and the first two levels of the corresponding structure chart resulting from the application of transform analysis. The remaining levels of the structure chart should be generated by applying the process described earlier assisted by transform analysis.

5.3.3 Transaction Analysis

The second technique used to aid the partitioning process is transaction analysis. A transaction in this context is an input to a system that initiates the performance of a function. Many microprocessor-based systems are actually transaction processing systems, and thus are suitable for partitioning using transaction analysis. For example, real-time microprocessor systems often react to inputs that occur with some variability. Another example of a transaction-based system is an interactive system which has a fixed set of valid commands. The fundamental concepts in transaction analysis are the identification of a transaction center in the DFD, the identification of subsequent transaction processing bubbles, and the use of these in building a structure chart. As shown in Figure 5-4, a process bubble in a DFD which receives an input data flow and selects a subsequent process based on the input type is a transaction center. The subsequent process bubbles which manipulate the input data are the transaction processes. Constructing a structure chart from such a DFD follows these steps (see Figure 5-4 for results of the process):

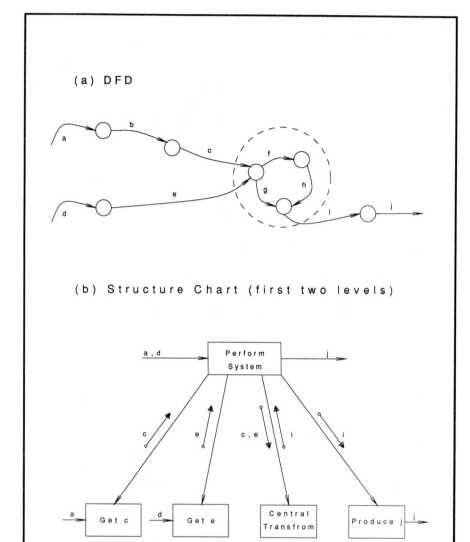

Figure 5-3.
Building a Structure Chart from a DFD
Using Transform Analysis

Based on Meilir Page-Jones, <u>The Practical Guide to Structured Systems</u>
<u>Design</u> (New York: Yourdon Press, 1980), pp. 192-194.

(1)   Select the superior process in the structure chart to correspond to the transaction center.

(2)   Select the subordinate processes in the structure chart to correspond to the transaction processes.

(3)   Build remaining parts of the structure chart by applying transform and transaction analysis to the remaining parts of the DFD.

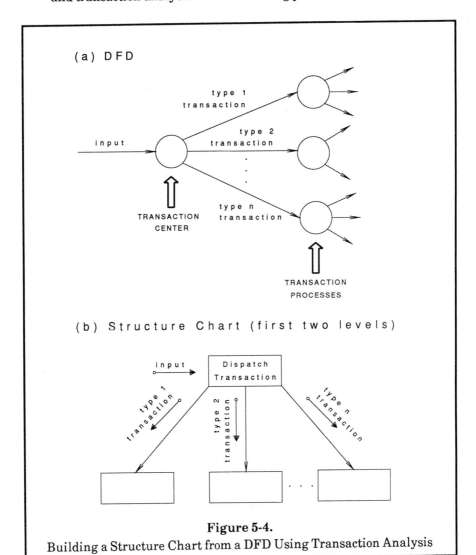

Figure 5-4.
Building a Structure Chart from a DFD Using Transaction Analysis

It is often the case that there is similarity of function among the various transaction processes. Even if this is the case, as a general rule one should not combine data flows as this would defeat the goal of partitioning the system clearly. It is, however, suitable for different transaction processes in the structure chart to reference common subordinate processes when this occurs naturally.

While transform analysis and transaction analysis are techniques that aid in the partitioning process, they do not guarantee a good design. It is useful to keep in mind the characteristics of a good design when developing a structure chart, and to use these characteristics to refine the techniques discussed previously. The remaining paragraphs of this section describe four important design characteristics: coupling between modules, cohesion within modules, module fan-out, and module fan-in.

5.3.4 Coupling

Coupling between modules deals with the relationships between modules in a structure chart and ultimately in the resulting program. More specifically, coupling is the degree of interdependence between modules. The rule to follow on this subject is

Minimize coupling between modules.

Minimal coupling is desirable for two reasons:

o   Low interdependence between modules makes it easier to isolate problems as they are more likely to be contained within a module rather than coexist within two modules or their interface.

o   Low interdependence between modules simplifies changes because changes are more likely to affect only one module or just a small number of modules.

The basic types of coupling[2] ordered from best (minimal coupling) to worst (maximal coupling) are

o   Data coupling

o   Stamp coupling

o   Control coupling

o   Common coupling

o   Content coupling

Two modules are <u>data coupled</u> if they communicate solely by passing parameters, and if each parameter is data information (not control information) that is either an individual data item or a table (array) each of whose elements are individual data items. Two modules are <u>stamp coupled</u> if this latter condition is relaxed to include parameters that have nonhomogeneous structures such as records that have several different data fields. An example of such a record is an employee data record which might contain

o   Employee's name (character data)

o   Employee's pay (a decimal number)

o   Employee's age (an integer)

o   Employee's dependents (list of character strings)

Stamp coupling is less desirable than data coupling because it dictates a fixed parameter structure which may limit its applicability in other situations. Two modules are <u>control coupled</u> if they communicate solely by passing parameters, yet one or more of the parameters are control items which control the logic of one of the modules. Common examples of control items are data switches and flags. Control coupling is undesirable because it implies that one module assumes knowledge of the internal flow of another module. Two modules are <u>common coupled</u> if they reference the same global data structure or item. Using common coupling makes programs difficult to understand because it may not be obvious which modules reference specific global data items and because it may not be obvious which data items are referenced by a specific module. Two modules are <u>content coupled</u> if one module refers directly to something contained in the other module, such as a data item, a statement label, or a statement

[2]Based on Page-Jones, <u>op</u>. <u>cit</u>., which explores these concepts in detail.

itself. Such direct control explicitly intertwines two modules and violates the basic precepts of structured design.

5.3.5 Cohesion

Cohesion is the degree of association of the functions which constitute a module. The general rule is to

Maximize cohesion within modules.

Strong cohesion within modules is desirable for three reasons:

o   Concentrating related functions together makes the system easier to understand than if the functions are distributed among modules.

o   Concentrating related functions together within modules reduces unnecessary intermodule references, an important consideration in the real-time performance of microprocessor systems.

o   Modules that perform complete, well-defined functions are more suitable for reuse in other systems.

Furthermore, cohesion goes hand-in-hand with coupling — a system with good cohesion within modules can exhibit good coupling between modules. The basic types of cohesion[3] ordered from best (maximal cohesion) to worst (minimal cohesion), are the following:

o   Functional cohesion

o   Sequential cohesion

o   Communicational cohesion

o   Procedural cohesion

o   Temporal cohesion

o   Logical cohesion

o   Coincidental cohesion

A module is <u>functionally cohesive</u> if it performs a single complete function that was well-defined in the requirements specification. A useful test to apply when designing a system is to try to name each module as a single inclusive verb-object pair. If you can do this for a module, then the module

[3]Based on Page-Jones, <u>op</u>. <u>cit</u>., which explores these concepts in detail.

is likely to display functional cohesion. An additional goal is for each direct object in the module names to be a single data structure, and for each data structure to be referenced only once in the collection of module names. In this situation, not only functions but also data structures are localized within modules. This is the fundamental concept of information hiding which can further improve the understandability and reusability of modules. A module exhibits sequential cohesion if it

o   Performs functions in a sequence predetermined by the requirements specification and

o   The output data for each function is the input for the next function

Sequential cohesion, while occurring naturally in many applications, is less desirable than functional cohesion because the sequence of functions limits reusability. In communicational cohesion a module's functions use the same input or output data. It differs from sequential cohesion in that the order of performing the functions is unimportant. A module exhibits procedural cohesion if it performs functions in a sequence predetermined by the requirements specification, yet the functions may otherwise be unrelated. A module with temporal cohesion performs functions that are related in time; the classical example is the initialization routine in business data processing. Procedural and temporal cohesion are significantly less desirable than the previous types of cohesion because the functions in these modules are less likely to be related. A logically cohesive module performs a set of related functions, however, it performs only one function at each invocation as selected from the calling module. The problem with a logically cohesive module is that it forces a single common interface for multiple functions. A module with coincidental cohesion is composed of functions which have no relationship to one another. Logical and coincidental cohesion are the least desirable because the calling module needs detailed knowledge of the logic of the module with such little cohesion.

5.3.6 Fan-Out and Fan-In

The fan-out from a module is the number of different modules it calls directly, i.e., the number of immediately subordinate modules in the structure chart. For example, the module named "Control the Process" in Figure 4-8 has a fan-out of four. The general rule to follow on this subject is

Limit module fan-out to seven or less.

A module whose fan-out is more than seven is likely to be responsible for too many functions to comprehend readily; such a module should be factored into two or more modules. On the other hand, a module with a fan-out of one or two may be the result of needlessly creating modules.

The fan-in to a module is the number of different modules that reference it directly, i.e., the number of immediately superior modules in the structure chart. For example, the module named "Average Values" in Figure 4-8 has a fan-in of two. In some microprocessor systems high fan-in is desirable because it can reduce the amount of code required to implement a system. While such code reduction is desirable, the desire to increase fan-in should be tempered by the following observations:

o   If a module with high fan-in executes as an independent process in a real time system, other processes may have to wait for it to perform a function for them. This can degrade the performance of the real-time system.

o   It is easy to fall into the trap of making minor changes to a module to increase its fan-in. Such changes may degrade the cohesion of the module and cause the passing of different parameters to it; both of these circumstances should generally be avoided even at the expense of more modules in the system.

5.4 Design Synthesis – Detailed Design

5.4.1 The Detailed Design Process

The third step in the design process is

Transform the structure chart or hierarchy chart
which describes the logical structure of how the software will work
into a PDL description of the physical structure of the final program.

Note that there may be a difference between the modules in the hierarchy chart or structure chart and the modules in the detailed design document because the hierarchy chart or structure chart may show logical organization while the PDL description shows physical organization. Most of the hierarchy chart or structure chart will be directly used in developing the detailed design document, so it is important to devote full attention to developing these logical structures. The modules described in the detailed design document, whether written in PDL or some other notation, should correspond exactly to the final code modules that constitute the microprocessor software system.

5.4.2 Developing the Physical Program Structure

The first step in detailed design is to develop
the high level physical structure for the program
using the hierarchy chart or structure chart
and implementation constraints as guides.

There are two fundamental approaches to developing this high level physical structure:

o   The physical structure corresponds exactly to the logical structure. In this case the top module in the hierarchy chart or structure chart plays the central role in the program. It is the first module to begin execution in the microprocessor software system, and it directs the performing of functions by calling or initiating other modules.

o   The physical structure consists of several substructures which may execute concurrently as separate processes. In this case the top module in the hierarchy chart or structure chart may not appear as a physical module, and the subtrees of the top module in the chart work as interdependent processes. The physical modules correspond to those of the subtrees of the top module in the hierarchy chart or structure chart, although the top modules in the subtrees may be deleted similarly. The passing of data and the manner of invocation among the processes should be determined at this point.

Due to the nature of the capabilities of microprocessors and the applications for which microprocessors are being used, it is often desirable to use multiple processes in the following situations:

o   There are multiple microprocessors to perform processes.

o   Functions are logically independent in time.

As an example of the differences between logical and physical structure, the hierarchy chart in Figure 4-1 shows the logical structure for a program, while the structure chart in Figure 4-8 shows the particular physical structure for the program.

5.4.3   Describing the Top Modules in the Physical Program Structure

Having developed the high level physical structure,

The second step in detailed design is to write
PDL descriptions for the top module(s)
in the hierarchy or structure chart.

As described earlier, the PDL description for each module specifies

o   The function the module is to perform

o   The interfaces to superior and subordinate modules

o   Data definitions

o   Algorithm definition

As this information will be the basis for actual code modules, it should be organized in a way that facilitates the writing of code modules. Consequently, the formats for code modules shown in Figures 2-2 and 2-3 should serve as a basis for the PDL description of a module.

In particular for PDL

o   The function the module is to perform is the first item in the prologue.

o   The interface to superior modules is summarized by the component header and described in detail by the lists describing inputs and outputs in the prologue.

o   The interface to subordinate modules is described by the list of called procedures in the prologue.

o   The data definitions (which show a direct correspondence from structure chart to PDL to code) follow the prologue. Note that data definitions include comments describing their meaning.

o   The algorithm definition expands upon the verb-object name of the module to describe in some detail how the module performs the desired function.

The creative part of the detailed design process is this last step of expanding a brief description of a function into an algorithm. This expansion need not be a difficult or random process for two reasons:

o The algorithm will be written in structured English so the designer need not worry about the detailed syntax of a particular programming language.

o The hierarchy chart or structure chart already specifies the subfunction modules to be used. With these as a basis, the algorithm development largely consists of ordering and selecting the subfunctions and performing the other smaller activities to provide a complete algorithm.

The algorithm expressed in PDL will be the basis for the coded algorithm expressed in some programming language. As a general guideline, each PDL statement should correspond to two to five higher level language statements. If a programmer requires more higher level language statements per PDL statement, then the design is likely to be too general, open for multiple interpretations, possibly misunderstood, and thus prone for error creation. If a programmer uses exactly one higher level language statement per PDL statement, then the design will frequently be constrained by the programming language and the programming activity may be a trivial boring exercise. With two to five higher level language statements per PDL statement, the PDL design document serves as a useful skeleton for the program.

As one describes the detailed design for a microprocessor software system, it is usually necessary to keep in mind the implementation constraints imposed by the microprocessor system or the application. Therefore,

When developing the detailed design,
allocate constrained resources to each module.

Microprocessors may constrain the program by limiting memory size and executing instructions slower than larger computers. Applications which utilize microprocessors may have stringent requirements in areas such as real-time response. The list of constraining resources may go beyond the various memory types (ROM for program storage, RAM for data storage, etc.) and time aspects (response time, real time utilization, etc.) to include factors such as the number of modules, total number of processes, and the number of active processes. By considering all resources that might constrain the system during the detailed design stage, then taking the resources available to a module and allocating them among the called modules, one can find problems earlier than if resource utilization considerations are postponed to the programming stage.

5.4.4 Completing Module Descriptions

Once the top level physical structure, the PDL for these modules, and resource allocation have been developed:

> *Complete the detailed design by writing PDL descriptions for*
> *and allocating resources to the remaining modules*
> *in the structure or hierarchy chart.*

The PDL description and resource allocation should be developed as described previously for the upper level modules in the structure or hierarchy chart. When writing the PDL descriptions for modules, there are several guidelines to follow. The coding techniques described in Chapter 2 should be used in the detailed design process as well. Another guideline to follow is to keep the PDL description for a module short, one or possibly two pages should be sufficient. In fact, the PDL processor will issue a warning message if a module is longer than one page. If the PDL description of a module is longer than one or two pages, then it should be decomposed into two or more modules. This may necessitate redoing the high level design, however, it is much better to perform the redesign at this point than to redesign after starting coding or debugging and discovering that modules are too big to understand readily. The lowest level modules in the hierarchy or structure chart are the ones most likely to need further expansion and decomposition. The techniques for performing this decomposition follow those used in high level design. In fact, these low level modules should be given special attention because they are likely to be the ones most frequently referenced in the execution of the microprocessor software system.

After the completion of the detailed design process, the PDL document will describe how the complete microprocessor software system will work. Of course, the operation of the microprocessor software system will perform some set of functions; these functions are specified by the algorithms written in PDL and summarized in the prologues of the modules. The set of functions thus described must correspond exactly to the functions described in the requirements document. The final step in the detailed design process is, therefore, to ensure the correspondence between the detailed design written in PDL and the requirements specification. If the FSM or DFD has been developed properly and the detailed design development has proceeded as described, then the correspondence should be straightforward to establish.

5.5 Design in Perspective

The previous sections have presented design as a straightforward process consisting of several steps performed sequentially. In reality, there are some practical considerations that modify this design process. The specification of details when documenting the lower level modules in PDL may necessitate changes in decisions made earlier. This is especially true when allocating resources to modules. Required changes may be small, they may cause a fundamental change in the high level design, or they may even require a change in the requirements if it can be shown that the requirements are unrealistic for the capabilities of the microprocessor system. The point here is that you should

>*Make design an iterative process in which decisions are*
>*periodically revisited, reviewed, and changed when necessary.*

Only a design that has withstood careful scrutiny after each level of detail has been added is ready for serving as a model for implementation. It is better to start a design over from the beginning than to proceed to implementation with a design that contains minor unsolved problems.

The design techniques described previously have used a top-down "breadth first" ordering. This means that all the details at one level will be described before proceeding to the next lower level in the hierarchy. In practice, it is sometimes appropriate to work from a middle level module downward to its detailed level in a depth first manner. This is shown in Figure 5-5. Depth first decomposition is appropriate when different individuals are working on different parts of the design tree or when the most detailed modules correspond to existing pieces of code. Of course, good design practices should not be sacrificed just to enable reuse of existing software, because "...conceptual integrity is the most important consideration in system design."[4]

The design process can be assisted by some automated tools in addition to the PDL processor. Graphical processors that print or plot DFDs, FSMs,

---

[4]Frederick P. Brooks, Jr., The Mythical Man-Month — Essays on Software Engineering (Reading, Massachusetts: Addison-Wesley, 1975), p. 42.

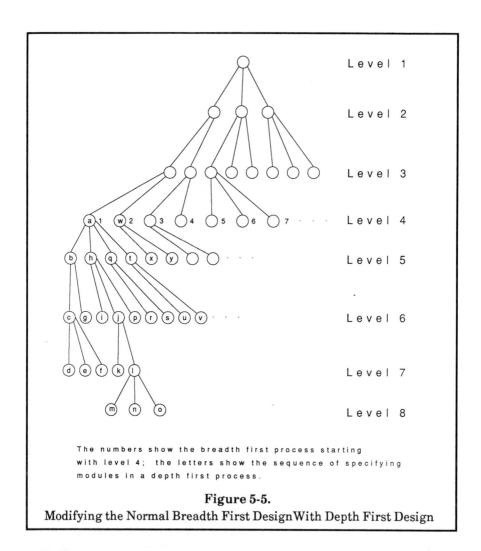

The numbers show the breadth first process starting
with level 4; the letters show the sequence of specifying
modules in a depth first process.

Figure 5-5.
Modifying the Normal Breadth First Design With Depth First Design

structure charts, and hierarchy charts can assist in the preparation of these
diagrams, however, most such programs serve as formatters rather than as
design aids. As with code modules, a good librarian can track the use of
design modules. In general there are few popular tools to assist in the
design process.

The design process can take a long period of time especially when the
design is iterated and reviewed properly. As described in Chapter 1,
however, this is not undesirable because the design activity should take
about thirty percent of the total project time. Such an investment is

worthwhile only if there are significant paybacks.   Indeed, a good design will more than compensate for the time invested for several reasons.

o   A good design simplifies coding and debugging.   Coding is straightforward because not only are all the modules defined in the design, but also the design describes the parts of the code module: the module header, the prologue, the data definitions, the algorithm, and the module terminator. In addition, PDL describes the algorithm so that only two to five higher level language statements are required for each PDL statement.   Debugging is simpler because iteration and review of the design document have eliminated many design errors.

o   A good design simplifies testing because it has already been reviewed and iterated upon to remove errors.   Furthermore, it allows test planning to proceed while coding is being pursued.

o   A good design simplifies maintenance because it carries the requirements specification to the coding stage in a straightforward way; it is organized in a hierarchical modular structure to facilitate change, and is expressed in small modules that make the system easy to understand.

It is also true that people are often willing to change and even scrap a design, but rarely ever scrap implemented code.[5]

[5]Michael Nekora, personal communication.

6

BASIC CONCEPTS OF REQUIREMENTS
SPECIFICATION AND ANALYSIS
FOR MICROPROCESSOR SOFTWARE

6.1 Introduction

Requirements specification is the most important activity in microprocessor software development. Requirements specification is the most important activity in microprocessor software development. Requirements specification is the most important activity in microprocessor software development. It is difficult to emphasize this point too much, yet requirements specification is often overlooked or done improperly when it is performed. The requirements specification for a software system describes *what* the software must do. When the specification process is performed improperly, the software designers are forced into making assumptions about what the software must do. Their assumptions are seldom entirely correct, and this causes errors in the later design and coding phases of microprocessor software development. Even worse, the assumptions are seldom documented, so the errors are even more difficult to find.

As illustrated in Figure 6-1, errors in microprocessor software systems are more likely to be found in later stages of product development. The reason for this phenomenon is that more verification is usually done in the later stages of software development; indeed, there is little verification, e.g., reviewing requirements and design specifications, performed before the debug and test stages. By these later stages, the errors or incorrect assumptions made in the requirements specification stage have been

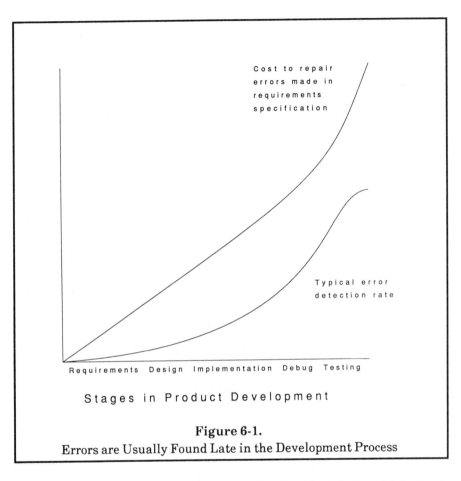

Figure 6-1.
Errors are Usually Found Late in the Development Process

perpetuated and magnified through the detail added during high level design, detailed design, and implementation. Thus, the errors made in requirements specification can be costly to repair (see Figure 6-1), especially in the time needed to redo the affected portions of high level design, detailed design, and implementation.

The purpose of the requirements phase of microprocessor software development is to prepare a specification, i.e., a definition, of *what* the software must do. This should be a subset of the system requirements; for microprocessor systems the first specification document often encompasses both hardware and software requirements. Information for the requirements development process will come from the customer, user, or related sources.

6.2 Characteristics of Requirements Specifications

The quality of the requirements specification is measured by the ease with which it can be used in the subsequent design and testing activities, and by the resulting facility with which the design and testing lead to quality microprocessor software systems that reflect the users' wants. Several characteristics of the requirements specification should serve as goals in the requirements specification process and thus, should be understood before initiating the development of requirements and should be kept in mind during requirements analysis and specification.

6.2.1 Fundamental Characteristics of Requirements Specifications

The following characteristics address the fundamental operational aspects of the microprocessor system to be developed. If the requirements specification does not exhibit these characteristics, then software developers (designers, implementers, and testers) will have to make assumptions about what is desired, which usually leads to errors in the system.

o   Completeness — *All* the functional requirements, performance requirements, and design constraints must be specified. In microprocessor systems especially, all assumptions must be documented since the user will often not understand computer systems and associated terminology.

o   Correctness — The requirements specification must accurately describe users' needs. Hence, communications between the software developers and the users (or their representatives) must be open and bidirectional.

o   Consistency — The various parts of the requirements documentation must not give or imply different specifications. Such contradictions would render the document incorrect.

o   Unambiguity — The requirements documentation must specify the requirements in enough detail so software developers do not have to make assumptions about the meaning of the requirements.

o   Testability — All the requirements specifications must be testable by the software development team. Furthermore, the testing required must be reasonable; for example, a requirement that implies a system test of a long period of time (months or years) is generally not reasonable. If a requirement is not testable, it is likely that requirement will cause the system to fail.

o   Relevance — The requirements specified must pertain to the problem at hand and must be traceable to the requests of the user. Overspecification can be as troublesome as underspecification.

6.2.2 Readability Characteristics of Requirements Specifications

The following characteristics address the ability of the various audiences who read requirements specifications to gather desired information quickly and accurately from the requirements specifications. These aspects are all too often overlooked in favor of the fundamental characteristics described earlier. When this happens, the requirements specifications may be as useless as if they were incomplete, incorrect, or inconsistent.

o   Conciseness — The requirements should be specified without excess verbiage and without irrelevant or unnecessary information. A concise specification facilitates finding desired information quickly.

o   Lack of Redundance — A redundant specification contains more than one description of the same requirement, possibly using different wording. Redundant specifications unduly increase the length of a requirements document, resulting in wasted effort and time on the part of a reader and writer. Furthermore, a specification containing redundancies is more difficult to change correctly when modifications are required.

o   Comprehensibility — The requirements specification should not use notation that is unfamiliar to the reader. The requirements specification should be precise and clear.

6.2.3 Ease of Writing Characteristics of Requirements Specifications

In addition to preparing requirements specifications for readers, one should approach the development of requirements specifications so writers can produce the documentation in an easy and timely way. Proper planning for the writing of requirements specifications has a beneficial effect not only on the resulting documentation but in its preparation as well.

o   Modifiability — A good requirements specification facilitates the inevitable changes caused by successive reviews and increased expectations. Thus the requirements specification must be well organized and indexed, so that someone other than the original authors can readily understand the specifications and make changes.

o   Subsetability — Requirements should be broken into parts (modules) so that several people can simultaneously participate in the development of the requirements specification and so that the entire system can be understood by more than one person.

6.2.4   Feasibility Characteristics of Requirements Specifications

Requirements specifications are the foundations upon which the software design and implementation are built. As such they determine the direction for the remainder of the software development process. The characteristics to be determined by this direction must be kept in mind as the requirements specification is being developed.

o   Manageability — The project to design, implement, test, and maintain the software being specified must be achievable within reasonable organizational constraints of the development team. Requirements that necessitate unrealistic plans in terms of people, schedule time, computer facilities, and other resources are doomed to encounter severe problems.

o   Freedom from unwarranted design detail — Requirements that unduly constrain the designers (for example, specification of a particular algorithm or data structure) can lead to suboptimal designs and eventually to inefficient or ineffective systems. The requirements writers should concentrate on understanding, formulating, and documenting the requirements rather than producing a rough design for the system.

Failure to consider these characteristics can lead to errors, as illustrated in Figure 6-2. The figure shows that errors in requirements specifications fall into a variety of categories. It also shows that straightforward techniques can significantly reduce the errors introduced in the requirements

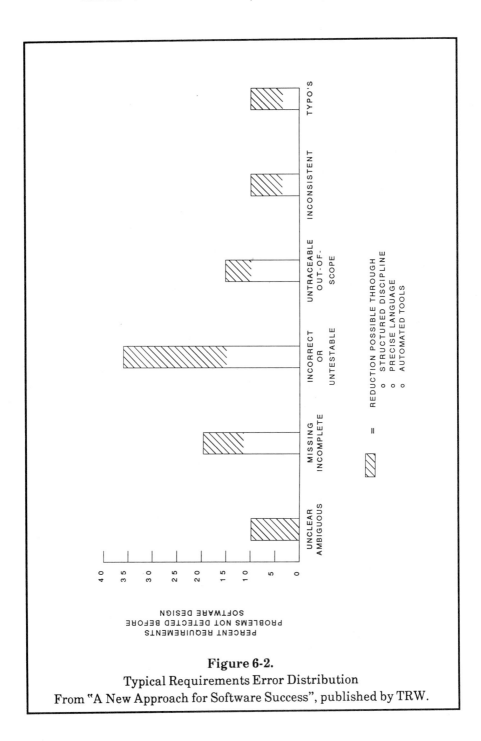

Figure 6-2.
Typical Requirements Error Distribution
From "A New Approach for Software Success", published by TRW.

specification process. This chapter and Chapter 7 will describe such techniques.

6.3 Users of Requirements Specifications

The various characteristics of requirements specifications described in the previous section have differing degrees of importance depending on the user of the specifications. For example, a person writing the specifications will be most concerned about the readability and ease of writing characteristics, while a developer will be more concerned about the fundamental and feasibility characteristics. Accordingly, the requirements specification, or the various sections or documents that constitute the requirements specification, must be written with several audiences in mind.

o   End users — End users are concerned with the interface presented by the microcomputer system. They will want to discern readily the usability features and external characteristics of the microcomputer system; these comprise not only the hardware aspects (switches, keyboards, displays, etc.) but also the software aspects as manifested in the presentation of input to the system, the commands to initiate processing, and the manner in which results will be output from the microcomputer system. The appropriate specification for users is relatively informal and emphasizes interaction with the system; indeed, a formal specification for users would often be incomprehensible, misleading, and as a result counterproductive.

o   Customers — While customers may often be end users, with microprocessor-based systems customers often represent the users and will define requirements based on the perceived desires of users. For example, the customers of microcomputer-based cash registers may be store owners or managers, while the users may be sales clerks. Customers are concerned with the features and functions the system is to support, and the performance the system is to achieve. To facilitate customer understanding, the requirements specification must be written using a style and terminology that are relevant to the customer and reflect the terminology of the customer's application area. For example, requirements specifications for microcomputer-based cash registers should be written in terms that a retailer readily understands.

o   Software designers — Since the purpose of software design is to transform a requirements specification into a design specification that describes how the software will implement the original requirements, the software designer wants a description of the functions to be performed, the performance to be achieved, and the design constraints which bound the software development and solution. Software designers will be most concerned with the following fundamental characteristics of requirements specifications: completeness, correctness, consistency, and unambiguity. In addition, software designers will be concerned with conciseness and comprehensibility, so they prefer documents that are more formal and contain less jargon than do customer documents. Finally, software designers will want to use their experience, knowledge, and creative talents to develop good designs; they do not want to be constrained by design decisions that have crept into the requirements specification. For example, it is generally inappropriate for a requirements document to specify the structure of a data item internal to a program.

o   Testers — Before testing is performed on a microcomputer software system, the testers should design the test plans. When these plans are executed, the testers should be able to determine whether or not the microcomputer system provides the features and performance required. The requirements specification must, therefore, be used as a basis from which to write test plans. To the tester, the fundamental characteristics of requirements specifications are critical, especially the testability characteristic.

o   Managers — The managers of the group responsible for developing the microcomputer software system want a requirements specification that they can read and understand, that they can use to negotiate a contract with customers, and that they can use to quantify and control the design constraints.

o   Requirements specification writers — The people who actually write the requirements specification must perform a difficult activity. They must take information from customers (often expressed in an informal and unstructured way), combine it with knowledge about the software development environment (capabilities of the microcomputer systems, capabilities of the development team, time constraints, and so forth) and produce requirements specifications that satisfy the needs of all the audiences. In addition, the requirements specification should display all the characteristics described previously, especially ease of writing characteristics that facilitate timely document preparation and updating.

The needs of these various users dictate different aspects and formats for the parts of the requirements specification process and resulting documentation.

6.4 Requirements Specification Process and Its Results

The requirements specification process, like the design process, consists of two phases: analysis and synthesis. In the analysis phase, members of the development team learn about the needs of the customers and users of the microcomputer system. In the synthesis or definition phase, this knowledge is structured and transcribed into the requirements documentation for communicating the information to others involved in the software development process.

This documentation, which is the result of the requirements specification process, comprises two major parts. The first part is the functional requirements for the microcomputer system. The functional requirements describe the functions the microcomputer system is to perform and the performance the microcomputer system is to achieve. It is important to note the system aspects of this documentation. Customers and users of microcomputer systems generally do not and should not concern themselves with the hardware specific aspects or software specific aspects of the microcomputer system. Indeed they may not even be aware that the system uses a microcomputer for control.

The functional requirements consist of two parts:

o   Customer requirements that specify, perhaps informally, the functions and performance the microcomputer system is to achieve. The degree of informality depends on the technical capabilities of the customer representative who will review the documentation. The specification should contain a high level description of the functions to be performed and the performance criteria to be met.

o   A user manual that describes in detail all the functions to be performed from an input/output perspective. That is, every permissible input or sequence of inputs to the microcomputer system should be described. For each input or sequence, the user manual should describe the output the system will generate. In cases where timing is critical the manual should describe the performance responses as well.

After the functional requirements have been specified and approved, the software requirements should be developed. These software requirements should be developed in conjunction with the hardware requirements, for the hardware and software aspects of microcomputer systems must be synergistic. In developing the software specification, it is necessary to address three areas.

o   The functions the software is to perform

o   The performance the software is to achieve given performance specifications for the microcomputer and associated hardware

o   The constraints that bound the development of the software system

The software requirements documentation also comprises two parts. The first part is a document that corresponds to the user manual in level of detail. This software system requirements specification should, therefore, describe in detail and somewhat formally:

o   All the inputs or sequences of inputs

o   All the functions performed as a result of the occurrence of these inputs

o   The outputs that are produced as a result of the functional processing

Similarly the performance criteria and development constraints from the viewpoint of the software system should be described.

The second part of the software requirements specification is the subsystem software requirements specification. This documentation is needed when the microcomputer hardware is modularized into clearly separable subsystems each of which has clearly identifiable requirements. An example is a multiple microcomputer process control system where each microcomputer performs a specific set of subfunctions, the combination of which constitute the functions of the entire system. The information in each of the subsystem software requirements specifications follows the same format as the information in the software system requirements specification.

Figure 6-3 summarizes the different parts of the requirements specifications for microcomputer systems.

1. Functional Requirements — an informal description of the functions and performance from a system viewpoint.

    1.1 Customer Requirements — a high level description concentrating on features.

    1.2 User Manual — a detailed description concentrating on inputs and responses.

2. Software Requirements — a formal description of the functions, performance, and development constraints from a software viewpoint given knowledge of the hardware system.

    2.1 Software System Requirements — a detailed description from the software system viewpoint.

    2.2 Subsystem Software Requirements — a detailed description from the viewpoint of each of the software subsystems that controls a hardware subsystem.

Figure 6-3. Parts of a Requirements Specification Document

6.5 Requirements Analysis

There are basically three ways for a microcomputer system development team to learn the desires of customers so they can prepare the necessary requirements documentation.

The first way for the microcomputer system development team to learn the needs of customers is to peruse documentation prepared by customers or a marketing group. This may be a formal document such as a request for proposal from a customer, or a general description of product goals from a marketing group derived from competitive analysis and a long-term product strategy. It may also be an informal document such as a wish list of desired system capabilities. In either case such documentation should be used as a starting point for obtaining additional information. It should not be used as a final requirements specification because it will usually fail to address some of the conflicting functional requirements, performance requirements, or developmental constraints that must be considered by the software development team. Using this documentation as a starting point, a more detailed requirements specification should be prepared and reviewed by the customer or marketing group.

The second way for the microcomputer system development team to learn the needs of customers is to interview the customers. Interviewing usually consists of an informal high level part and a formal detailed part. The informal high level interview of the customer management team should be used to determine initial direction and bounds on three criteria of interest in requirements specification. The following types of questions should be asked:

o   Functionality

   - What are the desired features and functions?

   - What features and functions are not needed?

   - What are the fundamental characteristics of the human interface to the microcomputer based system?

   - What are the basic modes of operation?

   - What are the special functions to be performed if the system fails (e.g., on a power outage)?

o   Performance

   - What is the desired response time for individual inputs to the system?

   - What is the desired system loading level?

   - What are the desired reliability and availability characteristics, such as response in overloaded conditions, mean time between failures, and mean time to repair?

o   Constraints

   - What is the goal for development cost?

   - What is the goal for scheduled delivery of the first system?

   - What is the cost goal for manufacturing subsequent copies of the system?

   - What is the physical environment in which the system is to work? For example, is it a high noise environment? Is it part of another computer system?

- To what extent will the system be modified, subsetted, or extended in the future?

- What are the tradeoffs or priorities among the different product goals?

While these questions are not intended to be exhaustive, they do give a flavor and direction of the type of high level questions that should be asked.

The formal detailed interviews should take place with people who will be users of the microcomputer-based system. From these discussions should come all the details necessary to write complete specifications. In these interviews the following types of questions should be asked.

o   Functionality

- What is the information that is to be input to the system, and what are the formats?

- What is the processing that is to be performed on this information?

- What are the outputs the system is to deliver and what are the formats?

- What are the subsystems that merit consideration as independent units, and what are their input, process, and output characteristics?

o   Performance

- What is the speed at which the inputs will enter the system?

- What is the speed at which the output responses exit the system?

o   Constraints

- Which of the functionality and performance characteristics may change in the future and how might they change?

In asking these questions of potential users, the software development team should try to interview a diverse set of people so the scope of their investigation will not be too narrow.

The third way for the microcomputer system development team to learn the needs of customers is to examine customers' existing systems. The existing systems may be manual, semiautomated, or completely automated. In any case, the functions performed in current systems will generally be a minimal set for the new system. Thus an understanding of the existing system will serve as a strong basis for understanding what the desired system is to be. In examining the existing system, one should o   Peruse documentation available on the system.

o   Talk with users of the system.

o   Use the system if possible.

Using the system provides firsthand knowledge that is difficult to obtain in any other way. Indeed, one of the great shortcomings of developers of microprocessor-based systems is that they fail to take the viewpoint of a typical user, and as a result, microprocessor-based systems often have a poor user interface and are considered failures for that reason.

Recall from Chapter 1 that about 25 percent of the development time for a project should be devoted to the requirements specification phase. Of this time some 40 percent to 50 percent should be spent in analysis to learn the desires of customers. In this analysis activity, all three of the techniques discussed previously should be used. The activities complement one another; it is difficult to get a complete picture of customers' needs without pursuing all three activities. To summarize this section:

> *Analyze requirements to determine customers' needs by*
> o   *perusing documentation from customers and*
>   *marketing groups*
> o   *interviewing customers and future system users*
> o   *examining and using existing systems*

Devote the time needed to completely understand customers' requirements.

7

SYNTHESIS OF
REQUIREMENTS SPECIFICATIONS
FOR MICROPROCESSOR SOFTWARE

7.1 Synthesis of the Functional Requirements

The purpose of the functional requirements documentation is to provide information desired by two groups — the customers and the users of the microprocessor-based system. For this reason the documentation comprises two parts — customer requirements and the user manual.

Developing the functional requirements consists of a number of steps. The first step is really a natural extension of the analysis activity described in the previous chapter.

The first step in the synthesis
of requirements specifications is
to organize the information obtained
during the requirements analysis activity.

In the analysis activity, a microprocessor system development team obtains information in a variety of ways; this information must be organized and categorized before a specification can be written. The information obtained during analysis should first be categorized into the three main topics to be covered in a requirements specification: functions to be performed, desired performance, and design constraints in building the system. At this stage the information should be categorized hierarchically. The major functions and subfunctions should be determined. The principal performance criteria classes and particular performance goals within those classes should be ascertained. The categories of design constraints and particular goals to achieve should be listed.

On the first pass through this organization process, a microprocessor development team will usually find that they lack certain information, and that there are holes in the document they are developing. When this situation arises, the development team should revisit the customers with specific questions to fill the information gaps. This should be part of an ongoing dialogue with the customers, a dialogue which should be maintained throughout the development process. An ongoing dialogue does not mean a continuous one. Customers have a lot of work to do in addition to interfacing with developers of a microprocessor system; they are usually happy to answer questions periodically, but not constantly.

In organizing the information for the customer requirements specification, a data base system can be very useful. With a good data base system, information can be put into categories and subcategories and cross-referenced easily. In fact, many of the sophisticated automated tools used to assist the developers of requirements specifications for large systems are special purpose data base systems oriented to requirements writing.

7.2 Writing the Customer Requirements Specification

Having organized the information, the second step is to outline and write the actual customer requirements document.

> *The outline of the customer requirements specification should follow these general guidelines:*
> (1)   *Review the information gathering and analysis.*
> (2)   *Describe the functions to be performed.*
> (3)   *Describe the performance goals.*
> (4)   *Describe the design and development constraints.*
> (5)   *Introduce the user manual and the software requirements specifications.*

The review of the information gathering and analysis functions serves two purposes. First, it shows the customer what information you have. Second, and probably more important, it shows what information you do not have. In situations where the development team has overlooked some source of information, it is important to discover and remedy the oversight immediately. For this reason the review of information gathering and analysis is an important part of the customer requirements document.

A description of the functions to be performed is the second part of the customer requirements specification. It is often considered to be the fundamental part of requirements documentation because it presents what the microprocessor system will actually do. Functions to be performed should be described on a feature-by-feature basis, where a feature may be considered to be a fundamental system action in response to a particular sequence of inputs. For example, an office-to-office call in a telephone switching system is a feature, a charge transaction in a point of sales terminal activity is a feature, and a feedback loop in a process control system is a feature. A useful technique for describing a feature in a microprocessor system is the stimulus-response sequence. Briefly, a stimulus-response sequence describes a feature as a sequence of user stimuli (inputs) followed by the desired system responses (outputs). For the customer requirements specification, stimulus-response sequences can be presented in a high-level way using terminology indigenous to the customers' application area. Such descriptions will not only present the ranges of functions, inputs, and outputs, but they will also serve as a logical compendium which the customer can review for completeness.

The performance goals for the microprocessor system constitute the third part of the customer requirements specification. Performance criteria may be grouped into several categories.

o   Normal performance — the expected performance of the system in normal operating modes. This would include criteria such as the number of inputs or transactions to be handled per second.

o   Abnormal performance — the expected performance of the system in critical situations, such as conditions of heavy system loading and the reliability of the system in producing correct responses.

o   Downtime performance — expectations as to frequency of system failure (e.g., mean time between failures) and duration of repair (e.g., mean time to repair).

For the customer requirements specification, these criteria must consider the entire microprocessor system (not just the hardware or just the software) and the environment in which it is to be placed. Environmental conditions that can affect performance include the consistency of the electrical power supply (e.g., blackouts and brownouts) and high electromagnetic noise.

Design and development constraints identify the boundary conditions for the implementation of the system. These constraints span a variety of factors:

o   Time — to system delivery, or phased delivery of systems with increasing functionality or performance.

o   Cost — the cost of delivering systems.

o   Customer interface — providing training and support through personal interactions and reference documentation, both before and after system delivery. System delivery must define the acceptance criteria which the customer will use to accept delivery of the system.

o   Physical environment — how the system is to interface with other manual, semiautomated, and automated systems to differentiate what is done by the microprocessor system and what is done by users.

All such factors should be considered, since they often have a greater effect on the achievability of a development project than just the functional criteria to be implemented.

The last part of the customer requirements specification is an introduction to additional requirements specification information, namely, the user manual and the software requirements specifications. These pointers are important because the user manual and software specifications describe the detailed specifications which precisely define the system to be implemented. They differ from the high level of the customer requirements document in that they are low level and refine details that are summarized in the customer requirements specification.

The customer requirements specification should be written to convey major concepts to the first customer contacts. Accordingly, the specification should not be lengthy; twenty-five pages constitute a long customer requirements document. The goal of a customer requirements document is to serve as an executive summary for the rest of the requirements documentation. It should use the terminology of the customer's application area, so that its contents can be grasped quickly, and so that it can serve as a review and contractual vehicle. The customer requirements specification should be reviewed carefully by the customer. Both the customers and developers must examine the requirements specifications to ensure that the characteristics described in the previous chapter have been met and that there are no conflicting requirements either within or among the three principal sections of the specification: functions, performance, and design constraints. Usually the review process will be an interactive one in which the customer makes comments and the microprocessor system development team changes the specification until both parties approve the document.

After approval, the document serves as a basis for succeeding requirements specification activities.

7.3 Writing the User Manual

Having written the customer requirements specification, the next step in the synthesis of the functional requirements is to write the user manual which will serve as a reference and training guide for users of the microprocessor system.

> *The outline of the user manual should follow these general guidelines:*
> *(1)   Introduce the microprocessor system.*
> *(2)   Describe the physical user interface.*
> *(3)   Describe the basic features of the system.*
> *(4)   Describe in detail the input/output sequences that constitute each feature.*
> *(5)   List separately the errors that can occur and the appropriate response actions.*
> *(6)   Provide an index to features, input/output sequences, and errors.*

The introduction to the microprocessor system should address the purpose of the system and outline the body of the document. It should describe the environment in which the system is to be used, addressing both the human interface and the interface to other computer-based systems. Because the user manual is not principally a training manual, it should describe previous training or information with which the user should be familiar. The user manual should also classify the different types of users and direct them to the sections of the manual in which they should be interested.

The physical user interface for the microprocessor system is composed of the physical devices through which data are entered into the system and the physical devices through which the system presents data. Some examples of input devices for microprocessor-based systems are the following:

o   A terminal keyboard

o   Buttons or switches on a user interface panel

o   A tape or disk drive

o   A communication line

Examples of output devices are

o   Simple displays such as light emitting diodes and liquid crystal
    displays

o   A CRT monitor

o   A printer

o   A tape or disk drive

o   A communication line

For most of these devices the physical structure of the data is important.
For example, the general format of commands or data entered into a
keyboard is significant even though pressing a particular key causes a
specific set of bits to be sent to a microprocessor. Similarly, the format of
information on a disk or tape and the timing of information coming across a
communication line should be presented to users so that they can avoid
simple I/O errors.

The basic modes of operation and features of the microprocessor
system should be summarized and categorized for the various types of
system users. Many microprocessor systems have users who may be
classified in three categories:

o   Users who configure or initialize the system

o   Users who use the system on a regular basis

o   Users who query the system to obtain information about its use

The user manual should be organized to simplify reference by separate
user groups and by levels of user sophistication within groups. Within these
categories, features should be described in some logical way.

The largest part of the user manual will be the detailed description of
the input/output sequences that constitute each feature. The descriptions
should be self-contained with the possible exception of references to the
physical environment or basic operational modes described earlier in the
document. Writing in such a self-contained style will facilitate referencing
the manual and reduce the need to look in several places for information.
The narrative for each feature should describe the exact form of the input,
the output with which the system responds, and the change of mode the
system makes, if any.

The fifth section of the user manual should be a separate listing of the errors that can occur and the appropriate response actions for each error. The microprocessor system should indicate the errors that occur in system operation by succinct clear messages; error numbers should be used only if the accompanying messages do not fully convey the problem and alternative actions. The user manual must expand upon the information presented by the microprocessor. It must be thorough so there is no doubt in a reader's mind about what has happened and what should be done next. This section of the user manual will probably be referenced frequently, so it must be organized for ease of access.

The final section of the user manual provides an index to features, input/output sequences, and errors. This section will often be the first one examined when a user needs the manual, so it must also be logically organized and complete. It is often useful to organize the index in more than one way, for example, by input/output sequence within a feature as well as wholly alphabetical. As an adjunct to an index a card which summarizes key material can be a useful pocket reference.

Like the customer requirements specification, the user manual should be written using the terminology of the application the microprocessor system supports. There is no general guideline on length; the user manual should provide all the information the various system users require and nothing more. For example, the user manual should not describe features of the hardware or software that implement the system. The user manual should also be reviewed and approved by customers and users as it describes the user/system interface.

7.4 Synthesis of the Software Requirements

7.4.1 Introduction

The purpose of the software requirements documentation is to provide information desired by three groups — software designers, testers, and managers. Rather than having separate documents for each of these groups, the software requirements documentation addresses the needs of each group by proper presentation and organization of information.

Developing the software requirements consists of a number of steps. The first step involves extending the information described in the functional requirements documents.

The first step in the synthesis of
software requirements is to classify
the functionality of the hardware and
the functionality of the software.

At this point it is not possible to determine detailed functions to be implemented in hardware and detailed functions to be implemented in software, but based on the functional requirements, it is appropriate to decide what the hardware capabilities will be (microprocessor selection, memory size, communication techniques, component speeds, associated circuitry, etc.). This will provide a basis for software definition.

Having defined the basic hardware functionality, one proceeds to

Define the details of the software
functions, performance, and constraints.

The first step in describing the software function is

List completely the inputs and outputs
that the software must accept and generate.

For each input and output item, several characteristics must be described. These include value range, accuracy, data representation, and so on. Figure 7-1 shows three excerpts from the "Software Requirements for the A-7E Aircraft."[1] Figure 7-1(a) introduces the descriptions of input and output data items; Figures 7-1(b) and 7-1(c) show sample input and output data items respectively.

The second step in describing the software functions is

Describe the functional transformations
that take the inputs and produce the outputs.

[1]Kathryn L. Heninger, John W. Kallander, John E. Shore, and David L. Parnas, "Software Requirements for the A-7E Aircraft," NRL Memorandum Report 3876, Naval Research Laboratory, Washington, D. C. (November 27, 1978).

A-7 Software Requirements   Section 2
Version 3

2. Input and Output Data Items

2.0 Introduction

    This section describes the individual data items communicated between the TC-2 and other devices in the aircraft. There is a separate subsection for each hardware device. Within each subsection, input items precede output items. The data items are alphabetized within each category.

Provided for each data item are (a) a standard acronym enclosed in brackets (/input/ and //output//) to be used throughout the document and during system development; (b) a verbal description of its significance or meaning in terms of the device with which it is associated; (c) characteristics of each numerical data item, such as range, accuracy, etc., or mnemonic names enclosed in brackets ($value$) for the possible values of each non-numerical data item; (d) the format of the data representation; and (e) the TC-2 instruction sequence that must be executed in order to read the item or transmit it to the external device. For numerical data items, the range gives the maximum and minimum values encountered in actual use. This may be smaller than the range of values that can be represented. Where such information is available and meaningful, the document describes any timing restrictions that must be observed.

Figure 7-1.
Excerpts from "Software Requirements for the A-7E Aircraft"
(a) Description of input and output data items

There are a variety of techniques or models with which one can describe the functional transformations of a microprocessor based system. These include

o   Stimulus-response sequences

o   Input-process-output sequences

o   Requirement nets

A-7 Software Requirements   Section 2.1.1
Version 3

2.1.1.4

Input Data Item: IMS Mode Switch   Class: DIW5
                   (IMS Control Panel)

Acronym: /IMSMODE/

Hardware: Inertial Measurement Set

Description: /IMSMODE/ indicates the position of a six-position rotary
             switch on the IMS control panel. This switch determines
             the IMS's mode of operations, as described in (33a,
             Section 3.4.1.5).

             Switch nomenclature: OFF; GND ALIGN; NORM;
             INERTIAL; MAG SL; GRID

Characteristics of Values

     Value Encoding: $Offnone$ (00000)
                       $Gndal$ (10000)
                       $Norm$ (01000)
                       $Iner$ (00100)
                       $Grid$ (00010)
                       $Magsl$ (00001)

Instruction Sequence: READ 24   (Channel 0)

Data Representation: Discrete input word 5, bits 3-7

Comments: /IMSMODE/ = $Offnone$ when the switch is between
          two positions.

Figure 7-1. (continued)
Excerpts from "Software Requirements for the A-7E Aircraft"
(b) A sample input data item

A-7 Software Requirements   Section 2.3.2
Version 3

2.3.2.2

<u>Input Data Item</u>:   Flight Path Angle

<u>Acronym</u>:   //FPANGL//

<u>Hardware</u>:   Attitude Direction Indicator

<u>Description</u>: //FPANGL// positions the horizontal needle of the ADI.
Positive direction is up when looking at the ADI. A value
of zero centers the needle.   The value -20 puts the
needle out of view.

<u>Comments</u>:   //FPANGL// is defined in Sec. 2.1.3.8, under FLR.

//FPANGL// is not assumed to be the Flight Path Angle by
the ADI. Other quantities can be displayed provided the
FLR is not in Terrain Following Mode.

Figure 7-1. (continued)
Excerpts from "Software Requirements for the A-7E Aircraft"
(c) A sample output data item

While these models are functionally equivalent, we are interested here in communicating information to software designers, testers, and managers. We must use a technique that best provides information to these users of the software requirements document, and that is supported by adequate tools. With the variability in the desires of different users and in available tools, there will be circumstances where each of these techniques may be applicable. We, therefore, give a brief description of each.

7.4.2 Stimulus-Response Sequences

Stimulus-response sequences describe system responses that result from user inputs or stimuli. Stimulus-response sequences use an algorithmic English-like notation as illustrated in Figure 7-2. To describe each stimulus-response sequence,

o   Start with some known state, such as the "idle state" in Figure 7-2.

o   From that state list each possible sequence of inputs. The inputs may be explicit external stimuli such as the "go-off-hook" input in Figure 7-2, or they may be implicit inputs such as "wait 500 milliseconds."

o   For each input in each sequence list the system response which consists of two parts: a physical output and a change of the state of the system. For example, in Figure 7-2 the telephone switching system responds to a "go-off-hook" signal with the output of a "dial-tone" to the caller and a change in state to the "dial-tone-state." Either the physical output or the state change may be null, i.e., for an input there may not be an output or a state change.

```
            IN idle-state
            WAIT FOR caller TO go-off-hook
            OUTPUT dial-tone TO caller
            IN dial-tone-state
            WAIT FOR caller TO Dial-Number
            IN number-dialed-state
            IF dialed-number HAS length = 7
            THEN IN local-call-state
                          .
                          .
                          .
```

Figure 7-2.
A Portion of a Stimulus-Response Sequence
for a Telephone Switching System

The third step in this process, i.e., listing the system response, merits a more detailed explanation. First, the response may depend on the system state so its description may include conditional clauses, such as the clause "If dialed-number..." in Figure 7-2. Second, the description of the response may involve some intermediate transformations. For such descriptions a properly constrained subset of English is useful. To avoid ambiguity and misunderstanding a set of keywords (including, for example, the capitalized words in Figure 7-2) should be defined at the beginning of the software requirements document. Other words that typically are used include ACCEPT, ASSIGN, DISPLAY, OUTPUT, and INITIALIZE. Although the use of a subset of English will introduce more formality in the software requirements, stimulus-response sequences defined in this way will be more effective in providing the desired information.

Of course it is unreasonable to consider sequences of all possible lengths in which any system input can occur at any time: there are an unlimited number of such sequences. To make the number of sequences manageable, one should use several techniques:

o   Group related inputs into a single input class. For example, in Figure 7-2, as in most microcomputer systems with a numeric key pad, the individual digits may be referenced by a generic input "digit."

o   Make the stimulus-response sequences short, so that they begin and end on specific states. Use such sequences within other sequences where appropriate, so that stimulus-response sequences have a hierarchical as well as a flow of control orientation. In Figure 7-2, "Dial-Number" is a stimulus-response sequence that starts in the "dial-tone-state," collects multiple dialed digits, and ends in the "number-dialed-state."

o   Ignore inputs that are invalid, or treat them in a simple consistent way such as issuing an error message. For example, in the telephone switching system of Figure 7-2 it may be appropriate to ignore "go-on-hook" inputs that are less than a few milliseconds in duration.

By proper selection, the principal sequences can be made to correspond to features of the microprocessor system being described. A requirements specification document for an office telephone switching system might include sequences for office calls, local calls, dictation calls, call forwarding, and so forth.

The use of stimulus-response sequences is perhaps the most appropriate technique for writing requirements specifications for microprocessor-based systems because their form is so amenable to various users of specifications.

o   For software designers, they provide a framework for generating the finite state machine or data flow diagram model of the system in the analysis phase of design (see Chapters 4 and 5).

o   For system testers, stimulus-response sequences provide a natural basis for testing features.

o   For managers, software requirements writers, and others who read requirements specifications, the prose-like format of the stimulus-response technique facilitates reading and understanding with little need for special training in a new notation.

In addition, the tools for assisting in the development and maintenance of stimulus-response sequences are relatively straightforward. A good text editing system, such as the ones available on many microcomputer support systems, provide a sufficient capability for easily entering and editing requirements specifications expressed as stimulus-response sequences. Advanced tools process stimulus-response sequences by checking for completeness, consistency, and redundancy and by transforming stimulus-response sequences into other representations, such as finite state machines.[2]

Defining the performance requirements within the context of stimulus-response sequences can be accomplished in two ways. The first way is to include the performance criteria in the sequences themselves. For example, in Figure 7-2 the third line could be changed to read:

OUTPUT dial-tone TO caller IN 500 milliseconds

The second way is to address the various categories described previously — normal performance, abnormal performance, downtime performance, and so forth — in a separate section. Note that the refinement required here is in the performance of the software system only; the performance of the microprocessor system will depend on both hardware and software performance. In the telephone switching system example, the following performance criteria are exemplary:

[2]Alan M. Davis, Thomas J. Miller, Esther Rhode, Bruce J. Taylor, "RLP: An Automated Tool for the Processing of Requirements," COMPSAC 79 Proceedings, IEEE Computer Society (November 1979), pp. 289-299.

o   Normal performance — the number of calls (or instances of each feature type) that can be handled and still meet the immediate response time performance requirements, such as providing a dial tone in 500 milliseconds or less.

o   Abnormal performance — the behavior of the system when the maximum number of calls is exceeded. Possible specifications for this situation, listed in decreasing order of desirability, are longer waiting time for dial tone, refusal to accept additional calls, and system shutdown (crash).

o   Downtime performance — the telephone switching system should be nonfunctional for at most "n" minutes per year due to software faults.

Similarly, the design and development constraints should be addressed, stating requirements for hardware and other needed support so that software constraints can be quantified. One of the advantages of the stimulus-response technique is that some features can be implemented and tested before others so a phased introduction of features can be accomplished. In many cases, this is not only desirable but useful for customers in bringing users up to speed with a new system.

7.4.3 Other Requirements Specification Techniques

Input-process-output (IPO) sequences are another textual technique for specifying requirements for microprocessor systems. With IPO sequences a system is defined as a collection of processes, which perform transformations on inputs to produce the desired outputs. Figure 7-3 shows an IPO sequence[3] similar to the telephone switching example in Figure 7-2. IPO sequences are most suitable for transaction oriented systems where real-time requirements are not critical and where there is little relationship among the transitions. Some tools have been developed to support the writing of requirements with IPO sequences. The Problem Statement Language/Problem Statement Analyzer (PSL/PSA) System[4] provides a

[3]Alan M. Davis and Tomlinson G. Rauscher, "A Survey of Techniques Used for Requirements Definition of Computer Based Systems," GTE Automatic Electric Journal, GTE Automatic Electric, Northlake, Illinois (September 1979), p. 169.

[4]D. Teichroew and E. A. Hershey III, "PSL/PSA: A Computer Aided Technique for Structured Documentation and Analysis of Information Processing Systems," IEEE Transactions on Software Engineering, vol. SE-3, no. 1 (January 1977), pp. 16-33.

language for describing IPO sequences and a processor that uses a data base to track consistency among data objects. The IPO sequence in Figure 7-3 is written in PSL. IBM's system, Hierarchy plus Input-Process-Output (HIPO)[5] also uses the IPO sequence technique.

```
Define Process:     Line Scan:
    Triggered by:   Caller-Goes-Off-Hook,
                    Caller-Idle;
          Makes:    Caller-Receives-Dial-Tone,
                    Caller-Not-Idle;



Define Process:     Digit-Collector;
    Triggered by:   Caller-Receives-Dial-Tone,
                    Caller-Dials-Local-#;
          Makes:    Local-Call-Successful;



Define Process:     Local-to-Local-Connector;
    Triggered by:   Local-to-Local-Connector;
                    Called-Party-Not-Busy,
                    Called-Party-Busy;
          Makes:    Receiving-Busy-Tone,
                    Receiving-Ring-Ringback-Tone;
```

Figure 7-3.
An Excerpt from an Input-Process-Output Sequence

Requirements nets are graphical descriptions of stimulus-response sequences. Figure 7-4 shows a requirements net representation that corresponds to the initial part of Figure 7-2. TRW has developed a system[6]

[5]"HIPO: Design Aid and Documentation Tool," IBM Technical Note #SR20-9413-0, 1973.

[6]M. W. Alford, "A Requirements Engineering Methodology for Real-Time Processing Requirements," IEEE Transactions on Software Engineering, vol. SE-3, no. 1 (January 1977), pp. 60-69.

called SREM that uses a Requirements Statement Language similar to PSL and requirements nets to define and check requirements specifications.

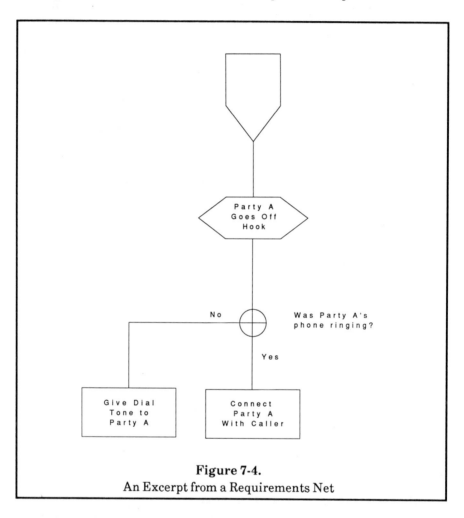

Figure 7-4.
An Excerpt from a Requirements Net

Although other techniques have been used successfully for stating requirements, they are not as applicable to microprocessor systems as the ones described previously.[7]

---

[7]A. M. Davis and T. G. Rauscher, <u>op.</u> <u>cit</u>.

7.4.4 Recommendations on Preparing Software Requirements

While these various techniques are useful and functionally equivalent, we recommend:

Use the stimulus-response sequence technique
to describe functional transformations.

This technique is preferred for people who are being introduced to requirements specifications for microprocessor systems because

o   The stimulus-response sequence technique is easy to learn and use.

o   It corresponds naturally to requirements writers' conceptual views of the systems they are specifying.

o   It can be used by designers, testers, and others who need to read requirements specifications.

o   There is a natural transformation to the finite state machine and data flow models used in microprocessor software design.

o   The minimum set of tools required to support stimulus-response sequences is simple, and advanced tools require only additional software processors.

The development of software requirements specifications should be an iterative process, not a linear one. It should be reviewed at major points with the principals involved, i.e., managers, customers, designers, and testers. Using such external reviews to complement the internal review process will help to identify problems at a point in the software development life cycle where their impact can be minimized.

7.5 Synthesis of the Subsystem Software Requirements

In microprocessor-based systems, there is often a well defined separation of hardware subsystems. When this situation occurs, then in the first step of the synthesis of software requirements (i.e., the classification of hardware and software functionality) the detailed software requirements should be written on a subsystem-by-subsystem basis corresponding to the hardware modularity of the system. In this case, one should proceed with the specification of subsystem software requirements in much the same manner as that described in the previous section. For example, the detailed functions performed by the various subsystems must constitute the functions to be performed by the system viewed in its entirety. There are two aspects which merit special consideration:

o   The interface among the software subsystems must be described. This can be accomplished within the stimulus-response sequence technique by having the response for one subsystem serve as the stimulus for another.

o   The allocation of performance and constraint requirements to the various subsystems and their interfaces must constitute the performance and constraint requirements of the entire system.

The descriptions of subsystems and interfaces can be straightforward when the hardware subsystems are controlled by separate microprocessors. Great care must be taken when several hardware subsystems will be controlled by one microprocessor due to interactions among the software subsystems.

8

TESTING
MICROPROCESSOR SOFTWARE

8.1 Introduction

As the penultimate phase in the software life cycle, testing plays a key role in the quality of the end product. This phase is the "last chance" to ensure that the user will get what he wants when he wants it. Thus testing may be defined as demonstrating that the software performs according to the user's reasonable expectations. This implies that the required functions have been implemented to meet the original specifications defined by the user. A counterdefinition has been proposed by Myers. He defines testing as "the process of executing a program with the intent of finding errors."[1] Myers feels that testers are more apt to find errors if they are considered successful when they demonstrate the existence of errors. If tests are considered unsuccessful when they manifest errors in the program, Myers argues the psychological effect on the tester and the programmer is negative. To avoid the controversy, we will define testing as the process of executing the program with two purposes:

o   To demonstrate that the software meets the user requirements

o   To find any errors that exist in the software

[1]Glenford J. Myers, The Art of Software Testing (New York: John Wiley & Sons, 1979), p. 5.

149

With this definition a test cannot be considered successful or unsuccessful but rather

o   A test will demonstrate that the program functions properly under particular circumstances or

o   A test will manifest the existence of an error

In selecting test cases, i.e., data input to a software system to determine its functionality and performance, some techniques place the emphasis on the demonstration of function while other techniques emphasize the discovery of errors. Generally both approaches are necessary to establish confidence in the reliability of the system.

Since testing traditionally comes at the end of the software development process, the temptation may be great to minimize testing if the project is late or over its budget. The cost of inadequate testing, however, can be quite expensive. The cost may include:

o   The cost of repairing a software error after installation. For many microprocessor applications where thousands of products containing the microprocessor software may be sold, this cost can be prohibitive. The common microprocessor practice of implementing the software in ROM aggravates this cost problem.

o   The cost of damages caused by the faulty software. Typical of microprocessor systems are the real-time and process control applications where faulty software can result not only in lost time, but also in lost revenue or even human endangerment.

o   The cost of lost business resulting from one's damaged reputation caused by a "buggy" product. Many companies build a reputation on quality products and they advertise this fact. The perceived quality of a new product and the company's reputation can be significantly affected by the software in a microprocessor-based system.

On the other hand, good test planning and implementation can reduce some costs. Proper test planning followed by testing performed as the microprocessor software development proceeds allows one to run a comparatively small number of test cases and still achieve reliability. This saves both personnel and machine costs. A good plan allows management to allocate the appropriate number of persons to the project at the appropriate times.

An important point to remember as we begin the discussion of testing is that "the amount of difficulty encountered at each testing step is inversely related to the thoroughness of the preceding steps."[2] Indeed, the debugging process, described earlier, and reviews of requirements, design, and code to be discussed later in this book, can all be considered a part of the testing process. Thus care taken during the early phases of the system development will pay off during the later phases of development.

8.2 The Testing Process

Traditionally, testing has been approached in an ad hoc manner. Tests were developed using intuition rather than formalism, and testing terminated when the programmers felt that the testing completed was adequate or when the time and/or money allocated to the project had been consumed. Although the problems of testing have not all been solved, a more formal approach to testing can ensure a higher quality software product at reduced cost. The testing process consists of four distinct phases:

(1)   Test planning

(2)   Test case selection

(3)   Test execution

(4)   Test review

We discuss each of these phases in the next four sections.

8.3 Test Planning

8.3.1 Testing Phases

In diagrams depicting the phases in the development of a software product, testing is always near the end. Yet test planning should begin much earlier and should be performed in parallel with the requirements, design, and coding activities. Before any specific test data are generated, the overall plan and goals of testing for the project should be determined. In this section, we will discuss the different phases of testing to which the software

2M. S. Deutch, "Verification and Validation" in Randall W. Jensen and Charles C. Tonies, eds., Software Engineering (Englewood Cliffs, New Jersey: Prentice Hall, 1979), p. 340.

should be subjected. During these phases, the modules that constitute the software system will be subjected to a hierarchy of tests. This hierarchy consists of the following four distinct sets of tests, each of which has its own sets of objectives and criteria:

(1)   Module Test

(2)   Integration Test

(3)   System Test

(4)   Acceptance/Installation Test

Module tests are generally performed after a module is coded to assure that the code implementing the module meets the design specification for the module. Integration testing addresses groups of completed modules. The objective of integration testing is to ensure the integrity of the system design, i.e., the solution structure. System testing involves tests of the complete system to demonstrate that the system satisfies the requirements, i.e., performs the functions required of it. The final tests, acceptance and installation tests, are generally tests performed, or at least specified, by the customer before the customer accepts the product for use. Acceptance tests are performed at the development site while installation tests are performed at the customer site. For commercially distributed microprocessor-based products, surrogates for customers usually perform acceptance and installation tests to reduce the activities the consumers have to perform.

The test plan should describe the kinds of tests to be performed at each phase and the criteria to be used to determine the test cases.

8.3.2 Approaches to Integration Testing

As one develops the design and test plan, an important consideration will be the approach used to integrate and test the system. In general, the possible approaches can be classified as incremental and nonincremental. An incremental approach implies the addition of one module at a time to the part of the system already tested. This has the obvious advantage of isolating the source of almost all errors that are manifested by the tests. Incremental tests can be performed in a top-down or bottom-up order. In the hierarchy chart in Figure 8-1, for example, a top-down test would first test module A. Once A has been verified, one of modules B, C, or D would be added to the system (currently just module A) and the system would again be tested. If one chose to add B, then after testing A and B together one

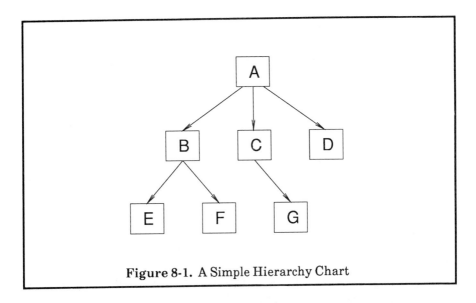

Figure 8-1. A Simple Hierarchy Chart

would next add C or D to the system. Continuing in this manner, one would add a module at a time until all modules were added and tested.

A bottom-up incremental test proceeds in the opposite direction. In this case, one would first test modules E, F, G, and D individually. One could then add module B to modules E and F and test the B-E-F subsystem. Continuing, one would add G to C and test. Finally, add A to the system for the final set of tests.

Selecting the bottom-up or top-down technique for incremental testing depends on the particular application. Top-down testing is advantageous when it is desirable to test the system structure early and to determine quickly if there are any major interface problems in the design. The top-down approach also allows the user to see a preliminary version of the system to ensure that the user's needs are being met. On the other hand, bottom-up testing is advantageous when there is a low-level module that has a critical effect on the real-time performance of the system. Using top-down testing, problems with such a module would not become apparent until near the end of the scheduled testing activities. In many systems using microprocessor software, there may be concerns related to critical high-level interfaces in the system involving several processors and critical timing concerns controlled by low-level modules. In this situation, it may be necessary to use a hybrid testing strategy, testing in parallel the critical low-level modules while also beginning a top-down incremental test to test the interfaces.

In testing modules using the top-down approach, one should use stubs for the modules which are called by the module being tested. For example, to test module A of the system in Figure 8-1, one should develop stubs for modules B, C, and D. Although frequently one sees stubs that simply print a message such as "Module B Called," a proper test of the calling module requires the stub to check the input parameters and return reasonable values for the output parameters. A simple table look-up technique can often be used to accomplish this. On the other hand, when testing proceeds bottom-up, drivers are required. To test module G in Figure 8-1, for example, it is necessary to have a driver which calls module G and passes it the appropriate parameters for the test cases that one wants performed. In general, writing drivers or stubs are tasks that are considered to be about equal difficulty. Thus neither method gains advantage on this point.

Nonincremental testing consists of two categories: phased testing and "big bang" testing.[3] The "big bang" approach is to combine all of the modules in the system after unit testing and subject the total system to testing. For a system of any significant size, this approach cannot be recommended because of the difficulty of planning tests to exercise the system thoroughly as a whole and the difficulty in locating any errors that are manifested by the tests. Phased testing is closer to the traditional method of testing. In phased testing, groups of related modules are tested as subsystems and then the subsystems are combined and tested. For example, given the hierarchy chart in Figure 8-2, modules F, G, and H might be tested and then added to module E for testing.

Meanwhile, modules K and L would be tested together and then added to module I for testing. Finally, these two groups of modules would be combined and subsystem testing would occur. Simultaneously, the other two subsystems could be similarly tested. The final system test would combine the three subsystems with module A for the final integration tests. An apparent advantage of this phased bottom-up approach is the amount of parallelism in the testing process. The time saved by this overlap can, however, be lost if one must spend considerable time solving interface errors that are discovered in the final phases of integration testing.

To summarize, integration testing should usually be done incrementally because of the relative ease of isolating errors and of generating appropriate tests for the most recently added module. Testing should generally be performed in a top-down fashion, however, some hybrid

[3]Myers, op. cit., p. 89

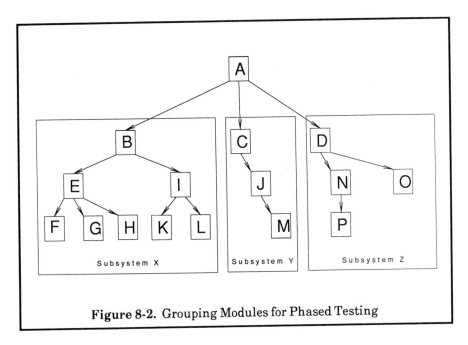

Figure 8-2. Grouping Modules for Phased Testing

of top-down and bottom-up testing may be appropriate on occasions where low-level modules will be crucial in the system's ability to satisfy the performance requirements.

8.3.3 Documenting the Test Plan

The test plan document, often called simply the "test plan" just as the requirements documentation is referred to as the "requirements," is the result of the first phase of the testing process, namely, test planning.

> *Prepare the test plan in parallel with the design activity.*
> *Organize the test plan so that it addresses:*
>
>   *(1)   the tests to be performed at each level*
>   *of the test hierarchy*
>   *- module test*
>   *- integration test*
>   *- system test*
>   *- acceptance/installation test*
>   *(2)   the criteria to be used to determine test cases*
>   *(3)   the criteria for terminating each level of testing*

For each type of test, the following sets of questions must be answered.

(1) WHO?

o   Who is responsible for performing each of the levels of testing?

o   Who is responsible for developing stubs and drivers required for testing?

o   Who is responsible for finding and correcting errors that are manifested in testing? How will the responsible party be notified of the errors? What documentation will that person want?

(2) WHAT?

o   What are the objectives of each of the levels of testing?

o   What criteria should be used to determine when to stop testing at a particular level?

o   What criteria should be used to design test cases?

o   What method of system integration is to be used?

(3) WHEN?

o   When will the test cases be designed, implemented, and executed?

o   When are each of the testing levels scheduled to begin and end?

(4) WHERE?

o   Where will the testing for each phase take place: in a lab, in a simulated environment, or in the customer's environment?

(5) HOW?

o   How will the tests be executed? Will a simulator, the final machine, or a testing tool be used?

o   How will modules changed as a result of finding errors in testing be tested?

8.4 Test Case Selection

As Glass points out, the purpose of using a formal methodology for the test case selection process is to "ensure that all tests planned are necessary and sufficient and that their results conclusively prove that the developed capability is complete, correct, and operable."[4] Although it is not possible to prove conclusively that the software is one hundred percent correct by testing, one can use formal techniques to estimate how well the test cases test the software, and thus determine an appropriate set of test cases to achieve the desired reliability. Most criteria used to measure the extent of testing may be classified as either black box or glass (white) box methods. Black box testing is a testing strategy where test cases are generated solely by analyzing the system requirements. In glass box testing strategies, test cases are generated by analyzing the logic of the code.

8.4.1 Glass Box Testing

One frequently bases testing criteria on some measurement of the amount of code that has been exercised by the test. Several measures have been developed to determine the extent to which the code has been tested. These measures include:

o   Statement coverage

o   Path coverage

o   Decision coverage

o   Condition coverage

o   Decision/condition coverage

o   Multiple condition coverage

Statement coverage measures the percentage of statements in the program that have been executed in a test. Although selecting data to obtain one hundred percent statement coverage is the desired goal, achieving this coverage may be an elusive goal because of special cases that are difficult to test. Even achieving one hundred percent statement coverage does not mean that all or even most of the errors have been found. Successfully achieving one hundred percent statement coverage means that every statement in a program is meaningful; it would not necessarily check, for example, that a test for equality in a conditional statement should be replaced by a test for "less than or equal to."

4Robert L. Glass, <u>Modern Programming Practices, A Report from Industry</u> (Englewood Cliffs, New Jersey: Prentice-Hall, 1982), p. 139.

A more stringent criterion is path coverage. Path coverage measures the percentage of unique paths that have been executed in a test. A path is a sequence of statements executed in a module between the entrance to the module and the exit from the module. The total number of paths is the number of all possible ways to get from the module entrance to the module exit. Covering all unique paths through a typical program is generally not feasible. The diagram in Figure 8-3 which is much simpler than most programs, has approximately 10^{20} unique paths through it[5]. This is more test cases than one can generally hope to run and check.

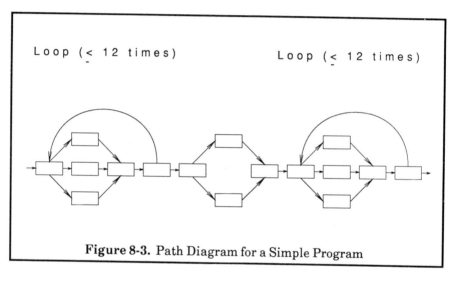

Loop (< 12 times)   Loop (< 12 times)

Figure 8-3. Path Diagram for a Simple Program

Because of the infeasibility of complete path coverage, one generally attempts instead to cover each path segment. A path segment is the sequence of statements executed between two adjacent potential branches in the code, thus path segments exist between all pairs of adjacent decisions in the code. Testing each path segment in a module is equivalent to testing each possible outcome of every decision, so path segment coverage is frequently called decision coverage. An example of the difference between decision coverage (or path segment coverage) and statement coverage can be seen in the following code:

IF A < 10 THEN A : = 100;

[5]M. S. Deutch, "Verification and Validation" in Randall W. Jensen and Charles C. Tonies, eds., <u>Software Engineering</u> (Englewood Cliffs, New Jersey: Prentice Hall, 1979), pp. 337-338. Reprinted by permission.

Using statement coverage this statement might be tested only with the value of A less than 10. Decision coverage, on the other hand, would require that this statement be tested with a value of A less than 10 and a value of A greater than or equal to 10.

Testing each branch from a decision point may still leave many undetected bugs. For example, in the segment

IF (A < 10 AND B = 5) THEN....

the test cases (A = 5, B = 5) and (A = 15, B = 5) would satisfy the criterion for decision coverage. Suppose, however, that the second condition should be B less than or equal to 5. The above test cases will not cause this bug to become apparent.

To detect such errors, one would require test cases that cause each possible outcome for each condition. This is called condition coverage. For the above example, this would require test cases with A less than 10, A greater than or equal to 10, B equal to 5, and B not equal to 5.

Notice that if one chooses test cases (A = 6, B = 8) and (A = 12, B = 5), the condition coverage criterion has been satisfied, but the decision criterion and even the statement coverage criterion have not been satisfied. Thus one generally requires both a criterion for testing all conditions and all decision outcomes. The test cases (A = 5, B = 5) and (A = 12, B = 7) satisfy this decision/condition criterion.

An even stronger criterion would require that all possible combinations of each condition in a decision be tested. The test cases (A = 6, B = 5), (A = 10, B = 5), (A = 6, B = 8), and (A = 10, B = 8) satisfy this multiple-condition criterion. The multiple-condition criterion would detect such errors as using a logical "and" operator when an "or" operator was desired.

It is interesting to note that is it possible to generate test cases that satisfy the most stringent of the coverage criteria presented and yet do not find the simple hypothesized bug in the above example. Some knowledge of the kinds of errors that are most frequently made, and a little common sense, can help when devising test cases to maximize the probability of detection of such errors. In particular, since many errors are caused by an off-by-one situation at a boundary, it is generally more profitable to pick boundary conditions for test cases rather than arbitrary test cases that satisfy the necessary conditions. In addition, the set of test cases generated for equality comparisons should include test cases with values less than the specified value and values greater than the specified value. Using these guidelines, a more complete set of test cases for the above example would be (A=9, B=5), (A=10, B=5), (A=9, B=4), (A=9, B=6), (A=10, B=4), and (A=10, B=6).

Generally, glass box techniques are most appropriate for module tests. It is usually only at this level that it is feasible to generate test cases to exercise the code sufficiently to satisfy the desired criterion. For multiple modules examined collectively the number of test cases usually required is so large, and the difficulty of generating the appropriate test cases to satisfy the criterion is so high, that glass box techniques become virtually unreasonable. It is also during module tests that one should be concerned about verifying the details of the code logic. During later phases of testing, one should have a more global test criterion.

Use glass box testing to obtain the desired
coverage of statements, paths, decisions,
and conditions in a module.

8.4.2 Black Box Testing

In black box testing one generates test cases without looking at the code that implements the system to be tested; instead, one generates test cases by examining system requirements. Since it is rare when one can test a system with all possible combinations of potential inputs, a methodology is required to select good test cases. A good test case is one that represents a wide range of possible input cases. To achieve this, one may partition the range of possible inputs into a set of equivalence classes. If one test case from an equivalence class detects an error, then every other member of the equivalence class would also cause a similar error. This is called equivalence partitioning.

To obtain the equivalence classes, one looks at the input specification. Each portion of the specification describing an input item will result in at least two equivalent classes, one containing the valid values and one containing the invalid values for that item. For example, assume that the specification states a particular measurement will be in the range 0 to 150. This results in three equivalence classes: (1) the valid values, which are in the range 0 to 150; (2) the invalid values, which are those less than 0; and (3) the invalid values, which are those greater than 150. In this case, the invalid values were divided into two equivalence classes because it is possible that values less than 0 are handled differently from values greater than 150.

After listing all equivalence classes, one needs to select test cases to cover each of the classes. First, test cases representing equivalence classes resulting from valid inputs should be devised. Frequently, one test case can represent several input classes. Second, test cases representing equivalence classes generated by considering invalid inputs should be devised. Each of these equivalence classes should have a unique test case. This is to ensure that all relevant tests are performed. It is frequently the case that a program will terminate after encountering the first error, and thus the test to handle additional inputs might never be performed.

An improved variation of equivalence partitioning is based on analyzing boundary conditions. As mentioned earlier in discussing glass box techniques, there is a much higher probability of an error occurring at a boundary point than at some other random point in the the set of possible input values. To account for this, boundary analysis requires using test cases from the boundaries of equivalence classes. Thus, if one has a partition for an integer input X with $0 \leq X \leq 150$, one would generate test cases with $X = 0$, $X = 150$, $X = -1$, and $X = 151$. When generating equivalence classes, one should not forget such conditions as no data (e.g., an empty input file).

A less formal but sometimes very effective technique to use for generating test cases is called error guessing. This method requires one to look at the specification and decide what aspects of the problem or solution might be error-prone. For example, a portion of the specification may be ambiguous or lacking in certain details. This may have resulted in a misinterpretation by the designer or programmer. As another example, an experienced programmer may know that a certain situation is frequently not handled properly, such as a queue overflowing.

Use black box testing augmented by glass box testing
to obtain the desired coverage of functions and performance
in integration, system, and acceptance/installation testing.

8.4.3 Testing by Program Modification

An additional testing technique that is often useful in microprocessor software is based on modifying the program. By purposely introducing errors into the program or changing slightly the functionality of the program, one can test the effectiveness of the test cases used to test the program. If the test cases do not detect the errors in the modified program, the test cases should be augmented. It is obviously crucial to document thoroughly the modifications to the program to avoid the possibility of releasing a mutated version of the system accidentally.

In addition to modifying the program, in some situations the environment should be modified to test the robustness of the system. For example, the timing cycle may be changed or the amount of available memory might be reduced. In many microprocessor-based products, the software expects inputs in certain time intervals. The length of the time intervals should be varied to ensure that the software is not too sensitive to moderate variations in the environment. The use of a simulator can facilitate testing the software under slight changes in the environment.

8.4.4 Test Case Documentation

For each test case, prepare a test document that describes
- *the input values required to perform the desired test*
- *the environment in which the test will run*
- *the expected results*

It is essential that the expected results be documented in order to minimize the chance of missing an error in the output because "everything looked good" to the tester. By requiring thorough documentation of all test cases, one avoids generating "throw away" test cases which are then not available later when further testing is required.

8.5 Test Execution

Test execution is the process of actually running the microprocessor software using as input the test cases generated during the earlier phases of the testing process. As with other phases of software development, documentation is important during test execution.

Keep a test log which records each test,
the results obtained, and follow on actions.

It is important that both final outputs and events that occurred during execution be noted. This is particularly true in real-time microprocessor systems. As an example, consider an oven that uses a microprocessor to adjust the temperature readout depending on the altitude. If during high altitude testing, the appropriate response is received after a two-hour period, the fact that it took two hours for the calibration is as important as the fact that the correct response was finally obtained.

8.6 Test Review

After the test cases have been run and the results recorded, the test log should be examined and test summary reports prepared. Test summary reports summarize the results of the test cases run, indicating what problems occurred. It is then necessary to trace back to the source of the problem, and determine what action to take. If the expected test results were wrong, then the test case documentation should be corrected and the test review repeated.

If the review of the test results show that the software
or the design is incorrect, make the appropriate changes
to the design, to the software, and to all relevant documentation;
after these changes, repeat the test execution and review.

If the results do not meet the requirements specified for the product, the ideal situation would require changing the system to meet the requirements followed by retesting and reviewing the results until the requirements are met. In practice, however, it may be too expensive, or perhaps even not feasible, to meet the original requirements. In this case, it becomes necessary to change the requirements to match the capability of the software.

Document carefully all changes to the software
made as a result of testing.

Comments in the prologue should describe who made the modifications, when they were made, and the purpose of the modifications, i.e., the test case which was handled incorrectly but which should now be handled correctly. The changed code should be commented out, and the new code inserted with relevant comments. Comments should also indicate the correspondence between the code changes and the description of the modifications in the prologue.

It is important that all modifications to code or documentation go through the same review and testing processes that the original documentation and code went through. This is to avoid the introduction of additional errors in the attempt to fix existing errors. It is frequently the case that corrections are more error-prone than the original code because fixes are frequently done hastily and under stress. By requiring a review of all modifications, the number of "quick fixes" that produce errors can be reduced.

8.7 Test Termination Criteria

A primary concern in testing is the question, "How much testing is enough?" Unlike coding, where the completion of the task is obvious, it is not obvious when software has been adequately tested. Frequently the only criterion used for terminating testing is the passing of a date on the project schedule.[6] If previous phases of the software development project have taken longer than expected, e.g., as a result of changing requirements, then the time allotted to testing may be more closely related to budget concerns or product delivery schedules than to the complexity of the problem and the number of errors in the code.

> *Specify the criteria for terminating*
> *each testing level in the test plan.*

The termination criteria might include any combination of the following:

o   The test cases satisfy some glass box criterion such as the decision/condition criteria, and no errors are found.

o   The test cases were generated using some black box technique such as equivalence partitioning and boundary value analysis, and no errors are found.

o   A specified number of errors have been detected.

o   A specified amount of time has passed.

o   The error detection rate has decreased below a specified level.

Each of the criteria has certain advantages and disadvantages. The glass box techniques are generally appropriate only for tests of individual modules or small subsystems. Even at the module level, it may be necessary to use tools to help in the generation of the test data. (Test tools will be discussed in the next section.) The advantage of criteria based on glass box techniques is the relative simplicity of demonstrating that the test does satisfy the desired criteria. The use of testing tools facilitates such testing.

---

[6]Myers, op. cit., pp. 122-128.

Black box techniques are most appropriate for the system tests. A major disadvantage of specifying black box criteria is that there is currently no way to verify that a set of test cases satisfy the desired black box criteria. Experience and care are needed to determine the equivalence classes.

If one could predict the number of errors in the software and how many of these errors could be found during each phase of testing, detecting that number of errors would be the best stopping criterion. Unfortunately, the number of variables that affect the number of errors in the software is so large that it will be almost impossible to predict the exact number of errors. Rough estimates of the number of errors in the software can be obtained from either experience or one of several models[7,8,9] developed for this purpose. Since these estimates are generally rough, some common sense should be applied to their use. For example, if the expected number of errors is found quickly, the software is probably more error-prone than the average and testing should be continued. On the other hand, after what appears to be thorough testing, the expected number of errors might not have been found. In this case, an independent group should certify that the tests do appear to thoroughly exercise the software. This will decrease the possibility of having had insufficient or inadequate test cases.

The final criterion is based on the assumption that one should continue a particular test phase until that level of testing is no longer effective. The effectiveness of the testing is measured by the number of errors found per unit of time. When the number of errors found per unit of time falls below some predetermined level, one moves on to the next level of testing. For example, suppose one has gathered the data in Figure 8-4 during integration tests. By week six, very few errors are being found using this type of test and so the next phase of testing should probably begin. Of course, there are several underlying assumptions made in this model which must be kept in mind. The primary assumption is that the code is being subjected to the same amount of testing each time period. If during one

[7]Glenford J. Myers, Software Reliability (New York: John Wiley & Sons, 1976), pp. 336-342.

[8]Linda M. Ottenstein, "Quantitative Estimates of Debugging Requirements", IEEE Transactions on Software Engineering, vol. SE-5, no.9 (September 1979), pp. 504-514.

[9]Linda M. Ottenstein, "Predicting Software Development Errors Using Software Science Parameters," 1981 ACM Workshop/Symposium on Measurement and Evaluation of Software Quality, Performance Evaluation Review, vol. 10, no. 1, pp. 157-167.

week, there were only two working days because of holidays or the computer used for testing was not available, the error rate may decrease below the specified level. This, however, would not necessarily mean that the software was thoroughly tested.

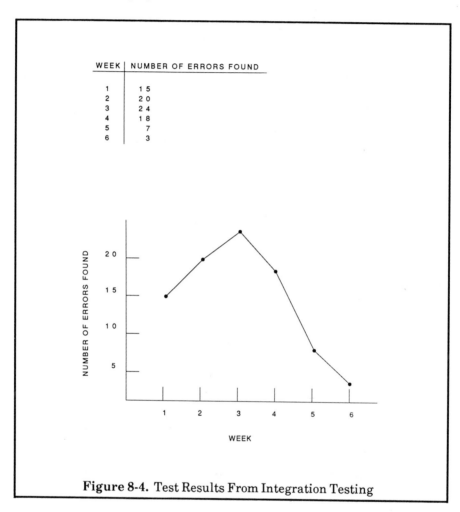

Figure 8-4. Test Results From Integration Testing

8.8 Testing Tools

Many types of testing tools can be used to aid in the testing process, however, these tools are not used as much as they should be. The tools currently available can be classified as static tools or dynamic tools. Static tools are programs that analyze the code to be tested, while dynamic tools analyze the executing program.

Static tools include syntax checkers which may point out error-prone or questionable syntactic constructs and check module interfaces for consistency of parameter usage. A static flow analysis tool can be used to detect potentially uninitialized variables and unreachable code. Generally, these tools are most easily used (and most economical) when they are included in the compiler.

Dynamic tools include test coverage analyzers, assertion checkers, and test drivers. A test coverage analyzer monitors the code as it is executed noting the frequency of execution of each statement. Statements with an execution frequency of zero were obviously not tested during that execution of the program. An automated test case generator could then be used to generate an appropriate data set to exercise the previously untested section of code. One problem with automatic test case generators is that they generate only the input data; it is up to a human to determine the correct output to make the data a test case.

Assertion checkers are debugging systems that allow the insertion of assert statements into a program. An assert statement specifies conditions on variables that should be true at a particular point in the execution of the program. If the conditions are true, execution of the program would continue. If not, the programmer would be informed of the problem. For example, suppose that if a system is functioning correctly, a parameter, A, to a particular module should always be positive. To be sure that this is what happens, the program would have the following statement at the beginning of the module:

ASSERT A > 0

If during execution, the module is called with a nonpositive value passed for A, the run-time system would detect the false condition in the assertion and execution of the program would terminate.

A test driver is generally used to perform module tests. A good test driver provides a language for specifying test cases including inputs and expected outputs. The driver executes the module with the provided inputs and notifies the user of any discrepancies between the specified outputs and the outputs actually obtained.

One of the most frequently used tools for testing microprocessor software is the environment simulator. An environment simulator is a system (usually computer controlled) that provides physical inputs (such as electrical signals in real-time control systems) and records physical outputs under the control of the tester. An environment simulator allows one to test the software in an environment more easily controlled than the actual environment in which the software will eventually be used. In addition to responding to the software being tested in the same manner as the actual environment would, a good environment simulator should provide some additional features. These include allowing the tester to monitor the system, to stop and examine the system, and then to have it proceed normally, and to modify the environment to determine the effect.

8.9 Testing in Perspective

Three final points to be made about testing are

o   Software testing, if done properly, can be a very rewarding experience. Unlike hardware which wears out, once a correct fix has been made to software, the fix is permanent; that particular bug will never occur again.

o   The proper synthesis of a program through the requirements definition, design, and coding stages significantly simplifies testing.

o   Testing does not prove the absence of errors in or the correctness of a program; it shows only that the program works correctly for the situations represented by the test cases.

Researchers working on program proof techniques are attempting to find ways to mathematically verify that a program is correct under all circumstances. Proofs have been done for small programs, but currently the techniques are too cumbersome to be used in general. In addition, the proof of a program only involves the static analysis of the code and a verification of its mathematical accuracy. In many real-time microprocessor applications, there are critical timing constraints between devices. The correctness of the timing could not be proven by static proof techniques.

8.10 Summary of Testing Principles

Test planning should proceed in parallel with the system design phase.

A test plan detailing the how's, why's, where's, and what's of the testing process should be documented.

Testing should consist of four levels — module tests, integration tests, system tests, and acceptance/installation tests.

Glass box criteria are generally appropriate for module level tests while black box criteria are used for higher level tests.

Integration testing should be done in an incremental top-down manner. An exception to this occurs when there are critical low-level modules that have a significant effect on the system's ability to meet its requirements. An example would be a low-level module that could significantly affect timing constraints. In this case, the critical modules should be tested bottom-up in parallel with the traditional top-down integration.

The results of all runs of test cases should be documented in the test log. This includes both outputs of the system and events that occurred during execution of the run.

A test summary report should be prepared summarizing the results of the test runs.

All changes that are made to the system, in the documentation or the code, should go through the life cycle process again including all relevant reviews to assure the correctness of the fixes.

9

MAINTAINING

MICROPROCESSOR SOFTWARE

9.1 Overview of Software Maintenance

9.1.1 Maintenance of Software in a Traditional Environment

Since software does not wear out like mechanical or electronic hardware, the meaning of software maintenance is quite different from the meaning of maintenance of other engineering products. A general definition of software maintenance is "the process of modifying existing operational software while leaving its primary functions intact."[1]

The modifications made to the software in the software maintenance process can be classified into two categories: repairs and enhancements. Repairs are necessary to correct errors in the original software that were not detected by testing, or to account for deficiencies in some other aspect of the system that can be accommodated by the software. This latter aspect of correcting for other deficiencies is especially important in microprocessor software. Enhancements are made to increase the efficiency of the system, to improve the user interface, or to adapt the system to changing requirements and desires.

Because of the extensiveness of the maintenance process, one should not be surprised that maintenance consumes a significant portion of

[1]Barry W. Boehm, "Software Engineering: R & D Trends and Defense Needs," in Peter Wegner, ed., Research Directions in Software Technology (Cambridge, Massachusetts: The MIT Press, 1979), p. 65.

resources allocated to software development. Figure 1-2 illustrates the role of maintenance in software development. It has been estimated that software maintenance has grown to consume over half the total cost of hardware/software systems. This evolution is illustrated in Figure 9-1. This percentage of cost allocated to software maintenance has grown as additional code is continually developed and put into a maintenance phase faster than existing code is retired.

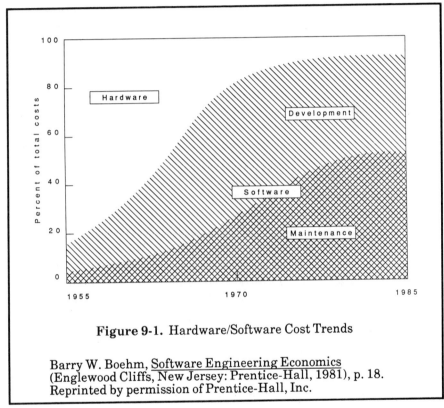

Figure 9-1. Hardware/Software Cost Trends

Barry W. Boehm, <u>Software Engineering Economics</u>
(Englewood Cliffs, New Jersey: Prentice-Hall, 1981), p. 18.
Reprinted by permission of Prentice-Hall, Inc.

In spite of the cost and time involved in maintenance, "software maintenance has been an area of management neglect, little prestige, and only crisis appearance in budgeting cycles."[2] Likewise, in academic circles, the maintenance phase of software development has been largely ignored. Unlike testing, for example, very little research has been done on maintenance techniques and associated tool development.

---

[2]Anne W. Laffan, "The Software Maintenance Problem," <u>Proceedings of the Eleventh Hawaii International Conference on System Sciences</u>, 1978, pp. 37-39.

9.1.2 Maintenance of Software in a Microprocessor Environment

The maintenance phase of software written for microprocessors is often significantly different from the maintenance of software written for large-scale machines. The reason for this is due to the medium in which the software is distributed along with the cost of change to software in that medium. In large systems, the customer pays a significant sum of money for the software which is typically distributed on a magnetic tape. When errors are detected, the developer makes corrections and prepares and distributes to customers a new tape with the updates. In many microprocessor-based products, such as consumer devices and office equipment, the software is burned into ROMs and must be treated like hardware. In these instances, the cost of installing software updates on products after they have been sold and delivered to customers is prohibitive because the hardware would have to be changed. Thus one may argue that there should be no maintenance phase for microprocessor software (i.e., that testing should be performed so that no changes are necessary). Even when repairs are not required in the field, however, most microprocessor software will require maintenance. Frequently, for instance, after a product has been in service for some time, the desire for improvements will become apparent. These modifications will be made to the software for the next release of the product. For new products, it is often better to update old reliable software from a similar product than to develop new software. Because of the demand for high reliability in many microprocessor-based products, careful modification of an existing reliable system may reduce the high cost of software development and increase reliability.

9.2 Reducing the Need and Time for Software Maintenance

Because of the cost of software maintenance, it is particularly important to reduce the amount of maintenance when dealing with microprocessor systems. Since the first aspect of maintenance is error correction, the first step toward reducing maintenance is to develop software with no errors; this eliminates the requirement for corrections later. The techniques described in previous chapters provide a foundation for developing error-free software. In addition to these techniques, it is important to maintain close communication with the customer or user of the system during the entire development process. Frequently developers are in so much of a rush to begin the project that not enough time is devoted to communicating with the customer. This poor communication can lead to a disparity between what the customer wants and what the developer delivers. Customers should not be pressured into making decisions too quickly, especially if they do not fully understand the consequences of their decisions. Developers should maintain contact with the customers throughout the development of the project to ensure that it is still conforming to the customers' wishes.

Developing a product that is as error-free as possible and meets the customers' specifications is only half the battle. Even if no errors are found, modifications will almost surely still be necessary. It is therefore important that the program be designed for modifiability. Several of the techniques described in previous chapters improve the modifiability of software. Modularization is the key to modifiability.[3] Design decisions should be isolated to individual modules. Parnas's information hiding techniques should be practiced.[4] Documentation should be well written, complete, and accurate. It is particularly during the maintenance phase that the effort put into modularization and documentation during earlier phases will pay off. Other preventive maintenance activities to be practiced include:[5]

o   Parameterization of program constants that could conceivably change.

o   Leaving a margin of any constrained resource for modifications. For example, do not use every byte of available memory.

o   Maintaining software standards.

To summarize this section:

> *Reduce the need and time for software maintenance by*
> - *using the techniques in previous chapters to develop high quality software*
> - *maintaining close communication with customers*
> - *designing software for modifiability*

[3]Anthony I. Wasserman, "Information System Design Methodology," University of California, San Franscisco, Medical Information Science, Technical Report 39 (November 1979).

[4]D. L. Parnas, "On the Criteria to be Used in Decomposing Systems into Modules," Communications of the ACM (December 1972), pp. 1053-1058.

[5]Robert L. Glass, Software Reliability Guidebook (Englewood Cliffs, New Jersey: Prentice Hall, 1979), pp. 158-159.

9.3 The Maintenance Process

The maintenance process should be as well controlled as the other phases of software development. The maintenance process is initiated by documented problem reports or requests for changes.

> *Review each problem report or request for change*
> *to determine if it warrants making modifications*
> *to the software and if so, to prioritize the work.*

When reviewing a particular request, one should consider

o   The remaining lifetime of the software. If the system is to be retired or replaced shortly, it may not be worth the expense to update the current system. If correct operation of the current system is critical, however, it may be worth updating so that it can serve as a backup to the new system in the future. Thus, the anticipated value of the updated system must be compared to the costs of the updates.

o   The applicability of the change to the function of the system. It may be appropriate to provide the requested function as a part of another system rather than as an addition to the current system.

o   The criticality of the request. If the software is difficult to modify and the bug is easy to work around, one may decide that it is safer to continue to work around the bug rather than risk introducing more severe problems.

As during the other phases of software development, documentation of the maintenance process is important. All problems and requests for changes should be submitted on a form so that they can be monitored to ensure that none are lost. After a decision to process or ignore is made, the result should be recorded and the initiator notified. If the decision is to update the software, an expected date of completion should be given. If a negative decision was made, the initiator should be informed of the reason for the rejection.

> *Programmers processing a change request or error*
> *report should follow these steps:[6]*
> > *(1)   Understand the objectives of the request.*

[6]S. S. Yau and J. S. Collofello, "Some Stability Measures for Software Maintenance," IEEE Transactions on Software Engineering, vol. SE 6, no. 6 (November 1980), pp. 545-546.

It is important to know exactly what the user is requesting.

(2)   *Study the relevant sections of the software*
      and documentation.

Since the maintainer may not be the original programmer, enough time should be allotted to allow complete understanding of the relevant portions of the software.

(3)   *Generate a proposal to meet the desired objectives.*

The proposal should be reviewed in a manner similar to that for newly developed software to ensure that it meets the specified objectives.

(4)   *Determine the portions of the system to be affected*
      by the change.

It is necessary to account for all possible side effects of the change, both internally and externally. Tests must be devised to establish that only the desired effects have been introduced by the modified software. External side effects that are desired must be documented while undesirable side effects should be eliminated.

(5)   *Run the tests developed during the previous phase to*
      show the desired effects and to demonstrate that
      anticipated undesirable effects do not occur.

This should be followed by regression tests. Regression testing consists of running test cases selected from those used for system integration testing to assure that the system still behaves as expected. Unlike earlier testing phases, during regression testing the most complex tests are run first. If they show no undesirable system behavior, the changes may be assumed to have introduced no new problems. If errors are manifested, then simpler tests are run to isolate the source of the problem. If earlier testing phases are done properly and the appropriate documentation kept, regression testing will be much less difficult.

(6)   *After testing has been completed, the change should be*
      approved, installed, and documented.

Program headers should include the name of the person making the modification, the date of the modification, and an explanation of why the modification was made. The new code should be marked as a revision with an explanation. Old code should be converted to comments with a date and explanation rather than be removed. This gives a historical perspective to future maintainers of the system.

9.4 Managing Software Maintenance

Several points merit special mention concerning typical management decisions about various aspects of software maintenance. The first pertains to the programmers to whom maintenance should be assigned. It is frequently the policy to assign maintenance tasks to new hires to give them time to learn the system before writing their own code. On the surface there appear to be advantages to this policy.

o   The new programmers have the opportunity to see and learn from code developed by more experienced programmers.

o   They are exposed to the company standards for code and perhaps most important, they become aware of the importance of standards, of good documentation, and of readable code.

There are, however, disadvantages:

o   New programmers often (but incorrectly) believe that maintenance activities do not require creativity. Unless the organization provides appropriate incentives, new programmers can rapidly develop morale problems because of the low prestige they attribute to maintenance. Low morale among new programmers hurts both the company and the individuals.

o   The inexperienced programmer is apt to bungle the maintenance task. Much of the results of the effort put into the prior stages of the development of a piece of software can be undone quickly by an inept maintenance programmer. For example, once the documentation and the code no longer match, the maintenance process becomes much more difficult.

o   Certain skills are needed in a maintenance programmer that not all programmers, and therefore not all new programmers, have. A maintenance programmer should be adaptable. One does not want a maintenance programmer that spends much of his time rewriting code to make it more understandable to him. A good maintenance programmer is one who can accept that others may do things differently and can maintain programs written by different programmers.

A second concern about the management of microprocessor software maintenance deals with the monitoring of the maintenance process. Depending on the organization structure, the monitoring task may be assigned to a maintenance manager or a change control board. This individual or group should review all requests for changes, should ensure that adequate retesting has been completed, should check that the appropriate documentation has been updated, and maintain an error tracking system. The error tracking system serves two purposes. It should monitor change requests to assure that they are being handled expediently. It should also monitor the locations in the system to which modifications are being made. If a particular module has been heavily modified, a review of that module should be performed. Heavy modification frequently indicates a major problem in the original design. Even if the original design was adequate, heavily modified code is difficult to maintain. It may, therefore, be more cost effective to redesign and recode a frequently changed portion of the system than to continue to update it.

A final management concern is interacting with the users during maintenance. It is frequently necessary to interact with users after change requests are received to ensure that the users' requirements are well understood. The person with whom the users interact can have a significant impact on the confidence the users have in the system and in the development team. Whether the person interacting with the users is the actual programmer or is an intermediary, it is important that the person be both empathetic and technically competent. Customer relations can have a tremendous impact on the users' satisfaction with a product, and during maintenance this relationship can be extremely important whether the customer is in another part of the company or an external user.

SUMMARY OF MICROPROCESSOR

SOFTWARE DEVELOPMENT

10.1 Introduction

In previous chapters we have described in some detail techniques for performing each of the phases in microprocessor software development: requirements specification, design specification, code, debug, test, and maintenance. We addressed the software development phases not in their sequential order but rather in an order more conducive to study by people with some experience in software development. Having examined the phases in some detail, it is now appropriate to review and summarize the principal points in microprocessor software development in their logical sequence. This chapter reiterates the key recommendations that were expressed in previous chapters as italicized imperative statements. These statements summarize the important points in developing microprocessor software.

10.2 Requirements Specification

Requirements specification is the most important activity in microprocessor software development. The result of the requirements specification process is a set of requirements specification documents that describes **what the** software must do. Requirements specification consists of two parts — analysis and synthesis:

Analyze requirements to determine customers' needs by
 o *perusing documentation from customers and marketing groups*
 o *interviewing customers and future system users*
 o *examining and using existing systems*

Devote the time needed to completely understand customers' requirements.

The first step in the synthesis of requirements specifications is to organize the information obtained during the requirements analysis activity.

The second step in the synthesis of requirements specifications is to write the customer requirements document.

The outline of the customer requirements specification should follow these general guidelines:
 (1) Review the information gathering and analysis.
 (2) Describe the functions to be performed.
 (3) Describe the performance goals.
 (4) Describe the design and development constraints.
 (5) Introduce the user manual and the software requirements specifications.

The third step is to write the user manual.

The outline of the user manual should follow these general guidelines:
 (1) Introduce the microprocessor system.
 (2) Describe the physical user interface.
 (3) Describe the basic features of the system.
 (4) Describe in detail the input/output sequences that constitute each feature.
 (5) List separately the errors that can occur and the appropriate response actions.
 (6) Provide an index to features, input/output sequences, and errors.

The fourth step, writing the software requirements, consists of two substeps:

*The first step in the synthesis of
software requirements is to classify
the functionality of the hardware and
the functionality of the software.*

*Define the details of the software
functions, performance, and constraints.*

To describe software functions:

*List completely the inputs and outputs
that the software must accept and generate.*

*Describe the functional transformations
that take the inputs and produce the outputs.*

To describe functional transformations for microprocessor-based systems, we make the following recommendation:

*Use the stimulus-response sequence technique
to describe functional transformations.*

10.3 Design Specification

The purpose of the design specification phase of microprocessor software development is to transform the requirements specification into a design specification that describes **how** the software will implement these requirements. The design specification consists of two documents: (1) a high level description of the structure of the software system to be implemented and (2) a detailed description of algorithms and data that can readily be transformed into implementable components in a computer programming language. As in the requirements specification process, design specification consists of two parts — analysis and synthesis. Design analysis consists of the following three steps:

*Analyze the system behavior by modeling it
with a data flow diagram or a finite state machine.*

To develop an FSM model of a system:
    (1) List all the possible system inputs.
    (2) List all the system outputs.
    (3) Determine the sequence of inputs that generate each output.
    (4) From the sequence determine states.

To develop a DFD model of a system:
    (1) List all the possible system inputs. These are the input data flows.
    (2) List all the system outputs. These are the output data flows.
    (3) Fill in the DFD body — adding processes, sources and destinations of data, data stores, and internal data flows — by working from inputs to outputs, or from outputs to inputs.
    (4) Label the process bubbles in terms of inputs and outputs.

Design synthesis produces the two aforementioned documents, and consists of two steps — high level design and detailed design. To perform high level design do the following:

> *Transform the DFD or FSM model of the system behavior*
> *into a structure chart or hierarchy chart*
> *which represents the logical structure*
> *of how the software will work.*

To draw a structure chart, first

> *Draw a single box (process module)*
>   o *whose inputs are the input data flows of the DFD or FSM*
>   o *whose outputs are the output data flows of the DFD or FSM, and*
>   o *whose name is a verb-object pair that describes the function of the microprocessor software system*

and then repeat the following steps

(1)   Partition the process described in a box into subprocesses, so that each subprocess performs a subset of the functions performed by the parent process in the DFD or FSM.

(2)   Draw a box for each subprocess on a horizontal line below the parent box and give it a verb-object name.

(3)   Assign each of the inputs and outputs from the parent process to the appropriate subprocesses, and create intermediate input/output data items as required, using the notation of Figure 4-7.

(4)   For each subprocess, expand the information about the processing function or data specification if required before proceeding to the next step.

There are two strategies for performing the partitioning activity in step (1):

Use transform analysis (or transform centered design)
and transaction analysis (or transaction
centered design) in partitioning.

Additional guidelines to follow in performing the partitioning activity are

Minimize coupling between modules.

Maximize cohesion within modules.

Limit module fan-out to seven or less.

The next step in the design synthesis process is detailed design.

Transform the structure chart or hierarchy chart
which describes the logical structure of how the software will work
into a PDL description of the physical structure of the final program.

The first step in detailed design is to develop
the high level physical structure for the program
using the hierarchy chart or structure chart
and implementation constraints as guides.

The second step in detailed design is to write
PDL descriptions for the top module(s)
in the hierarchy or structure chart.

When developing the detailed design,
allocate constrained resources to each module.

Complete the detailed design by writing PDL descriptions for
and allocating resources to the remaining modules
in the structure or hierarchy chart.

To keep the design specification process in perspective:

Make design an iterative process in which decisions are
periodically revisited, reviewed, and changed when necessary.

10.4 Coding

The two fundamental tenets of good program presentation style are

Make the program self-documenting.

Specify explicitly; unspecified assumptions will be misinterpreted.

Most coding presentation techniques are special cases of these two tenets.
In developing program components, for example:

Use the general form shown in Figure 2-2
for each component in a self-documenting program.

Examining the parts of the standard program component, we make the
following recommendations.

Component header:

Make the name in the component header descriptive.

Prologue:

Use the format in Figure 2-3
for the prologue of a program component.

Declarations:

Declare all variables.

Use descriptive names for variables.

> *Group logically related variables together,*
> *e.g., loop variables, temporary variables.*

> *Comment each variable to describe its purpose.*

Initializations:

> *Set the initialization apart*
> *from surrounding portions of code.*

> *Comment initializations that are not obvious.*

> *Use defined constants to replace*
> *common numeric specifications.*

Paragraph documentation:

> *Set off paragraphs of code*
> *by liberal use of white space (blank lines).*

> *Extract paragraph documentation*
> *from the design document.*

> *Within paragraphs, comment only*
> *code whose meaning is not obvious.*

Paragraph code:

> *Group statements logically.*

> *Indent statements within*
> *loop and selection blocks.*

> *Put multiple statements on one line*
> *when they constitute a simple concept.*

In implementing the design as paragraphs of code there are several guidelines whose use will make the meaning of the code paragraphs more understandable. Fundamental to these is

> *In implementing algorithms*
> *use structured programming.*

In the narrow sense "structured programming" means using only three flow of control constructs: sequential execution, selection, and repetition. In the broad sense "structured programming" includes the following guidelines:

Limit control flow constructs to those
which have a single entry point and a single exit point.

Avoid nesting repetitive loops too deeply.

Avoid THEN-IF and null ELSE constructs.

Minimize the number of control paths
through program components.

Avoid programming tricks.

Avoid side effects.

Avoid global data.

Avoid aliases.

Eliminate or isolate system dependencies.

10.5 Debugging

Debugging is the initial procedure of executing a program component or set of components to determine if it is operating as expected. A fundamental aspect of debugging is

Instrument program components
before starting the debugging process.

Instrumentation is the addition of code to a program component itself to assist in debugging. There are several useful instrumentation techniques that should be used in debugging microprocessor software.

Provide information on control flow
in all program components.

Check data passed to a program component
for validity and reasonability.

Provide information about the values of important variables
at certain points in program components.

Comment the code added for instrumentation.

When debugging uncovers problems and changes are made in the code to fix these problems:

Comment the code changes which are intended to fix problems.

In order to debug a particular program component it is usually necessary to link it with other components in the system.

Proceed in a top-down manner in coding and debugging.

Use stubs and drivers to link
a program component for debugging.

For debugging to be successful, one must select appropriate test data:

Generate sets of test data to exercise
not only the normal cases
but the boundary conditions
and special cases as well.

There are several common programming mistakes for which test data should check:

Check that variables have been properly initialized.

Check that variable values are not affected
by references to other program components (side effects).

Check that single data elements
in a data structure with multiple elements
are referenced properly, e.g., valid subscripts in arrays.

Check for off-by-one errors,
e.g., performing loops one time too few or one time too many.

The mechanics of the debugging process have a major impact on the efficiency of finding and correcting errors; thus:

Plan your debug sessions:
prepare sets of test data and
develop objectives each set is to test,
before starting a debug session.

Use system debug time wisely;
avoid spending all your time on one problem,
get the proper instrumentation data,
and proceed to other problems.
If you are trying to solve one problem,
have a plan for isolating it.

Keep a log book, recording what was tested and changed,
where in the program changes were made,
who made them, when they were made,
and why they were made.

The debugging process, however, is not a substitute for properly performing the other steps in software development.

Do not substitute instrumentation
and other techniques for proper problem analysis.

One common microprocessor software debugging technique is greatly overused:

Machine language patching
should almost never be performed.

Appropriate debugging tools can simplify the debugging process.

Use a library system for controlling versions
and configurations of components, test data, and documentation.

For sophisticated microprocessor-based products,
debug the software on a simulator
controlled by the product microprocessor.

One should be careful not to develop an overdependence on tools, i.e., tools should not become crutches.

10.6 Testing

Testing is the semiformal process of demonstrating that the software meets the user requirements. It actually starts early in the software development process.

> *Prepare the test plan in parallel with the design activity. Organize the test plan so that it addresses:*
> *(1) the tests to be performed at each level of the test hierarchy*
> > *- module test*
> > *- integration test*
> > *- system test*
> > *- acceptance/installation test*
> *(2) the criteria to be used to determine test cases*
> *(3) the criteria for terminating each level of testing*

Testing techniques may broadly be characterized as glass box techniques, which examine the code itself, and black box techniques, which test the functional and performance characteristics of one or more program components.

> *Use glass box testing to obtain the desired coverage of statements, paths, decisions, and conditions in a module.*

> *Use black box testing augmented by glass box testing to obtain the desired coverage of functions and performance in integration, system, and acceptance/installation testing.*

After using these techniques to select test data,

> *For each test case, prepare a test document that describes*
> > *- the input values required to perform the desired test*
> > *- the environment in which the test will run*
> > *- the expected results*

Next the tests are performed according to the test document, and reviewed.

> *Keep a test log which records each test, the results obtained, and follow on actions.*

Unlike previous phases in software development, testing does not have a clearly distinguishable end-point. Therefore,

> *If the review of the test results show that the software*
> *or the design is incorrect, make the appropriate changes*
> *to the design, to the software, and to all relevant documentation;*
> *after these changes, repeat the test execution and review.*

> *Document carefully all changes to the software*
> *made as a result of testing.*

> *Specify the criteria for terminating*
> *each testing level in the test plan.*

10.7 Maintenance

Whether it involves correcting problems or adding new features, software maintenance can become a very time consuming activity. However, one can

> *Reduce the need and time for software maintenance by*
> *- using the techniques in previous chapters to develop*
> * high quality software*
> *- maintaining close communication with customers*
> *- designing software for modifiability*

The maintenance process is initiated by documented problem reports or requests for changes.

> *Review each problem report or request for change*
> *to determine if it warrants making modifications*
> *to the software and if so, to prioritize the work.*

If the review results in the decision to process a change request, then

> *Programmers processing a change request or error*
> *report should follow these steps:*
> *(1) Understand the objectives of the request.*
> *(2) Study the relevant sections of the software*
> *   and documentation.*
> *(3) Generate a proposal to meet the desired objectives.*
> *(4) Determine the portions of the system to be affected*
> *   by the change.*

(5) *Run the tests developed during the previous phase to show the desired effects and to demonstrate that anticipated undesirable effects do not occur.*

(6) *After testing has been completed, the change should be approved, installed, and documented.*

11

INTRODUCTION TO
MANAGING MICROPROCESSOR
SOFTWARE DEVELOPMENT

11.1 Preparation for Managing Microprocessor Software Development

Chapters 2 through 9 have described the process of developing microprocessor software; Chapter 10 summarized the development process, presenting the phases in the logical sequence in which they should be addressed. One of our fundamental tenets of management (often eschewed by management theorists) is that a manager must understand the process he is managing. For the present area of interest this implies:

A microprocessor development manager must understand the microprocessor software development process.

Thus, the novice microprocessor software development manager should carefully review the summary presented in Chapter 10 before progressing into the remaining chapters in the book. Management's ignorance of the microprocessor software development process is one of the principal reasons that microprocessor software development projects develop problems.

As described in Section 1.3, the management of microprocessor software systems development is a microcosm of general management principles, and thus comprises the following activities:

(1)   Planning — formulating and scheduling activities to achieve the desired objective

(2)   Organizing — building a staff and establishing effective working teams to perform planned activities within a working environment for the purpose of achieving an objective

(3)   Actuating — directing and influencing group members to achieve not only individual objectives but group objectives as well

(4)   Controlling — evaluating group performance against plans, and developing and implementing alternative plans if required

Rather than examine these activities for the general case, the remaining chapters in the book, Chapters 12-19, examine specific topics within these activities where software managers must go beyond the general guidelines of standard management (or even standard engineering management) practices. The techniques presented thus provide additional knowledge to make a good manager into a good microprocessor software development manager.

11.2 Planning Microprocessor Software Development Projects

Chapter 12 addresses the critical problem of planning microprocessor software development projects. The planning process should produce a high level project plan that estimates project effort, cost, and schedule, as well as a detailed plan for the individual phases of microprocessor software development. We review some techniques for estimating software effort and describe a particular constructive cost model developed by Boehm that has been shown to be effective in estimating microprocessor software development projects. The model demonstrates the effect that a variety of product attributes, computer attributes, personnel attributes, and project attributes have on the effort required to complete a microprocessor software development project. For developing detailed project plans we describe the activities and milestones in the project development phases and additional tools and resources that should be obtained and scheduled. We conclude the chapter with a list of aspects that have been pitfalls on many projects.

11.3 Organizing Microprocessor Software Development Projects

We divide the subject of organizing microprocessor software development projects into staffing, described in Chapter 13, and organization structure considerations, described in Chapter 14. In staffing, we advocate that managers should devote substantial time to recruiting and staffing projects with people having a variety of experiences. Recruiting microprocessor software developers involves

o   Pursuing several sources to obtain job applicants

o   Screening applicants by reviewing résumés

o   Interviewing applicants to determine desirability of hiring

The staffing activity does not end with hiring; indeed, the development of personnel is even more important to the long-term growth of the organization. As software developers are generally not motivated by company loyalty, we review classical motivation theory and recent findings regarding motivation of software personnel. We describe several management actions by which software developers may be motivated to achieve their own goals and in so doing achieve the goals of the organization. These actions include both short-term operational issues and long-term developmental issues. The final topic on the subject of staffing is evaluation, which when used constructively can be an important part of motivation and development.

Our examination of organizing microprocessor software projects, which is the subject of Chapter 14, first considers three classical organization structures — functional, project, and matrix — in light of the characteristics of software development and software personnel. Reviewing the advantages and disadvantages of these structures leads to a discussion of organization structures designed specifically for software development teams. Experience with software staffing and organizing is now rich enough so that we can describe common pitfalls to avoid and techniques to use to improve capabilities of team members.

11.4 Actuating Microprocessor Software Development Projects

In Chapters 15 through 18 we examine selected topics from the subject of actuating microprocessor software development projects, i.e., providing the direction to achieve the plans developed earlier. A significant part of this activity involves the normal day-to-day direction of the tasks described in the first part of the book and planned according to the principles described in Chapter 12. This normal day-to-day direction to accomplish tasks does not differ significantly from other engineering management, so we concentrate in Chapters 15 through 18 on four topics which differentiate the microprocessor software development process from other activities.

Chapter 15 addresses the subject of software reviews. This subject may be considered a part of controlling software development projects; however, due to its constructive nature in the software arena, we address it as an actuating activity. Although there are different types of reviews for activities in the different phases of software development, there are fundamental elements common to all software reviews. We describe the roles of the members of review teams and note that most software development projects spend too small a proportion of their time on reviews.

Facilities required for microprocessor software development, described in Chapter 16, differ significantly not only from other engineering development activities but from other software development activities as well. The principal types of facilities we address are office facilities and equipment facilities. Thoughts on the design of office facilities and the effect they have on productivity have changed in the past decade due to new research done in this area and due to distinctive ideas used by the Japanese. Equipment facilities, such as computer and software tools, have also changed dramatically in the past decade with the development of the personal computer, the engineering workstation, and software tools for these systems. Our experience in facilities planning is that seldom are cost/benefit tradeoff analyses performed to determine the propriety of facilities acquisition.

Chapter 17 addresses microprocessor software development for a particular class of systems — embedded products. The motivation for examining the integration of microprocessor software into embedded products is

o   This product class represents an important application of microprocessors.

o   The interaction between the microprocessor software and the rest of the system differs from most other software applications.

o   Senior managers of embedded product development projects seldom have experience in microprocessor software management.

Given this situation, managers should devote special attention to providing technical direction and interacting with other managers. Chapter 17 addresses these topics in detail for the phases in the software development process.

Most microprocessor software development organizations view the completion of products or projects as the most important goal; a concomitant goal should be developing microprocessing software technology so that future products or projects may be completed more effectively. Developing microprocessor software engineering technology is the subject of Chapter 18, and is addressed in four areas:

(1)   Microprocessor software methodology, where the key is adapting the fundamental concept of the software life cycle to a particular application.

(2)   Architecture, where the keys are classifying the functionality of the hardware and software, and making tradeoffs among operating system, diagnostics, and application software.

(3)   Tools to assist in the development of microprocessor software itself and to assist in the management of the software development process.

(4)   Personnel whose development enables the realization of methodology, architecture, and tools.

11.5 Controlling Microprocessor Software Development Projects

When software projects are not properly controlled, the following problems may arise:

o   Schedule overruns

o   Cost overruns

o   Reliability or performance shortfalls

In Chapter 19 we state the fundamental tenet that microprocessor software projects that fail to meet their original objectives do so principally as a result of inadequate management. Common management problems are examined in some detail. An actual microprocessor-based product development project, in which the authors participated as reviewers, illustrates these common management problems. The chapter concludes with recommendations for improving software management.

12

PLANNING

MICROPROCESSOR SOFTWARE

DEVELOPMENT PROJECTS

12.1 Introduction

From a management viewpoint, the most common cause of problems in software projects is the lack of a consistent, complete, and reasonable plan. This is true for a wide variety of problems ranging from schedule slippages to failure to satisfy the customer's requirements.

There are two principal objectives to the planning process:

o First, an overall project plan, which includes estimates of the effort, cost, and schedule required to develop and maintain the desired system. This is used to determine the feasibility and desirability of the project.

o Second, after a project's feasibility has been determined, a detailed plan is developed. This plan contains a set of measurable milestones which will be used to determine if the project is staying on schedule. To be useful, a milestone must be a demonstrable event. For example, "publication of functional requirements" or "successful compilation of a module" are appropriate milestones. "Completion of 50 percent of the coding" is not a useful milestone because it is not verifiable.

12.2 Initial Project Scheduling and Costing

Developing good initial estimates for the resources and time required for software development in a microprocessor-based system can be both difficult and vital to the success of the project. Reasons for requiring good estimates include:

o   A software manager must be able to specify a realistic schedule and budget for his portion of the project when dealing with the overall project development team. Frequently, a project architect decides the software is required at a specific time, and so schedules the software completion for that date. The software manager then requires quantitative methods for determining if the proposed schedule is feasible. If it is not feasible, he must have the data to demonstrate the need for either more time or reduced requirements.

o   Software is often the pacing item in microprocessor development projects, even though it may not be the most expensive, because it controls the operation of the system.

o   During the overall system design phase, reasonable software cost estimates are required in order to make realistic hardware-software tradeoffs. For example, it may appear that reducing the amount of memory in a system would reduce the price of the product. This could, however, dramatically increase the time and cost needed to develop the software to fit in the limited memory, offsetting any savings in the hardware costs. Additionally, a delay in the software may delay the introduction of the product and allow a competitor to get an edge in the marketplace. Since hardware is tangible and software is not, the temptation is great to minimize the cost of the hardware and let the software take care of any resulting problems. Only with good estimates of the cost of the software can the appropriate balance be struck.

o   When a schedule is found to be unrealizable late in a project, the delay in product development may be the least of management's concerns. In microprocessor software development, for example, software engineers may have to work harder to compensate for a problem that they did not create. Facing a difficult situation like this, working long hours, and possibly missing vacation can cause morale problems. This could encourage good people to look elsewhere for a job where the pressure is less. It is also reasonable to expect less reliable work from tired and overworked software engineers with the result that either the debugging and testing time will increase or the product will not be as reliable as desired.

Unfortunately, there are no foolproof estimating techniques for planning software development time and costs. Most estimates currently used are based on experience and historical data. Many large companies that have been developing software for years build a data base as projects are developed to aid in later estimates. Since many developers of microprocessor software are just beginning to develop large amounts of software, they have no previous history to fall back on. Even if some members of the staff have had experience estimating software costs in other environments, care must be taken when translating that experience into estimating the development of microprocessor software in a new environment.

An illustration of the difficulty of estimating software costs can be found in a report by Siba N. Mohanty. Mohanty presented nineteen different published models for estimating software costs and then used twelve of the models to compute the cost of a hypothetical system. The estimated costs ranged from $362,500 to $2,766,667 for the same software project. The differences can be attributed to both the different factors that are accounted for by each model and the different environments in which each model was calibrated. This emphasizes the risk involved in estimating costs based on data or experience gathered in another environment. As Mohanty summarizes, "it is highly unlikely that any two models will estimate the same cost for a given project. We also observe that, even today, almost no model can estimate the true cost of software with any degree of certainty."[1] The most reliable way to develop software cost estimates currently is to determine what factors influence and how much these factors influence the cost of software development at a given facility. By measuring the factors which have been incorporated into published models and building a data base of these project characteristics and cost, one may improve cost estimating at a particular installation.

Such a study was presented by C. E. Walston and C. P. Felix.[2] Data were gathered from projects developed by the IBM Federal Systems Division over several years and then analyzed. The factors that they found to correlate significantly with programming productivity as well as change in the mean productivity rate are shown in Table 12-1.[3]

[1] Siba N. Mohanty, "Software Cost Estimation: Present and Future," Software Practice and Experience, vol. 11 (1981), pp. 103-121.

[2] C. E. Walston and C. P. Felix, "A Method of Programming Measurement and Estimation," IBM Systems Journal, vol. 16, no. 1 (1977), pp. 54-73.

[3] Ibid.

Table 12-1.
Variables that Correlate Significantly with Productivity
(Note: DSLPMM is delivered source lines per man-month)

Question or Variable	Response Group Mean Productivity (DSLPMM)			Productivity Change (DSLPMM)
Customer interface complexity	<Normal 500	Normal 295	>Normal 124	376
User participation in the definition of requirements	None 491	Some 267	Much 205	286
Customer originated program design changes	Few 297		Many 196	101
Customer experience with the application area of the project	None 318	Some 340	Much 206	112
Overall personnel experience and qualifications	Low 132	Average 257	High 410	278
Percentage of programmers doing development who participated in design of functional specifications	<25% 153	25-50% 242	>50% 391	238
Previous experience with operational computer	Minimal 146	Average 270	Extensive 312	166
Previous experience with programming languages	Minimal 122	Average 225	Extensive 385	263
Previous experience with application of similar or greater size and complexity	Minimal 146	Average 221	Extensive 410	264

Table 12-1. (continued)
Variables that Correlate Significantly with Productivity
(Note: DSLPMM is delivered source lines per man-month)

Question or Variable	Response Group Mean Productivity (DSLPMM)			Productivity Change (DSLPMM)
Ratio of average staff size to duration (people/month)	<0.5 305	0.5-0.9 310	>0.9 173	132
Hardware under concurrent development	No 297		Yes 177	120
Development computer access, open under special request	0% 226	1-25% 274	>25% 357	131
Development computer access, closed	0-10% 303	11-85% 251	>85% 170	133
Classified security environment for computer and 25% of programs and data	No 289		Yes 156	133
Structured programming	0-33% 169	34-66% -	66% 310	132
Design and code inspections	0-33% 220	34-66% 300	>66% 339	119
Top-down development	0-33% 196	34-66% 237	>66% 321	125
Chief programmer team usage	0-33% 219	34-66% -	>66% 408	189
Overall complexity of code developed	<Average 314		>Average 185	129

Table 12-1. (continued)
Variables that Correlate Significantly with Productivity
(Note: DSLPMM is delivered source lines per man-month)

Question or Variable	Response Group Mean Productivity (DSLPMM)			Productivity Change (DSLPMM)
Complexity of application processing	<Average 349	Average 345	>Average 168	181
Complexity of program flow	<Average 289	Average 299	>Average 209	80
Overall constraints on program design	Minimal 293	Average 286	Severe 166	107
Program design constraints on main storage	Minimal 391	Average 277	Severe 193	198
Program design constraints on timing	Minimal 303	Average 317	Severe 171	132
Code for real-time or interactive operation, or executing under severe timing constraint	<10% 279	10-40% 337	>40% 203	76
Percentage of code for delivery	0-90% 159	91-99% 327	100% 265	106
Code classified as non-mathematical application and I/O formatting programs	0-33% 188	34-66% 311	67-100% 267	79
Number of classes of items in the data base per 1000 lines of delivered code	0-15 334	16-80 243	>80 193	141
Number of pages of delivered documentation per 1000 lines of delivered code	0-32 320	33-88 252	>88 195	125

As an example of a cost estimating model, we will briefly describe Boehm's Constructive Cost Model,[4] COCOMO, which is actually a hierarchy of models. The top level model provides quick, rough estimates. The second level model takes into account more factors in an attempt to provide better estimates. Each model has three separate sets of equations to account for three types of project development modes: organic, semidetached, and embedded. In an organic development mode, the software is developed by a small group of programmers who are experienced both in the particular type of application to be developed and in the development environment. A semidetached mode of development is an intermediate stage between organic and embedded. In a semidetached mode either the project members are less experienced than in an organic mode or the project has a mixture of organic and embedded mode characteristics. Embedded mode software is usually part of a large complex project and must operate within tight constraints imposed by the other components of the system. Since much microprocessor software is part of an embedded system this model is often most appropriate to adapt to the microprocessor environment. Many of the other models have been developed using data from large-scale systems on mainframe computers and do not account for the extra difficulty encountered in an embedded environment.

The top level organic COCOMO model provides the following estimates for the effort and development time required for software projects:

$$MM = 2.4 \times KDSI^{1.05}$$

$$TDEV = 2.5 \times MM^{0.38}$$

In these equations:

KDSI is thousands of delivered source instructions in the software system

MM is the required effort (in man-months) for the software development project

TDEV is the required development time (in months) for the software development project

[4]Barry W. Boehm, Software Engineering Economics (Englewood Cliffs, New Jersey: Prentice-Hall, 1981). Figure 12-1, Table 12-2, and Table 12-5 are from Boehm's book pages 76, 118, and 485 and are reprinted by permission of Prentice-Hall, Inc.

This model is appropriate for small- to medium-size programs (64 KDSI or less) in an environment where programmers have experience with the kind of project to be developed.

In the semidetached COCOMO model:

$$MM = 3.0 \times KDSI^{1.12}$$

$$TDEV = 2.5 \times MM^{0.35}$$

As can be easily seen from Figure 12-1, the additional complexity and size of the program or reduced experience of the programmers increases the expected estimated effort significantly.

In the embedded COCOMO model:

$$MM = 3.6 \times KDSI^{1.20}$$

$$TDEV = 2.5 \times MM^{0.32}$$

This model accounts for the additional effort and time required due to the additional constraints imposed on an embedded system. See Figure 12-1.

Key assumptions included in the COCOMO model are

o   The delivered source instructions are the program instructions including formatting statements, data declarations, and control language statements. They do not include comments or utility software. Utility code should, however, be counted if it is developed using the same process as delivered program software.

o   The development period covered by the model begins at the design phase after the requirements have been specified and ends at the end of the integration and test phase.

o   The requirements specification is not substantially changed after the requirements phase.

This last assumption can frequently be the cause for the large discrepancy between estimated completion time and actual completion time, particularly in embedded systems typified by many microprocessor applications. Frequently, as other components of a microprocessor-based system are developed, problems emerge and the solution selected is to change the software requirements to solve the problem. A change in the software requirements after the design has begun is the most common cause for software projects to be late. Unfortunately, many managers do not recognize and understand this problem.

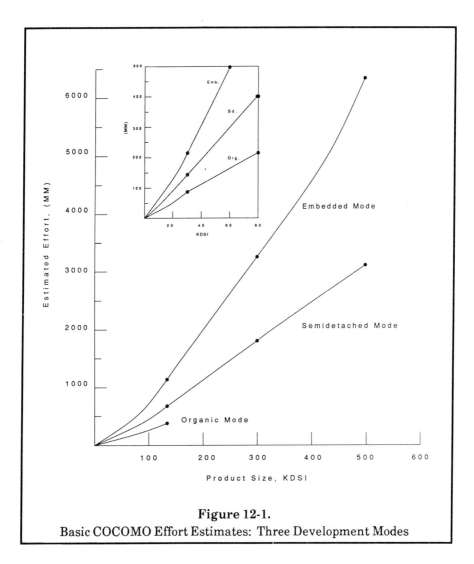

Figure 12-1.
Basic COCOMO Effort Estimates: Three Development Modes

The equations presented previously should be used only for rough estimations. In a study of sixty-three projects, the actual results showed that the estimates were within a factor of 1.3 only 29 percent of the time and within a factor of 2 only 60 percent of the time. These models should, therefore, be used with caution.

The intermediate COCOMO model takes into account an additional fifteen factors that have been found to affect the cost of a software product. These factors are listed in Table 12-2. In this model, the basic computations for man-months are modified by an effort adjustment factor. This effort adjustment factor is the product of values for each of the fifteen factors accounted for by the model.

The nominal effort equations for the intermediate model are

$$\text{Organic} \qquad MM_{nom} = 3.2 \times KDSI^{1.05}$$

$$\text{Semidetached} \quad MM_{nom} = 3.0 \times KDSI^{1.12}$$

$$\text{Embedded} \qquad MM_{nom} = 2.8 \times KDSI^{1.20}$$

The total effort is then computed from

$$MM = MM_{nom} \times \prod_{i=1}^{15} (\text{effort multiplier})_i$$

where the effort multipliers are obtained from Table 12-2.

Carefully examining Table 12-2 reveals some reasons why the development time of microprocessor software can so easily be underestimated. Suppose one estimates the development time for the software in a new product based on previous experience. If the previous experience were not with embedded software, one may not consider the added difficulty that will be encountered because of the high reliability, very high execution time constraints, and very high main storage constraints that are normally a part of an embedded environment. The multipliers for these factors are 1.15, 1.30, and 1.21, which implies an 81 percent increase in effort over a nominal project for just these three factors.

Two of the many additional points noted from examining Table 12-2 are

o   The use of modern programming practices and the use of software tools as espoused in this book can improve one's situation from the usual very low rating to a very high rating. This results in an effort reduction of more than 50 percent.

o   The use of good people can reap significant benefits. For example, very highly rated programmers can cause the effort to be reduced by one-half compared to using very poorly rated programmers. Thus, when hiring it is important to perform a cost/benefit analysis in making the tradeoff between the quality and expense of applicants. Note that this does not imply assigning only the "best" people to a project; we examine staffing in Chapter 13.

Table 12-2.
Software Development Effort Multipliers

	Ratings					
Cost Drivers	Very Low	Low	Nominal	High	Very High	Extra High
Product Attributes						
Required software reliability	.75	.88	1.00	1.15	1.40	
Data base size		.94	1.00	1.08	1.16	
Product complexity	.70	.85	1.00	1.15	1.30	1.65
Computer Attributes						
Execution time constant			1.00	1.11	1.30	1.66
Main storage constraint			1.00	1.06	1.21	1.56
Virtual machine volatility		.87	1.00	1.15	1.30	
Computer turnaround time		.87	1.00	1.07	1.15	
Personnel Attributes						
Analyst capability	1.46	1.19	1.00	.86	.71	
Applications experience	1.29	1.13	1.00	.91	.82	
Programmer capability	1.42	1.17	1.00	.86	.70	
Virtual machine experience	1.21	1.10	1.00	.90		
Programming language experience	1.14	1.07	1.00	.95		
Project Attributes						
Use of modern programming practices	1.24	1.10	1.00	.91	.82	
Use of software tools	1.24	1.10	1.00	.91	.83	
Required development schedule	1.23	1.08	1.00	1.04	1.10	

This model, like any other empirical model, should be used only as a guideline. If common sense dictates that certain other factors are important in a particular environment, they should be considered. After some experience using the model, it is appropriate to calibrate it to a particular environment.

We characterize our experience with real-time embedded microprocessor products in large companies by summarizing a "typical" product development activity in Table 12-3. Note that the product of the effort multipliers is 4.53, which means that the effort required is *over four times* the effort required for the nominal case. Taking this analysis one step further, we note from Table 12-4 that the development of 64 kilobytes of software (assuming that one higher level language statement generates on the average 2 bytes of code) requires

o   Over 69 man-years of effort

o   Over 21 months of calendar time

Understanding all the factors that affect microprocessor software development is thus critical to planning the schedule of a microprocessor-based product.

12.3 Detailed Project Plan

After the initial project plans have been completed and the project has been approved, the detailed plan must be prepared. The detailed plan will be used for scheduling manpower and facilities, and monitoring the project. Although we begin our discussion of the detailed plan with the discussion of the requirements phase, the requirements must be completed before the initial estimates discussed in the previous section can be made. One should not expect to estimate the cost or schedule for a project for which the requirements are unknown or unclear.

The detailed plan requires scheduling time periods and personnel for each of the following activities in the software development life cycle (one must be careful to include time for both the activity and the associated documentation).

(1) Requirements Definition

From a planning point of view, there are two reasons for performing requirements analysis. The initial purpose is to obtain the necessary information to estimate the cost of the project so a feasibility analysis can be done. Once the decision has been made to go with the project, a more thorough requirements definition should be done so that the project can be implemented. The steps in requirements definition that should be planned include:

Table 12-3.
Effort Multipliers for a "Typical" Real-Time Embedded
Microprocessor Software Product Development Project

Cost Driver	Rating	Characteristic	Effort Multiplier
Reliability	High	Major financial loss if product recall is caused by software failure	1.15
Data Base Size	Low	Most microprocessor software uses small data bases	.94
Product Complexity	Very High	Reentrant code, interrupt handling, communication, command processing	1.30
Execution Time Constraint	High	70 percent of available execution time used	1.11
Main Storage Constraint	Extra High	95 percent of available main storage used	1.56
Virtual Machine Volatility	High	Major change in virtual machine every two months during product development	1.15
Computer Turnaround Time	Nominal	Computer turnaround time less than four hours	1.00
Analyst Capability	Nominal	Average capability of the team in analysis ability, efficiency, and communication ability	1.00
Applications Experience	Nominal	Three years average experience	1.00

Table 12-3. (continued)
Effort Multipliers for a "Typical" Real-Time Embedded
Microprocessor Software Product

Cost Driver	Rating	Characteristic	Effort Multiplier
Programmer Capability	Nominal	Average capability of the team in programming ability, efficiency, and communication ability	1.00
Virtual Machine Experience	Low	Less than four months average experience with virtual machine	1.10
Programming Language Experience	Nominal	One year average experience with programming language	1.00
Use of Modern Programming Practices	Low	Experimental use of some modern programming practices	1.10
Use of Software Tools	Very Low	Basic microprocessor tools: assembler, linker, monitor, batch debug aids	1.24
Required Development Schedule	Low	15 percent acceleration compared to TDEV formula	1.08
		Product of effort multipliers	4.53

Table 12-4.

Effort and Time Required to Develop 64K of Microprocessor Software
in a Typical Product Development Environment

$$MM_{nom} = 2.8 \times KDSI^{1.20}$$
$$= 2.8 \times 32768^{1.20} \quad \text{assuming 2 bytes per higher}$$
$$\text{level language statement}$$
$$= 184$$

$$MM = MM_{nom} \times \prod_{i=1}^{15} (\text{effort multiplier})_i$$
$$= 184 \times 4.53$$
$$= 835$$

$$TDEV = 2.5 \times MM^{0.32}$$
$$= 2.5 \times 835^{0.32}$$
$$= 21.5$$

(a) Obtaining information — This will usually involve several iterations of making contact with the customer to get information and then synthesizing this information into a form suitable for further analysis.

(b) Preparing documents — The time required to prepare the requirements specifications documents must not be minimized. The completeness and accuracy of these documents will have a significant bearing on the success of the project. The steps involved in preparing the documents include outlining the document, making section assignments, section writing, reviewing the sections, combining the sections, and conducting a final review.

(c) Releasing documents — Before the documents are released, they should be reviewed with the customer, rewritten to meet the customer's specifications, reviewed again, and eventually approved. After final approval by the customer, the documents are released.

(2) Test Planning

Tests should be devised to exercise each feature described in the requirements specification. Test planning can be done in parallel with design and coding.

(3) Design

Design requires two phases: an analysis phase and a synthesis phase. During the analysis phase, the requirements specification is transformed into a description that summarizes the operation of the system, such as a hierarchical finite state machine or data flow diagram. Time must be allocated to allow for reviews and the solutions of problems at each level. The synthesis phase consists of developing the structure of a system, first in the form of a simple hierarchical graph structure and then in a detailed textual description. Again reviews must be scheduled at each level; indeed, documents must be reviewed and approved before they may be considered complete.

(4) Coding and Debugging

This phase consists of the actual writing of code and the debugging of the individual modules. Again reviews are important; code walkthroughs should be included in the schedule. As described previously, this is generally the shortest phase in the development process.

(5) Testing

This phase requires time and manpower for the integration and testing of the modules. After the software is integrated, the system integration tests are performed. Test results must be thoroughly reviewed. This phase is typically the longest phase in embedded microprocessor systems development because of the interaction with and control of other subsystems by the software.

(6) Product Delivery or Release

Time must be allocated for the preparation of the software for distribution. This includes copying the software to ROM, EPROM, or tape and copying the associated documentation.

When the plan is being devised, milestones must be scheduled which can be easily verified to ensure that the project is on schedule. Among the milestones for a microprocessor software development project are the following:

Requirements Definition

    Initial contact with customer

    Initial draft of requirements complete

    Customer review and approval of initial draft

    Revised draft of requirements complete

    Customer approval of requirements specifications

    Release of requirements definition

    Completion of user documentation

Test Planning

    Tests designed to test each functional specification

    Tests designed for module integration

    Tests designed for module testing

Design

    Completion of three levels of hierarchy chart

    Completion of textual description of all modules

Coding

    Successful compilation of all modules

    Successful completion of module tests

Testing

    Successful completion of integration

    Successful completion of functional tests

In addition to planning for the actual product development, the necessary tools and resources must be obtained and scheduled. Software support tools to consider include:

o   Text editor for documentation

o   Design language

o   Editor

o   Operating system

o   Compiler

o   Linker

o   Debugger

o   Data base manager for test plans and test results

o   Librarian for managing modules and configurations

Hardware support tools to consider include:

o   Microprocessor development system, minicomputer, or large system

o   Simulator

o   Data collector

All tools should be planned for and obtained early enough so that the developers can become familiar with the tools before they need to use them in one of the software development phases.

12.4 Pitfalls to Avoid When Planning

Various aspects of microprocessor software development require special attention during planning and execution to ensure that the project stays on schedule. Some of these are listed below.

o   Changing Requirements

Because of the embedded nature of most microprocessor applications, requirements frequently change when problems occur in other parts of the system. Developers must anticipate changes in their plans, or when changes are made, the schedule and cost estimates must be updated. The overall system architect should be aware of the cost of changes to the software requirements and should weigh carefully the merits and disadvantages of solving non-software problems by changing the software requirements late in the software development cycle. The COCOMO model accommodates this effect with a factor called "requirements volatility," described in Table 12-5.

Table 12-5.
Requirements Volatility Effort Multipliers

Rating	Project Rework Due to Requirements Changes	Effort Multiplier
Low	Essentially none	0.91
Nominal	Small, noncritical redirections	1.00
High	Occasional moderate redirections	1.19
Very High	Frequent moderate or occasional major redirections	1.38
Extra High	Frequent major redirections	1.62

o   Parkinson's Law Corollary — Code will expand to fill the memory available.

Since the cost per instruction can increase dramatically as the utilization of memory approaches the limit (see Figure 2-1), it is necessary to resist the frequent temptation to sneak in a few more features. In microprocessor systems this is usually a severe constraint, unlike large computer systems where virtual memory is often a solution.

o   How Much Code Syndrome

Design and review steps should not be rushed to begin coding. Management frequently desires to see code as an indication of work accomplishment, however, starting the code phase before proper design and review usually leads to larger delays later in the project.

o   Inadequate Time for Testing and Product Integration

In microprocessor software systems the time required for testing and product integration is often longer than with traditional software systems because

- The hardware is developed as the software is developed. There is not a stable base for software debug, thus lengthening the debug time.

- The microprocessor software is a small part of a large electromechanical system. Software debug is constrained by the rate at which the rest of the system is debugged.

As a conclusion to this chapter, we reiterate Brooks's Law which we stated in Chapter 1. "Adding manpower to a late software project makes it later."[5] This law expresses the difficulty inherent in coping with a bad schedule. Once a software project is late, it is extremely difficult to get back on schedule; thus, it is critically important to set a good feasible schedule with measurable milestones, and to check it frequently to determine if the project is on target.

[5]Frederick P. Brooks, Jr., The Mythical Man-Month — Essays on Software Engineering (Reading, Massachusetts: Addison-Wesley, 1975), p. 25.

13

STAFFING

MICROPROCESSOR SOFTWARE

DEVELOPMENT PROJECTS

13.1 Introduction

Staffing involves people. It involves making contacts with the right people, hiring them, and providing a stimulating and rewarding environment for them in which to produce and to develop. It involves determining the kinds and numbers of personnel required on various projects. It involves motivating people to produce to their capacity and to enjoy and feel rewarded by their work.

In a volatile field like software development, the hiring and retaining of good, qualified people can be quite challenging. In this chapter, we begin with a discussion of techniques for recruiting new personnel. This will be followed by discussions on aiding the development of current personnel and on evaluating personnel.

13.2 Recruiting

For many reasons, a manager whose responsibilities include managing microprocessor software development will be involved in recruiting. These reasons include:

o   The rapidly expanding use of microprocessors increases the demand for software development personnel.

o   The current job market encourages mobility of software development
     personnel.

The current job market situation, compounded by the newness of
microprocessor technology and the small number of experienced
microprocessor software engineers, can make recruiting the appropriate
people for a particular job quite difficult. Recruiting can involve a great
deal of time and effort in order to attract the right people, and managers
should recognize recruiting as an important part of their job.

Most projects should involve a broad mix of people whose expertise and
experience can complement each other. Computer scientists, electrical
engineers, computer engineers, and software engineers are all required to
provide a balanced perspective when developing a microprocessor-based
product. In addition, it is important to have a range of experience levels and
backgrounds in terms of types of products and types of projects to get the
best insights into solving new problems.

In this section, we describe where to seek applicants and how to
evaluate them.

13.2.1 Sources

There are seven principal sources of job applicants for microprocessor
software development personnel:

o   College Campuses

o   Computer Science Conference

o   Open Market

o   Internal Job Changes

o   Personal References

o   Employment Agencies

o   Job Fairs

There are advantages and disadvantages associated with each source and
different tactics are required to attract the best people from each source.

College campuses are probably the best source of new engineers and
scientists. Although new graduates usually require an orientation period,
graduates from a good school can bring new ideas from the academic world
into the industrial environment. Since colleges have academic programs
that vary significantly in emphasis, one should learn about the curriculum

and the faculty when deciding where to recruit. For example, if one is looking for someone to work on an operating system for a microprocessor, one would probably be disappointed recruiting at a school that stressed data processing applications and COBOL. Information on teaching emphasis is more difficult to obtain and usually requires talking to students, former students, or faculty. Some academic programs stress a project orientation while others stress a theoretical orientation. In many situations one may want a mixture of both.

After determining the appropriate schools at which to recruit, it is important to establish a relationship with both the placement office and at least one faculty member. The placement office can help with the logistics of recruiting while the faculty member can provide information about the program and references for students. Valuable information can be obtained about potential recruits over lunch with a faculty member. A student may have a transcript that looks quite similar to the transcript belonging to a top-notch software engineer hired last year, but may also have a personality that is not conducive to working in a team environment. The faculty member may also know additional students that would be worth contacting.

When attempting to establish a good relationship with a faculty member there are several points to remember. Although a manager may feel that his time is extremely valuable, faculty members are also under time pressures. In general, a manager has much more to gain from the time invested in discussions with faculty than the other way around. Thus it may help to cement good relations with the faculty, if they feel that the school also benefits from the relationship, or if they feel that the company is an exceptionally good place for their students to work. Such programs as summer employment and cooperative programs for the students or the donation of equipment or scholarship money can reap benefits.

The Employment Register offered in conjunction with the Computer Science Conference sponsored each year (usually in February) by the Association for Computing Machinery is an opportunity to interview a range of people. Most applicants are near graduation (B.S., M.S., or Ph.D.) although there are also experienced applicants. Almost all new graduate applicants attending the conference have degrees in Computer Science. The educational background of the experienced applicants is usually broader but most are seeking positions in a computer science related application. Books containing one-page résumés of the applicants are published for distribution at the conference, along with books containing one-page descriptions of job openings at companies attending the conference. During the conference a large room is reserved for interview tables which are assigned to employers. Applicants can then approach potential employers for initial interviews.   Mailboxes are also provided to facilitate communications between applicants and potential employers. Fees for the conference are quite reasonable. There are several advantages to recruiting at the Computer Science Conference. It allows one the opportunity to interview many applicants with diverse backgrounds at one location in a few days. In addition, one has the opportunity to learn much about schools and other companies from the recruiters and attendees at the conference.

To obtain applicants from the open market, one must generally place advertisements in appropriate publications. Ads placed in the professional journals, such as the <u>Communications of the ACM</u> and the IEEE Computer Society's <u>Computer</u> and <u>Micro</u> magazines, are more likely to lead to applicants with broad general backgrounds in terms of education and experience. Ads placed in trade journals are more apt to result in applicants with a specific, technical background. We prefer the general background when building a long-term microprocessor software group.

To get the most for one's advertising dollar, ads should be as realistic and as informative as possible. This frequently means that they are written by the managers involved with the project, not by ad writers. Information in an advertisement should include the types of positions that are available, the type of products and projects that are being developed, the level of experience required, and starting salary guidelines that might apply. The more information included in the ad, the less time and expense will be wasted on applicants who are either not qualified or not interested in the job. For example, it is rather wasteful to spend a large sum of money to fly a promising applicant in for an interview only to find out that he will not work on embedded defense systems or that he finds software for microwave ovens beneath his station. If one is looking for experienced personnel, such as a senior technical consultant, a project leader, or a manager, the expected experience and the anticipated duties should be included. If one wants an experienced programmer, the amount and type of experience should be specified. There are tradeoffs, however, in becoming too specific. A good software engineer with a broad background may be able to learn a new language or operating system quickly and bring good ideas to the project from a different perspective. Similarly, if one specifies three years' experience, one may not receive any applications from recent graduates. If recruiting is difficult, consider broadening the potential applicant pool to include strong applicants with less than the desired amount of experience.

Another potential source of applicants is through internal job changes. Many companies are currently finding themselves in a situation where the technical mix of people in their employ is no longer the technical mix that is required. As products have changed from being mechanically oriented to microprocessor controlled, the technical skills required to develop and build these products have changed. In many situations, it may be appropriate to offer employees an opportunity to retrain in a new discipline. In particular, it may be advantageous to both the employer and the employee to have, for example, some of the mechanical engineers retrain as software development engineers. In general, this process requires a period of formal education. One cannot expect an engineer who has written a few lines of assembler language to suddenly be able to write large, complex control programs that run in real time and are highly reliable. The technical training may be done either internally or externally. In either case, it may be advantageous to be done at no expense to the employee and that the employee be given time off to attend classes.

A good source of potential job candidates is through personal references from current employees. Many companies offer bonuses to encourage employees to recommend the company to others. In general, a personal reference by an employee implies that the employee, who knows both the company and the applicant, thinks that the two are compatible. If one has a good opinion of the employee making the recommendations, the fact that the employee feels the applicant would be a good colleague is valuable information when deciding whom to hire. When a bonus system is used, one wants to ensure that the amount is not so large as to tempt people into inappropriate decisions in their recommendations.

Employment agencies, commonly called flesh peddlers or headhunters, should be used with caution. A well-established firm that knows the organization may be quite helpful in finding the right type of person for a particular job. On the other hand, some operations may be out to make a quick profit by distributing all the résumés they receive to any company they can. By establishing a good relationship with someone reliable in the employment business and by carefully specifying the type of experience and background desired, one can obtain good applicants with minimum risk.

A job fair is usually set up by an employment agency in a city to give local people an opportunity to interview with representatives from a number of companies. In theory, the agency has made contact with many employees who are unsatisfied with their current position and/or may be interested in looking for a new position. Appointments are arranged by the agency for the applicants to interview with the participating companies. In reality, it is often the case that many of the applicants are not very interested in changing jobs but are primarily curious to see what salary offers they might receive. If the salary offers are high enough, then a job change might be considered. Since, in general, buying people is not a good practice, job fairs can be an expensive way to recruit with minimal benefit.

13.2.2 Résumés

The initial screening of applications should be based on the résumés. Items to study on a résumé are the education, experience, job history, and professional activities of the individual. As computer software development has become more established, one should be looking for education in computer science, computer engineering, or a related field for all but the most experienced applicants. Those not educated in a computer related field should have evidence of the relevant background from professional seminars or work experiences. The amount of education and type of education one wants to see will depend on the kind of position for which one is hiring. Broadly speaking, someone with a high school or technical school education will be a technician; a B.S. degree generally indicates a broader background and the ability to be somewhat creative. For positions requiring innovative design, creativity, or leadership, an M.S. or Ph.D. may be appropriate. Unless the position involves a large amount of research, the differences between an M.S. and a Ph.D. background may not be important. In addition to the degree, the courses that the individual has taken are important. When evaluating the experience portion of an application, the aspects to consider are the types of projects and products with which the person has been involved, and the specific responsibilities the person had. If, for example, one is looking for a group leader, someone with leadership experience on a slightly different type of project may be more appropriate than someone with experience coding on a very similar project.

One should generally not look for specific experience with the particular microprocessor that the project is to use. A good software engineer with a broad background should be able to pick up the necessary details of a new microprocessor quickly. Someone with a narrow background and extensive experience on only one system may have a hard time adapting to a new processor if the project requirements change or the next project requires a different processor. Between the education and the experience of the experienced applicant, one should find that the applicant has gained knowledge of software methodology, software architecture, and software management issues.

Additional valuable information about the applicant can be obtained by examining job changes and the motivation for the job changes. A highly motivated person, for example, may find it necessary to change jobs frequently to continue to grow toward his potential. On the other hand, someone who finds it difficult to work effectively with others may also change jobs frequently. In the appropriate environment, the first type of individual may become a productive long term employee while the second type would probably not. Another sign of growth interest is professional activities. Membership in a professional society is often a sign of interest in staying current in one's profession.

A good guideline in hiring is that one should hire people for more than one specific project, one should hire people who can contribute to the company for a long time period. Thus, one should look for people who will be appropriate not only for the current job, but will also be suitable for future ones. The best type of individual is one who will grow with the company.

13.2.3 Interviews

Because of the time consumed by an on-site interview, applicants should initially be screened by telephone. During the phone interview, questions about the résumé can be clarified, and more information about the applicant's specific responsibilities on his projects can be obtained. A few relevant technical questions can be asked to be assured of the depth of the applicant's technical background. One may also want to explore reasons for frequent job changes or of periods of time not mentioned on the résumé.

If the phone interview goes well, an on-site interview should be scheduled. The on-site interview should be well-planned to ensure its success. Two aspects of the interviewing process must be kept in mind at all times.

o   The interviewers should obtain as complete a picture as possible of the candidate's technical knowledge, skills, and personality to determine his or her appropriateness for a job. This is particularly important in a field such as microprocessor software development, which is so volatile that one must be particularly concerned about technical obsolescence.

o   In addition, the applicant must get enough information about the potential job to allow him or her to make an informed decision if tendered an offer.

Because of the high potential for well-qualified applicants to get several job offers, one would like to have the recruit leave the interview with as favorable an impression of the company as is realistic to increase the chance of an acceptance of an offer.

From management's point of view as much information about the individual as possible should be obtained from the interview. Using a team of people to conduct the interview brings more insights into the decision-making process. The team should be organized with each member knowing the time he or she is to meet with the applicant and the areas on which to focus discussions. Avoid the situation where each interviewer asks similar questions and no one asks certain important questions. If many applicants are to be interviewed, a structured interviewing process may be advisable. In structured interviewing, a predetermined set of questions is asked of each candidate in a specified order by specified people. Because of the similarity of the interviews, the candidates can then be compared more easily and more objectively. The interviewing team should consist of the potential manager, project leaders, and some coworkers. This ensures that the applicant will be evaluated both as a coworker and as a subordinate. If possible, the final decision should be made by consensus. In addition to bringing the most information to the decision-making process, group decisions on recruiting have the additional benefit of building team morale.

Several techniques can be used to improve the applicant's image of the company. Perhaps the most important is to select representative group members to constitute the interview team. Because many companies have similar fringe benefit packages and salary structures, applicants frequently make decisions on where to work based on the people with whom they expect to work. Because of this, it is wise to put good technical people on the recruiting team. As we will discuss in the next section, software developers are highly growth oriented. They will, therefore, be attracted to work at the place that seems to have the best technical people associated with it. It is folly in times of high demand for computer specialists to decide that one's best people are too valuable to waste their time with recruiting. All offers made should be followed through. A phone call or two made to the applicant after the offer to reaffirm the company's interest and to answer any remaining questions that the applicant may have about the position, the company, or the community, can be quite beneficial.

The recruiting process requires much time and a great deal of paper work. Careful records must be kept to track the applicants and interviews. One person should be in charge of maintaining the records to ensure that all applications are responded to promptly, that all interviews are scheduled and all the necessary parties meet the applicant at the appropriate time, and that follow-up phone calls and letters are made by the appropriate persons. Only by taking care and ensuring that the applicants feel that they are valued by the company will recruiting efforts be successful.

13.3 Development

A manager's responsibilities include staffing "not merely to get today's job done but, more importantly, to insure that the human resources of the company will develop so as to enable it to enjoy increasing prosperity."[1] Hiring appropriate people is just the beginning. The next step is to motivate the employees and to allow them to grow in their jobs to increase their value to the company.

Software developers are generally not motivated by company loyalty. The frequency and type of job changes among computer professionals is support for the premise that they have a low dedication to their employer and a much higher dedication to their profession. This, however, also implies a high internal drive to grow. The proper environment could, therefore, be advantageous to both the individual and the company. The individual in an environment conducive to growth would have his growth desires met and would thus be encouraged to stay. The retention of such individuals particularly in times of high demand is a definite benefit to the company.

Two of the factors which affect the professional development of an individual, motivation and accessibility of technical information, will be discussed in the following sections.

13.3.1 Motivation

Several theories have been proposed by behavioral scientists to explain what motivates employees. In this section we discuss several of these theories and some related findings of behavioralists; we conclude with some recommendations for companies developing microprocessor software.

Abraham Maslow in the 1940s formulated a theory based on need satisfaction.[2] According to Maslow, unsatisfied needs are the source of human motivation. Needs are hierarchical. Lower level needs must be met first. Once a lower level need has been met, a person is motivated by the next level of need. For example, once a person's basic salary needs have

[1]James J. Cribbin, Effective Managerial Leadership (American Management Association, Inc., 1972), p. 3.

[2]Abraham H. Maslow, Motivation and Personality (New York: Harper & Row, 1954).

been met, increasing his salary will probably not provide long-term motivation. The hierarchy of needs from lowest to highest are

o   Physiological Needs — Based on survival such as having sufficient food, water, and shelter.

o   Safety and Security Needs — Based on establishing a secure environment in which one is assured safety and the continued satisfaction of basic needs.

o   Social Needs — Based on the individual's desires to be liked and to belong.

o   Ego Needs — Based on the individual's desire to be special.

o   Self-Actualization Needs — Based on the individual's desire to achieve his full potential both at work and in his life as a whole.

A primary element of the theory is that the needs are hierarchical. Providing an opportunity for the individual to achieve his potential when he feels that his job is in jeopardy may not be a strong motivator.

In the 1950s, Maslow's theories were expanded by Herzberg.[3]   He argued that merely eliminating causes of dissatisfaction on the job did not automatically result in motivation. Instead, he felt that there are two types of factors that affect an employee's motivation: dissatisfiers and satisfiers. The dissatisfiers, also called hygiene factors, are related to the working conditions and include such things as salary, security, company policies, interpersonal relations, and status.   Meeting an employee's needs concerning these hygiene factors will result in no dissatisfaction. According to Herzberg, however, this is not the same as satisfaction.   To achieve satisfaction, one must work toward satisfying higher order needs. These factors, called satisfiers or motivators, are related to the job itself and appeal to a person's desire for growth.   They include achievement, recognition, the work itself, responsibility, and potential for advancement. Once the dissatisfiers are met, it is essential to provide opportunity for growth in order to provide motivation to work. A key to providing these opportunities for growth is through job enrichment, also called "vertical job loading."   Vertical job loading involves giving an employee additional responsibility, independence, and authority.   Frequently it also implies

    [3]Frederick Herzberg, Work and the Nature of Man (Cleveland: The World Publishing Co., 1966).

giving him more control over the product that he is developing. This should not be confused with job enlargement, i.e., "horizontal job loading."[4] Horizontal job loading implies additional work without any additional freedom or authority.

Studies have been undertaken to relate the concepts of motivational theories to software developers. One, by Jacs Fitz-enz,[5] obtained the following ranking of motivating factors for this group (from highest to lowest in importance):

o   Achievement

o   Growth Possibility

o   Work Itself

o   Recognition

o   Advancement

o   Technical Supervision

o   Peer Relations

o   Relations with Subordinates

o   Salary

The second study by J. Daniel Couger and Robert Zawacki[6] found that programmers had the highest growth need and the lowest social need of people in 600 job categories surveyed.

An important point that managers should learn from these theories is that "employees join and remain with a firm principally to satisfy their own needs, wants, and ambitions, even as the corporation thought of its own needs when it hired them. The real challenge of the manager-leader is to change a relationship that began on a basis of self-interest into one that produces mutual need satisfaction for both parties."[7]

[4]Gary Slaughter, "Managing the Maverick," Computerworld (1982).

[5]Jacs Fitz-enz, "Who Is the DP Professional?" Datamation (September 1978), pp. 124-129.

[6]J. D. Couger and R. A. Zawacki, "What Motivates DP Professionals?" Datamation (September 1978), pp. 116-123.

[7]Cribbin, op. cit., p. 153.

Specific recommendations to use in a software development environment include:

o   A manager should be a technical as well as an administrative leader and should also be aware of motivational theory. Without the appropriate technical background to understand what an employee is doing, it is difficult for the manager to assign job enriching tasks to a subordinate. Likewise, recognition of an employee by a manager who is not knowledgeable in the area may be viewed with skepticism.

o   An equitable salary program should be established. Although salary may not be a motivator, it can easily become a dissatisfier. This is difficult in many areas of the computer industry because of the high demand for computer professionals. A particularly difficult problem occurs when starting salaries increase significantly from year to year. This may result in compression of the salaries of experienced employees since the average annual percentage raise is not as high as the percentage increase in starting salaries. Under these circumstances an older employee may feel that his years of service to the company are not being recognized and the only way for him to get the salary that he deserves is to go elsewhere. This can result in the loss of some of the company's best, most experienced personnel. Some "solutions" to this problem have been proven not only ineffective but demotivating. One tactic is *en masse* promotions of groups of people with similar experience, so that their salaries are increased significantly but are still in line with company policies for particular job levels. By promoting everyone automatically, the sense of achievement and recognition that should go with a promotion is lost. There is no longer a way for an individual to satisfy his higher level needs. Perhaps a better way to solve the problem is to provide annual marketplace adjustments to salaries, separate from merit increases. The marketplace adjustment informs the individual that his increased value to others is recognized. His merit raise informs him of the value of his performance.

o   A proper working environment must be established. This makes sense from both a productivity point of view and a motivational point of view. A person with a strong desire to grow in his field will not only be less productive, but will also be frustrated working with outdated equipment and inadequate tools. Facilities required in a good working environment include computers, appropriate software tools, library facilities, and office conditions. Chapter 16 discusses facilities in greater detail.

13.3.2 Accessibility of Technical Information

Because of the rapid changes in computer hardware and software technology, the high growth need for software professionals, and the need for a company to obtain any competitive edge possible, a continuing education program and easy access to current technical information is vital. A continuing education program should probably include several of the following items: formal courses, informal courses and videotapes, seminars, guest lectures, and consultants. Each of the different forms of obtaining information is suited to particular situations. For example, a videotape might be developed and used to introduce new staff members to company programming standards while a guest lecturer who is actively doing research in the area would be a better source for the latest information on appropriate testing methods to use. An educational program should have several different targets. One aspect of it should be geared toward developing employees technically. This should increase productivity because of both increased technical skills and increased motivation. Another aspect of the program should be aimed at developing potential managers from the software developers. A third aspect of an educational program should be aimed at educating nonsoftware managers about software. Many companies that are now using microprocessors have a large number of managers who know little about computers and software but must deal with microprocessors in the development of the products under their control. Special courses or seminars should be developed to give them an understanding of the special aspects of software development.

13.4 Evaluation

Because of the increasing importance of the software engineering activity in a microprocessor-based product development environment, evaluations of the members of a software development team should be given careful consideration. Evaluations should be based on the individual's total performance in contributing to the team effort. When evaluating performance in achieving assigned tasks, be careful to measure more than just lines of code produced; many other activities are also important in the production of software. In fact, the number of lines of code is only a partial measure of the amount of coding an individual has done. For example, a particular programmer may have a special capability for being able to handle complexity well and may, therefore, always be assigned the most difficult modules. If he does not product code as quickly as someone writing straightforward code, he should not automatically be evaluated lower. Other signs of contribution to the group effort include preparation for and participation in design and code reviews. When evaluating a microprocessor software manager, one should measure more than the effort put into the job. Performance evaluations for managers should include measurements of meeting schedules, anticipating problems, interfacing with other managers, and contributing to total product efforts.

14

ORGANIZING MICROPROCESSOR

SOFTWARE PROJECTS

14.1 Organization Theory

In this section we discuss classical organizational theory and relate it to software development by presenting some of the advantages and disadvantages of the various organizational structures in the microprocessor software environment. The three basic types of organizational structures that we discuss are functional organization, project/product organization, and matrix organization.

14.1.1 Functional Organizations

A functional organization divides responsibility along lines of technical specialization with a manager for each specialty group. In a microprocessor software development environment, one possible functional organization would have functional groups for operating system development, applications software development, diagnostics software development, and microprocessor software tools development. Advantages of a functional organization include:

o   The ability to identify and take advantage of commonality among several projects. For example, duplication of tool development effort can be eliminated if a single tools group develops and standardizes all tools.

o   The ability to devote resources to study current technology of
      particular interest to the group to ensure that state-of-the-art methods
      are being employed by group members. An applications group might,
      for example, look at new review techniques while a quality assurance
      group would have an interest in keeping up on new testing
      methodologies.

o   A higher retention of employees. Software engineers often identify
      with their profession or organization rather than a project. This
      eliminates the high attrition which normally occurs under some other
      organizations, particularly project/product organization, as a project
      draws to a close.

o   A potential for greater emphasis on the individual rather than the
      project. A long-range perspective can be taken regarding the interests
      and potential of the individuals in the group as well as the costs of
      education, training, and the acquisition of tools to increase
      individual's productivity and satisfaction.

Disadvantages of a functional organization include:

o   The limited ability to give individuals an opportunity to develop
      broader skills. An applications software engineer, for instance, will
      have little opportunity to learn about operating system software
      development.

o   The difficulty in controlling individual projects. Since all projects are
      under the control of one overall manager, the amount of information
      that he must manipulate can be overwhelming. The result is that
      individual project details are frequently missed and as a consequence
      schedules, budgets, and quality may suffer.

14.1.2 Project/Product Organizations

In a project/product organization, a team is formed for each project or
product under a project manager. This manager has direct responsibility
for completion of the project. The team consists of the appropriate mix of
people required to complete the project. For example, a team might consist
of hardware design engineers, applications software engineers, operating
system programmers, and a technical writer. Advantages of the project
organization include:

o   High motivation of the team members during project development. Team members identify closely with the product. It is not surprising to hear a team member refer to the product as "our baby."

o   Better project control. One individual is responsible solely for the management of the project. The result is that the project is more carefully monitored and understood. Decisions can be made more quickly by a more thoroughly informed individual compared to a functional organization.

o   Opportunities for growth. Team members may be exposed to a wide range of problems during the course of the development of the project, and therefore, develop a more global perspective.

Disadvantages of the project organization include:

o   High attrition at project end. In the search for a new opportunity at the end of the project, software engineers are likely to look for positions outside the company while evaluating other projects within the company.

o   Difficulty of sharing resources. Because of the distribution of knowledge about the projects, there is little incentive to share resources among projects. Different teams may, for example, develop similar debugging tools, thus duplicating effort. Similarly, it is difficult to take advantage of any economies of scale across projects.

o   Little concern for long-range goals. Because a manager is concerned with completing the current project, there is little incentive to plan for the future, to expend resources on training, or investigating and obtaining state-of-the-art techniques and tools. As a project nears completion, the project manager is likely to try to perpetuate his group by proposing follow-on projects, which may not maximize the net present value of the firm.

14.1.3 Matrix Organizations

The matrix organization is an attempt to combine the advantages of both the project/product organization and the functional organization with the goal of optimizing over both long- and short-term constraints simultaneously. In a matrix organization, functional managers direct functional groups while project managers concentrate on project development. Workers can be assigned to projects in one of two ways.

Either the project manager can subcontract portions of the project to functional groups or members of functional groups can be temporarily assigned to project groups. In either case, individuals remain associated with the functional group to which they belong. Thus, theoretically, an employee does not feel the loss of identity that comes at the end of the project.

The advantages of a matrix organization include:

o   The attempt to optimize more than one constraint.

o   Higher retention of employees.

o   Some of the advantages of functional organization such as the ability to detect commonality among projects, a concern for training, and obtaining state-of-the-art tools.

o   Some of the advantages of project organization including good product control.

o   The ability to control manpower utilization better. For example, someone who is very good at design may be assigned to the project only for the design phase.

o   The opportunity for individuals to develop along either the functional dimension or the product dimension.

Disadvantages of the matrix organization include:

o   The potential for conflict among competing managers.

o   The two-boss syndrome, which occurs when an individual receives different directions from the project manager and the functional manager.

o   The requirement for greater project planning to get a project completed under the matrix organization. Rather than allowing a small group of individuals a free hand to complete the project, each portion of the project must be specifically defined and contracted for.

14.2 Organization of Programming Teams

In selecting an organization for microprocessor software development, one should examine the costs and benefits of different organizations, including organizations designed specifically for programming teams. Several methods have been suggested for organizing programming teams. Perhaps the most widely discussed, if not the most widely used concept is that of the chief programmer team.[1,2] First presented by Harlan Mills at the IBM Federal Systems Division in 1971, the chief programmer team method has been used with varying degrees of success since then. A chief programmer team consists of a chief programmer who has complete technical responsibility for the project, a backup programmer, and several other team members. The chief programmer is expected to be a highly experienced and competent programmer. His job is to develop requirements, design, and implement the entire system. The backup programmer should also be a highly competent programmer, although perhaps less experienced than the chief. The backup programmer's primary job is to maintain close contact with the chief programmer on all aspects of the system development. He advises the chief programmer and ensures a smooth transition of leadership to the backup programmer if the chief programmer becomes unavailable. In addition to the chief and backup programmer, the team should also consist of

o   A program librarian — He or she will enter, edit, and maintain all project files in the program development library. These files include requirements documentation, design documentation, source and object code, test plans, and so on. An important aspect of the chief programmer team concept is that all code is publicly owned, not privately owned by individual programmers, and is available in the program development library. The use of a program development library increases management's ability to monitor project progress reliably.

o   An administrator — Although the chief programmer should be the manager of the team, his greatest contributions to the project are to be technical. It is, therefore, important that he not be overly concerned with administrative duties. The result is that most large projects will need an administrator to handle administrative duties relating to people, furniture, space, and equipment.

[1]Harlan Mills, "Chief Programmer Teams, Principles, and Procedures," IBM Federal Systems Division Report FSC 71-5108, Gaithersburg, Maryland, 1971.

[2]F. Terry Baker, "Chief Programmer Team Management of Production Programming," IBM Systems Journal, vol.11, no.1, 1972.

o   A tester — As an aid to the chief programmer, the tester develops necessary test cases to test code along with building any required stubs or drivers.

o   An editor — Although the chief programmer is responsible for all documentation, the editor can take rough drafts and spend the time to clean them up, reworking the documents into final form.

o   Additional programmers — Depending on the size of the project, several additional programmers may be assigned to the team to implement well-specified functions requested by the chief programmer. The chief programmer is ultimately responsible for the project and therefore is expected to review all code.

o   A toolsmith — As development progresses, a chief programmer will need many tools such as compilers, editors, and interactive computer facilities. The toolsmith's responsibility is to provide the necessary tools. This may be done by locating the desired tools from other sources, implementing unavailable tools, or redesigning interfaces to existing tools to satisfy the requirements of the chief programmer.

Other members of the team include secretaries for clerical support and a language specialist to answer any ambiguities that may arise regarding the implementation language specifications.

Given the appropriate resources, in particular very highly qualified chief programmers, chief programmer teams can be very effective in accomplishing a job. The organization is designed to minimize the amount of time wasted by the most technically competent team members. All team members except the chief have specific supporting roles to play. The organization also minimizes costly communications.

There are, however, several problems inherent in this type of organization. In particular, it requires chiefs but does not provide a way for the grooming of chiefs. The backup programmers are expected to be nearly as experienced as chief programmers. The additional programmers, on the other hand, can be fairly inexperienced. They typically remain fairly inexperienced, never developing a global perspective as the project progresses. Furthermore, there is little professional growth opportunity when a company has a number of chief programmers.

Because of the staff constitution, many organizations find that as a general rule the chief programmer team is not workable. It can, however, be quite appropriate for certain time-critical projects given the right individuals and circumstances.

A more informal approach to team organization is presented by Weinberg. Weinberg feels that "In programming, the way a team organizes for work is most strongly determined by two factors — the organization of the target system and the composition of the team."[3] Frequently, team members will organize themselves and the software to take advantage of the various strengths of the different team members. This situation works best in an environment where egoless programming is practiced so that perceived skills nearly match actual skills. In a less structured environment as described here, it is not uncommon for team leadership to shift during the course of the project as a different member's expertise becomes of more importance. In order to monitor progress in this type of environment, the use of a program production library is necessary to ensure code visibility and to ease communication among team members.

14.3 Software Organization Pitfalls to Avoid

Three classical problems often occur in software development organizations. The first is the "indispensable programmer" syndrome. This may occur when a programmer becomes solely responsible for some important aspect of a project. By clever coding or ignoring standards, a programmer can make his code incomprehensible and unmaintainable by anyone but himself; thus the programmer becomes "indispensable." A person like this should be fired immediately. The short-term cost to overcome this problem is much less than the long-term cost of allowing the situation to continue. Occasionally, the system allows someone to become indispensable almost against his or her will. For example, a particular individual may be extremely good at programming a particular type of control system and, therefore, is always given these types of assignments. The result may be that no one else in the organization is familiar with these particular programs. In this situation, it is advantageous to have a trainee work with the indispensable programmer. One does not want to wait until the indispensable programmer decides that he is bored with his role in the organization and quits before others are exposed to his type of problems.

The second problem, called the "best people" syndrome, relates to the proper utilization of the individuals working for the organization. As a rule, project managers prefer to have just the best people in the organization on

[3]Gerald M. Weinberg, The Psychology of Computer Programming (New York: Van Nostrand Reinhold Company, 1971), pp. 69-70.

their teams, and can promise fast and quality results if they pick their teams. Obviously not all teams can be formed this way. If one tries, the best people may become overworked and decide to go elsewhere where the pressure is less. Meanwhile, the less experienced people will be underutilized. In almost all situations, teams should comprise a group of individuals with a mix of backgrounds. This allows the inexperienced people to learn from their more experienced counterparts. Although this may not be the most efficient way to complete a particular project, it maximizes the long-term goal of developing employees. It is important to remember the truism that half of the people in a software development organization are below the group average.[4] By allowing those below average to learn from the best developers in the group, the performance of the group as a whole will increase.

The third classical problem in microprocessor software organizations is based on the observation that the design structure of a software product closely resembles the organizational structure of the software group that developed it. This natural tendency arises from the desire of each software engineer to have control of a specific module and from the desire of a manager to structure software development tasks into separately manageable components. In some cases a software development organization may be appropriate as a model for the design of the software product itself, however, this is not generally the case, and a manager must be careful not to compromise software design to facilitate its implementation by his or her current staff.

14.4 Improvement of the Software Organization Team Members

Another concern when organizing microprocessor software projects is the introduction and utilization of new technology. In many companies currently developing microprocessor software, the software expertise is minimal. It is thus vitally important that the organization allow for the introduction and spread of modern software development techniques. One possible way to aid this process is to establish a small core of good software engineers to develop tools. The tools group can then introduce improved

---

[4]We casually refer to this statement as the second law of software management. The first law, of course, is Brooks's law.

software methodology techniques to the applications and diagnostics programmers as well as help in the education of management.

Another concern is the desire to organize in order to facilitate the reusability of design and code as new versions of products are developed. With proper planning and the appropriate knowledge on the part of project team members, the operating system and other software tools can frequently be carried from one project to another. In addition, one would like to achieve reusability of the applications programs with minimal modifications. This requires both well-written software and a well-organized software development group to be aware of the reusable software.

15

REVIEWING MICROPROCESSOR

SOFTWARE PROJECTS

15.1 Introduction

Although formal reviews are used to provide management, and at times potential customers, with an indication of the progress of the project under development, the main purpose of the review process should be to ensure the quality of the final product. Hence, reviews should be constructive; the intent is to find errors for the purpose of improving the system, not to find guilt. The creative tone of one-on-one reviews should be extended to formal reviews. Keeping this perspective makes it more likely that the potential benefits to be achieved from conducting reviews will be realized, and that the potential system problems will be eliminated.

A formal review should be conducted at the conclusion of each significant phase of the software process to ensure that the deliverable to the next phase is accurate and complete. In all but very small projects involving only a few weeks of effort, formal reviews should be held at major milestones in each phase, and informal reviews even more frequently. Although code reviews are the most well known, reviews during other phases of development are vitally important in determining the quality of the final microprocessor software system.

15.2 Phase Reviews

Reviews should be conducted during each phase of the software development process.

o   Requirements Reviews. The purpose of requirements reviews is to determine the extent to which the requirement specifications meet the standards set for the characteristics described in Chapter 6:

   -   Fundamental characteristics: completeness (of function, performance, and constraints), correctness, consistency, unambiguity, testability, and relevance.

   -   Readability characteristics: conciseness, lack of redundancy, and comprehensibility.

   -   Ease of writing characteristics: modifiability and subsetability.

   -   Feasibility characteristics: manageability and freedom from unwarranted design detail.

o   Design Reviews. The purpose of design reviews is to determine that design documents, both graphical and textual, meet standards that will lead to code implementation that is efficient, reliable, and maintainable. Reviews should investigate the extent to which designs are hierarchical, modular, consistent, and realize the requirements developed earlier; the design characteristics are discussed in Chapter 4.

o   Code and Debug Reviews. The purpose of code reviews is to determine that

   -   The code realizes the design and hence ultimately the requirements of the system.

   -   The code meets standards for presentation, such as self-documentation, and algorithm implementation, such as structured programming. Chapter 2 describes guidelines for these.

   Debug reviews are usually informal reviews whose purpose is to find the cause of a specific problem a microprocessor software engineer encounters in debugging.

o   Test Reviews. The principal review during the testing phase of microprocessor software development occurs after test cases have been run and results recorded. At that time, reviewers determine whether or not the system performed to expectations. If it did not, then changes must be made and earlier activities must be revisited. In large projects, reviews should address test plans and test case selection in addition to test execution results.

o   Maintenance Reviews. During the maintenance phase it is important to review each problem report or request for change to determine if it warrants making modifications to the software. If these reviews result in the decision to change the system, then reviews described earlier should be repeated as microprocessor software engineers make changes to requirements specifications, design documents, code, and tests.

15.3 Formal Reviews

15.3.1 Characteristics and Objects of Formal Reviews

A formal review[1] is characterized by the following features:

o   A formal review team, with well-defined roles for team members, conducts the review.

o   The review team prepares a written record of the proceedings of the review.

o   The review procedure follows a set of guidelines and standards.

o   Review team members have responsibility for the quality of the result.

In medium and large microprocessor software development projects, formal reviews should be conducted during all phases.

o   In the requirements phase, reviews should address the functional requirements (customer requirements and user manual) and software requirements (software system requirements and software subsystem requirements). If the system being developed is large, reviews should address the decomposition of the requirements and large sections of the requirements as they are written.

---

[1]The material in this section is based on work done in the Software Systems Design Section at Xerox Corporation in the early 1980s and summarized in the document "Technical Review Guidelines", by Dave Cropek, Frank Goetz, and Leslie Swanson.

o In the design phase, reviews should address graphical and textual designs developed for each parent module and its children.

o Similarly in the coding phase, reviews should address each parent module and its children.

o In the test phase, reviews should address the test plans, cases, and results for comprehensible subsets of each of the four testing levels — module test, integration test, system test, and acceptance/installation test.

15.3.2 Roles of Review Team Members

A formal review team consists of a team leader, the author of the product under review, a number of reviewers, and a recorder. Each of these team members has responsibilities before, during, and after the review.

The team leader is responsible for verifying that the appropriate material is ready prior to the target date for distribution. If all appropriate material is not available, the leader should request that the author provide the necessary material. If it is not possible to obtain the necessary material in time, the leader should notify management and reschedule the date for the review. The review leader should ensure that this material is distributed to all team members in time to allow for preparation. Depending on the situation, the review leader may request a written response to the review material or initiate a discussion with the reviewers on an individual basis to ensure that all team members are thoroughly preparing for the review. The review leader should also select the member of the review team who will be the recorder. During the review, the leader's main role is to moderate discussion ensuring that all relevant topics are discussed thoroughly. The purpose of the review should be clearly stated, as different types of reviews are held through the course of a project. The review leader should monitor and assist the recorder to verify that all relevant points are being recorded. The leader with input from the team members should determine if a follow-up review is required. After the review, it is the review leader's responsibility to ensure that all review results have been sent to the appropriate parties, so that action items may be traced.

The author prepares the package for the review and distributes it to team members well in advance of the review, typically three working days or more. The package includes the object being reviewed, e.g., a code module, and relevant material, e.g., an approved design document that describes the code module. The package should indicate to reviewers the relation of the object being reviewed to the rest of the system. During the review the author should give a brief presentation of his package, then respond to questions raised by the team. After the review the author should respond to the comments and questions raised in the review, incorporate changes into the product, and resubmit it for review if required.

The recorder's responsibility during the review is to record all relevant comments made by review team members. The notes taken should identify clearly the comment made, the team member who made the comment, and the section of the document to which the comment was related. After the review, the recorder should have the notes transcribed and distributed in a timely manner.

Prior to the review, each member of the review team is responsible for thoroughly reviewing the review package. The reviewer's goal is to find errors and ensure consistency in the software product. If the reviewer has difficulty finding the time to prepare properly, this should be discussed with the review leader and the individual's manager. When it is not possible to rearrange priorities to allow the reviewer adequate time to prepare, an alternate review team member should be assigned the task. During the review itself, each reviewer should make sure that all of his or her questions and comments are raised. Discussion should be conducted in a professional manner, remembering that it is the product under review, not the developer. The kind of statement made during the review is typified by the comment, "The comments at the beginning of the module don't follow the standards." Reviewers should also remember that the purpose of a review is to find problems, not to solve them, and that there are many different ways to solve problems correctly, not just their own.

15.3.3 Selecting the Review Team

Managers should give some attention to their selection of team members, as the mix of people has a significant effect on the quality of the review. Both technical and nontechnical factors should be considered in the selection process. A review team should consist of a small set of people (typically four to eight) with different perspectives on the project. Consideration should be given to the following types of individuals:

o   Representatives from the previous development phase. For example, during the requirements specification review a representative of the user community can provide useful insights, and during a design review a member of the team which wrote the requirements specification can help assure completeness. In general, such representation helps ensure that the documents produced in the previous phase were correctly interpreted by the current team.

o   Representatives from the team responsible for the next phase. For example, during a design review, a member of the implementation team should be included. This person focuses on the completeness and understandability of the documents produced.

o   Representatives from other teams that are producing subsystems which will interface with the software under review. In the microprocessor environment, this implies someone from the hardware development team participating in the review of the software design.

o   Colleagues on the software development team. People from this group usually constitute the majority of the review team. They provide comments on interfaces to other parts of the software system and on consistency of the application of standards and guidelines.

In addition to being a representative of some appropriate group, it is important that the individuals assigned to the review team have the following attributes:

o   An understanding of the importance of the review process

o   An understanding of the objectives of the current review

o   The ability to evaluate objectively the product under consideration, and not the author of the product

o   The ability to associate with other review team members in a professional manner

o   A willingness to follow the procedural guidelines for reviews

Review team leaders should have:

o   The ability to maintain control of the review session, keep the discussion on track, and ensure that all relevant topics are covered

o   Experience and familiarity with the overall project and development environment

o   No difficulties interacting with any of the review team members that might interfere with the review process

Recorders should also have

o   Familiarity with the product under review, the review process, and the jargon used in these

o   Conscientious writing skills and legible handwriting

o   Previous review experience

o   Effective communication skills

Although it may be possible to set up a formal review team that is always responsible for reviews, there are reasons to share the responsibilities for reviews among all software development team members. The review process can be an educational one. Review team members see approaches toward problem solving taken by others. They can improve their communication skills, and they are exposed to phases of the project in which they are not directly involved. In an environment where a permanent review team is given responsibility for all reviews, an unhealthy adversarial relationship could develop between the producers and the review team.

15.4 Informal Reviews

Although we have concentrated primarily on formal reviews in this chapter, the review process should not be restricted to formal reviews. In a team environment, the peer review process is an ongoing activity. Informal reviews of various types should be a natural activity. Informal reviews can range from impromptu get-togethers with one or two colleagues to a more formal structured walkthrough as subphases of a project are completed.

Informal reviews, especially one-on-one interactions, often have a fundamentally different objective from formal reviews. Rather than finding errors and checking consistency, informal reviews stimulate the creative process by giving reactions to design concepts or combining different perspectives to form new insights. The next chapter describes facilities for encouraging this creative aspect of microprocessor software development.

15.5 Role of Management in the Review Process

We have included the review process in our discussion of managing microprocessor software development because it is an important vehicle for ensuring the quality of microprocessor software systems. Nevertheless, we find that in most microprocessor software development projects personnel devote much too little time to reviews. The natural tendency for individuals is to concentrate on their own specific tasks, thus deemphasizing reviews, and causing problems in overall system correctness, completeness, and consistency. Managers can enhance the role of the review process and the quality of their products through the following actions:

o   Allocating time in project plans for reviews. This includes time for preparation for reviews and time for conducting the reviews. Our guideline is that microprocessor software engineers should devote 20 to 25 percent of their time to reviews.

o   Providing incentives for software development team members to participate in reviews. As software development is a team activity, personnel should be rewarded based on their team as well as their individual contributions. Thus rewards to individuals should be based on their contributions to reviews, the progress of the team as a whole, and the quality of the product.

By incorporating such actions into their activities, managers can encourage better reviews and as a result more effective product development.

16

FACILITIES FOR MICROPROCESSOR

SOFTWARE PROJECTS

16.1 Introduction

Our presentation to this point has concentrated principally on the *techniques* that should be used to develop microprocessor software and to manage this development activity. In this chapter we depart from this theme to focus on *facilities* that should be provided to produce software for microprocessor-based products. Appropriate facilities — in the form of computer hardware and software and physical surroundings — complement development and management techniques to provide a complete environment for the effective production of microprocessor software.

Facilities are an important factor in microprocessor software development for several reasons:

o   Computer hardware and software facilities can simplify much of the clerical work of microprocessor software engineers — work such as creating and editing requirements and design documents, putting programs into computer readable form and editing them, and keeping historical records of test results. This simplification of work can save substantial personnel time.

o   Computer-based debugging systems can assist microprocessor software engineers by providing information about the operation of their programs. This information leads to the faster development of operational software systems.

o   Office facilities can assist microprocessor software engineers by encouraging useful communication and discouraging unnecessary interactions.

Thus, appropriate facilities reduce the time and effort required to complete microprocessor software products, and this corresponding increase in productivity of microprocessor software engineers is a major objective of many organizations.

Facilities should support the wide variety of personnel associated with the microprocessor software development activity. This includes, but is not limited to

o   Software engineers who write and debug code

o   Requirements specification writers who determine customers' requirements and write and edit the specification documents

o   Software designers who translate the requirements documents into a form for software engineers to develop code

o   Software testers who prepare test plans and exercise them to demonstrate that the software meets users' requirements and to find any errors that exist in the software

o   Software maintenance personnel who correct and augment microprocessor software products

o   Software engineering managers who prepare software development plans and review project progress

o   Product managers who review software development status and its role in product development

o   Product planners who integrate software development plans into product development plans

o   Secretaries who support the aforementioned personnel by performing both technical and administrative tasks

Thus, appropriate facilities will address the requirements of people performing a variety of activities, both as individuals and as a group forming a development team.

Naturally there is a cost, usually a significant cost, associated with providing appropriate facilities for the number and variety of people involved in microprocessor software development. The objective of providing facilities is to reduce the effort, and hence the time, of microprocessor software development. There is therefore a tradeoff between the cost of facilities and the effort required to complete a microprocessor software product. Figure 16-1 illustrates this tradeoff. As shown in the figure, with no facilities the effort required to produce microprocessor software is very high. Who would think of developing microprocessor software without some kind of computer support such as a compiler, editor, and loader? Indeed, the task would be virtually impossible. As the facilities improve, the effort required decreases rapidly at first, then the rate of decrease slows. The reason the effort curve flattens is that after a necessary set of facilities is provided, additional facilities reduce the effort required by a smaller amount. The lowest point on the effort curve corresponds to the minimum effort achievable for a project. In the extreme, the time required to learn how to use additional facilities is more than the time the new facilities save, and the effort actually increases. The cost of facilities naturally increases as more and better facilities are provided. The cost curve in Figure 16-1 increases faster than linearly because very elaborate facilities are much more expensive than simple ones. For example, an organization could provide each software engineer with a mainframe computer; however, that would be much more expensive and only a little more productive than providing each engineer with a sophisticated workstation.

The correct approach in determining the facilities to acquire is to perform a cost/benefit analysis that comprehends both the near-term and the long-term costs of facilities acquisition and effort reduction. In Figure 16-1, the dotted line represents the sum of the effort and cost curves for increasing facility capabilities; the optimal set of facilities occurs where the dotted line reaches its minimal value.

In this chapter we describe two fundamental types of facilities. The first type is computer facilities, and the second type is office facilities. Although not obvious at first glance, both types of facilities support, and hence reduce, the effort required in all the software development phases and for all the personnel associated with the development of microprocessor software products.

16.2 Computer Facilities

16.2.1 The Purpose of Computer Facilities

There are three goals in providing computer facilities for developing microprocessor software:

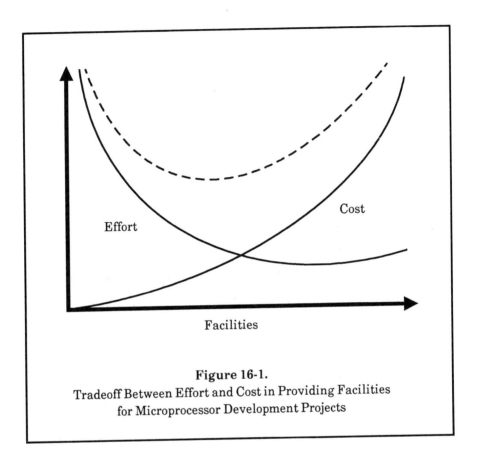

Figure 16-1.
Tradeoff Between Effort and Cost in Providing Facilities
for Microprocessor Development Projects

o   To assist in the production of microprocessor code during the coding, debugging, and testing phases of development. In these phases, computer facilities assist in the translation of design into executable microprocessor code and in the location of errors in the code.

o   To assist in the preparation of documents used in the software development process. The list of documents includes project planning documents, requirements specifications, design specifications, error lists, test plans, and reviews.

o   To assist in the automation of office and administrative operations like word processing, filing, calendar management, budget development, cost management, scheduling and announcing meetings, and distributing reports.

16.2.2 Computer Hardware Facilities

There are several types of computer hardware facilities that can be used to assist in the production of microprocessor code.

o   Personal computers are generally single-user desktop microprocessor-based systems. For projects requiring more than a man-month of effort, a personal computer (PC) should have an internal hard disk with a storage capacity of ten million bytes or more to simplify the management of program modules. Modern PCs have the capability to perform common code production operations (compiling, linking, simulating, and so forth) on the order of minutes or seconds. Equipped with a printer to provide listings and reports and with a floppy disk drive to prepare software for transport, modern PC costs start around two thousand dollars. Leading suppliers of PCs include IBM, Compaq, Kaypro, Leading Edge, and AT&T; a number of other vendors sell PCs appropriate for much microprocessor software development.

o   Minicomputers are larger than personal computers and provide more power in terms of instructions executed per second, internal random access memory, and disk storage. With this additional power, minicomputers typically support multiple users simultaneously and perform common code production operations in seconds, perhaps three to ten times faster than PCs. The user interface to a multiuser minicomputer is the computer terminal, with a keyboard and screen similar to those used for personal computers. Well-known suppliers of minicomputers include Digital Equipment Corporation, Data General, Hewlett-Packard, Prime, and IBM.

     A particular type of minicomputer, called the personal workstation — or more simply just a workstation — offers minicomputer power with a high resolution graphics screen for a single user. The cost of workstations, starting at well under ten thousand dollars, makes them very attractive for microprocessor software development. Leading suppliers of workstations include Xerox, Apollo, Sun, and Digital Equipment Corporation.

o   Mainframe computers are large, powerful systems designed to support multiple users simultaneously. They provide immediate access to large amounts of on-line disk storage, facilitating centralized control of software artifacts. As with minicomputers, users interface to mainframes via computer terminals. Mainframes are typically an order of magnitude more powerful than minicomputers, and their costs are higher — hundreds of thousands to millions of dollars. Well-known manufacturers of mainframe computers include IBM, Burroughs, Sperry, Control Data, and Amdahl.

o   Microprocessor development systems are PC-based or minicomputer-based systems that provide a wide range of capabilities designed specifically for the development of microprocessor software. They contain a CRT display, a keyboard, and a floppy disk drive. In addition to functions like compiling and linking, microprocessor development systems (MDSs) provide the capability to download software from the host development computer into the target microprocessor system and run the software under user control. A debugging program in the host computer assists the user in tracing the execution of his microprocessor code. Some MDSs provide the capability for in-circuit emulation (ICE), where the target microprocessor is replaced by a connector to another microprocessor-based system that can be stopped, examined, and controlled with great precision by the user. MDSs may also provide a data collection capability to record information about the execution of instructions and the occurrence of I/O events; this information can be later examined to aid in the debugging process. Two manufacturers of microprocessor development systems are Hewlett-Packard and Tektronix.

o   Simulators are computer-based systems that make the program appear to be running in an actual environment. In order to simulate the actual conditions where the system will operate, simulators provide input signals to the microprocessor running the software developed. This is an effective vehicle for debugging and testing, especially for real-time, microprocessor-based products. Since they are designed for particular products, simulators are special purpose; however, they can often be modified to support the members in a family of products. Advanced simulators provide the capability of being reconfigurable under software command.

Despite the variety of computer hardware facilities available, the costs and benefits of various alternatives are discernible so that managers can perform detailed analyses to determine appropriate facilities for their organizations.

Many of the facilities described for the production of microprocessor code serve as a basis for facilities for document preparation. The fundamental requirements of processing capability, keyboard input, CRT display, large internal memory, and large disk memory apply as well to the entering, editing, storage, and retrieval of documents. The capabilities of personal computers and workstations, coupled with advanced printing capabilities such as desktop laser printers, have spawned the new industry of desktop electronic publishing. Larger laser printers connected to minicomputers and mainframes provide documentation capabilities for supporting even large organizations. A key point to note is that most of the computer hardware facilities used to aid the production of microprocessor code can also be used in the preparation of documents in all phases of the microprocessor software development process, regardless of whether the computer hardware is a personal computer, a minicomputer, or a mainframe computer.

The facilities for document preparation, in turn, form a foundation for office automation requirements. Personal computers, minicomputers, and mainframe computers all have the capability to support the office automation requirements of individuals. Supporting all the members of a software development team, however, requires communication among the facilities used by individuals. If all the team members use the same mainframe computer, then intercommunication is usually straightforward. For team members who use personal computers or workstations, however, there is a requirement for a communication link among systems. Local area networks, such as Ethernet, have been developed to provide communication capabilities for people using a variety of different systems for a variety of purposes:

o   Retrieving software modules from a file server

o   Moving code from a workstation to a microprocessor development system

o   Distributing a document to several team members for review

o   Notifying team members of a scheduled review meeting

o   Filing reports in a central location

o   Forwarding expense reports to administrative personnel

o   Printing reports for review at a meeting

Figure 16-2 shows a topological diagram of a network for microprocessor software development and support. Note from the figure that the facilities connected by the network provide capabilities to all team members for all phases of the microprocessor software development process.

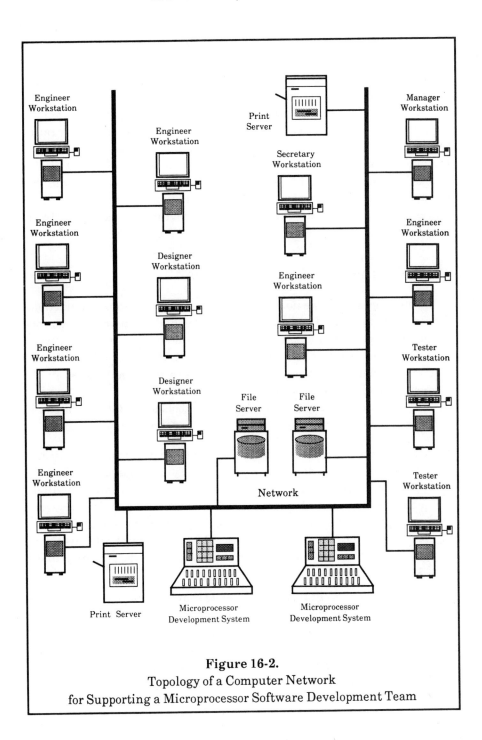

Figure 16-2.
Topology of a Computer Network
for Supporting a Microprocessor Software Development Team

In examining the utility of facilities, it is natural to ask the question, "How much effort does computer hardware save?" The COCOMO model gives us a partial answer to the question. Consider in Table 12-2 the computer turnaround time factor, defined as the time between the user's submission of a job and the user's receipt of the job completed by the computer. The difference between the low rating (when the computer turnaround time is greater than twelve hours) and the very high rating (when the computer turnaround time is less than five seconds) is over 32 percent! Thus, the time required to complete a software project can be reduced by almost a third by providing a computer hardware system that has a very high rating in computer turnaround time. This improvement is representative of results obtained by improving computer hardware facilities.

16.2.3 Computer Software Facilities

In the previous section we noted that, except for some specialized functions, the same computer hardware facilities could be used for microprocessor code production, document preparation, and office automation. It is the software in these systems that enable them to perform multiple functions. In this section, we mention several types of software tools that assist in the production of microprocessor software.

Perhaps the most widely used software tools are those that assist in microprocessor code production during the coding and debugging phases.

o   Editors are programs that allow the user to create and manipulate text (such as source code) on a computer. Typical operations are file creation, storage, retrieval, and modification (additions, deletions, changes, moves, and so on). Syntax-directed editors further assist microprocessor software engineers by informing them of some syntax errors during the editing process. Editors are most effective in an interactive mode. Simple editors are inexpensive, typically under $100 for personal computer versions.

o   Compilers are programs that translate source programs expressed in a higher level language into the microprocessor machine language. Compilers produce listings of the statements in programs and the errors found during translation. Commonly used languages for microprocessor coding include Pascal, C, and COBOL. Several compilers that produce code for microprocessors have been developed to run on personal computers. These compilers range in cost from a few hundred to a few thousand dollars.

o   Linkers and loaders are programs that combine separately compiled software modules and load them into the microprocessor memory or the simulated microprocessor memory. These programs are usually available as part of compiler packages or microprocessor development systems.

o   Debuggers are programs that often interact in real time with the microprocessor hardware to provide the capability to initiate program execution, interrupt program execution, inspect and change program code, and inspect and change program data.

o   As we describe in more detail in Section 18.3.2, an operating system is a collection of programs that appears to extend the basic capabilities of a computer. Operating systems facilitate the production of code by providing capabilities to create and manipulate files, sort and retrieve them from disks, and sequence the execution of other programs. Simple operating systems for personal computers cost under one hundred dollars.

Although code production tools were the first software tools used and are still the tools most frequently used in microprocessor software development, more attention in recent years has been given to other phases of software development. As a result, other software tools play an increasingly important role.

o   In the requirements phase, the goal is to produce requirements documents; a simple tool such as a word processor can greatly facilitate document production. A good word processor for a personal computer costs well under a thousand dollars. A requirements analyzer tool checks requirements documents for consistency, completeness, and correctness when the requirements are expressed in a form that can be analyzed mathematically, e.g., a finite state machine. A requirements traceability tool assists in the tracing of requirements through subsequent stages of microprocessor software development.

o   Tools for the design phase fall into two categories. Graphical processing tools translate high-level design specifications into graphs such as structure and hierarchy charts. Text processing tools, such as PDL described in Chapter 4, translate detailed design specifications into design documents. In addition to providing formatting to facilitate reading, these tools can check for design consistency, thus enabling microprocessor software engineers to find errors earlier in their development work.

o   Testing tools, described in more detail in Section 8.8, fall into two categories. Static tools are used in conjunction with compilers to analyze the code to be tested. They perform functions like checking the syntax of interfaces and detecting code that cannot be reached during program execution. Dynamic tools are used in conjunction with debuggers to analyze programs being executed. These tools perform functions such as counting the number of times each statement is executed and comparing actual program outputs to expected outputs. Tools to perform these functions are now available on personal computers.

o   Maintenance tools concentrate on record keeping for the maintenance phase. They help software engineers differentiate requests, prioritize their work, and control releases of software. While the range of capabilities of such error tracking and configuration control tools varies considerably, the simple tools for personal computers can have a significant beneficial effect on the maintenance of small-to-medium size programs.

The software tools designed to support document preparation may be considered a subset of the tools to assist in the automation of office and administrative operations. Word processing systems or word processing programs running on personal computers provide basic capabilities for document preparation, both documents developed as part of the software life cycle and documents developed in the normal conduct of business. Word processing programs on personal computers provide capabilities for document creation, editing, storage, retrieval, and printing. More sophisticated desktop publishing systems provide capabilities for

o   WYSIWYG editing ("what you see is what you get"), which provides the capability to print exactly what the computer monitor shows — including fonts, spacing, and graphics

o   Multiple character fonts — both in style and size

o   Graphics acquisition capability through drawing and scanning external documents

o   Automatic index and table of contents generation

o   High resolution printing with laser printers

Office automation capabilities, provided on a variety of workstations, extend these basic functions:

o   Electronic filing enables users to store documents (text, code, designs, and so forth) on a computer system for later retrieval. Going beyond the fundamental save and retrieve capabilities, they provide hierarchical capabilities. Thus, a user can store a document in a labeled electronic folder; the folder can be stored in a labeled electronic file drawer; the file drawer can be stored in a labeled electronic file cabinet; and so on. Such facilities simplify the management of a large number of items.

o   Electronic spreadsheets are programs that present users with a two-dimensional worksheet into which they can enter text, numbers, and formulas. It is easy to make changes to numbers and recalculate all the formulas in the spreadsheet. Such functions facilitate the preparation of financial and other reports, permit sensitivity analyses to be conducted quickly, and simplify the generation of month-over-month comparison reports.

o   Another useful office capability is the forms processing extension to word processor or publishing systems. The additional function provided is the ability to design commonly used office forms and fill in the variable positions quickly.

o   Electronic mail provides the capability to send information from one workstation to another. A modern network, such as the one illustrated in Figure 16-2, can transmit information at rates of ten million bits per second and more. Thus, multi-page documents, which typify the microprocessor software development environment, can be transmitted electronically in seconds. Electronic mail reduces telephone tag by sending messages to users and storing them for retrieval when the recipient returns. Electronic mail enables users to send documents to several people quickly, and to retrieve comments from several people without having to visit each one personally.

When electronic mail is combined with electronic filing, publishing, and other capabilities to form an office automation system, all the personnel associated with a software development project have a common set of tools to assist them in their work.

As with computer hardware facilities, the utility of computer software facilities can be determined from the COCOMO model. Consider in Table

12-2 the factor called use of software tools (described in more detail in Section 18.4). The difference between very low use of software tools and very high use of software tools is over 49 percent! Thus, the time required to complete a software project can be reduced by almost half by providing and using appropriate software tools.

16.2.4 Integrated Computer and Support Systems

In the previous two sections, we have discussed computer hardware facilities and computer software facilities separately; however, they must be considered to be part of an integrated system that supports a number of users for a variety of functions. In considering the system as a whole, it is important to note that the hardware/software system is actually providing a huge data base that facilitates manipulation of a variety of artifacts associated with microprocessor software development and management:

o   Plans

o   Documents

o   Code modules

o   Test results

o   Maintenance logs

The hardware/software system is complicated, not only by additional items to control, but also by the histories and versions of all these items. Advanced data base systems provide capabilities beyond those of software goals described earlier to manage

o   The variety of software programs

o   The numerous types of artifacts created by the team

o   The evolution of these over time

For example, a sophisticated data base system would ensure that a compilation would include all and only the latest versions of modules; and a progress report for a manager would include the latest status on development activities reporting to him. Such a data base has to manage numerous disparate hardware and software facilities.

An integrated computer system to facilitate microprocessor software development must be supported to be effective. Support encompasses a variety of activities:

o   Repair. When a system is inoperable due to hardware or software
      failure, it not only reduces productivity through lost time, it also
      affects morale. While repairs can be expensive, managers should
      perform tradeoff analyses to determine the appropriate level of
      support for their system.

o   Upgrading. As new or enhanced tools become available for acquisition
      (through external purchase or internal development), managers
      should determine the potential benefits of incorporating them into
      their system. If they are cost effective in providing greater benefits,
      then the tools should be installed and supported.

o   Training. The addition of tools to the system and new personnel to the
      software development team creates a demand for training personnel in
      tool use. Training is useful as it increases users' knowledge of the
      facilities and hence productivity in pursuing their work. In addition to
      formal training, it is beneficial to provide assistance to users who
      generate questions as they pursue their development activities. Such
      assistance not only aids the engineers, it also points to problems in the
      system and provides insights into future improvement directions.

Thus, support plays an important role in providing facilities to software
development team members.

      Given the variety of facilities available, it is natural to pose the
question: "What facilities should I get for my project?" As with most
economic questions, the answer is, "It depends." It depends on the number
of people, the amount of software to be written, the future use of the
facilities, the cost of money, and a variety of other factors. For medium-size
projects, we prefer a system comprising

o   A network of workstations with print servers, file servers, and
      connections to simulator and debug facilities

o   Software tools to support the software life cycle and to provide office
      automation capabilities

o   A support group that can develop new tools

Such a system can be built from commercially available components, is
reliable, and is easily expanded and upgraded. In addition, it gives each
workstation user substantial computing power, yet it makes users
appreciate the system's limitations. Such a system, when developed with

the appropriate cost/benefits analysis, can provide a productive, yet cost effective, environment for microprocessor software development.

16.3 Office Facilities

16.3.1 The Purpose of Office Facilities

To appreciate the goals of providing office facilities, it is useful to examine the fundamental personal and interpersonal activities that software engineers, managers, and other team members use to realize software products:

o   Creative thinking. A significant portion of software engineers' time is devoted to the creation of designs and algorithms and to the review of other engineers' work. An important management activity is the creation of plans to accomplish overall project objectives.

o   Clerical activities. Software engineers and their support personnel perform many clerical activities, such as typing documents and programs into a computer system, running programs, retrieving printed output, and accessing file systems.

o   Communication. Several types of communication occur during the normal conduct of microprocessor software development activities. Software engineers interact with each other on a one-to-one basis to gain feedback on conceptual ideas and stimulate their creative thought processes. Software engineers meet as groups to conduct reviews of requirements documents; design documents, code, test plans, and test results. Large groups of software engineers meet for classes, project meetings, and other gatherings.

o   Machine interaction. Microprocessor software engineers and support personnel (such as technicians and test personnel) spend significant time interacting with the microprocessor-based systems or simulators for which they are developing software.

o   Services. Members of microprocessor software development teams require access to both ordinary services and special services such as technical information libraries.

This list of fundamental activities provides a foundation for the requirements for office facilities to support microprocessor software development:

o   Creative thinking is best conducted in an environment of privacy and comfort, to reduce the effects of unnecessary interruption, and spaciousness, to facilitate the manipulation of material recorded on a variety of media. Office facilities that support creative activities like microprocessor software development require security to protect the investment in new concepts.

o   Clerical activities require immediate access to computers, terminals, files, and so on, to reduce the time engineers devote to noncreative activities.

o   Communication requirements comprehend a variety of levels — facilities for one-on-one communications, conference rooms for group communications, and electronic communication.

o   Machine interaction requires an environment, such as a laboratory, that can accommodate the microprocessor-based system being developed, the test and debug equipment associated with it, and the number of personnel who may work on it at one time. Such environments may also have requirements for temperature and humidity control.

o   Services have additional space and power requirements, but vary depending on their special nature.

With this basic understanding of facilities requirements, we can proceed to describe appropriate facilities for microprocessor software development.

16.3.2 Offices

The office of a microprocessor software engineer should be private, comfortable, and secure. It should provide access to terminals and files and facilitate one-on-one communications. We recommend the following:

o   An enclosed office with floor-to-ceiling walls, soundproof walls, carpeting on the floor, and a closeable door. Such an office should house *one* engineer.

o   The size of the office should be at least ten feet by ten feet to accommodate furniture and room for interaction with at least one additional person.

o   A standard set of furniture which can be arranged to the software engineer's personal tastes:

- A desk that accommodates a personal computer or computer monitor, provides a moveable keyboard stand, and offers no leg room obstructions.

- Tables or hanging work surfaces that offer sufficient space to accommodate working with large computer fanfold paper.

- Files, bookshelves, and storage drawers to accommodate computer listings, notebooks, reports, and personal items.

- An ergonomic chair for use by the principal office occupant.

- An additional chair for use by a person visiting the office for interpersonal communication.

- A wall-mounted whiteboard for writing concepts, that facilitates easy writing and review.

Figure 16-3 shows the interior of a typical software engineer's office. The figure is adapted from one of the pioneering studies on facilities design to support software development.[1]

o   The office should have a personal computer or workstation connected to a local area network that connects to other software engineers' computers and other services as shown in Figure 16-2.

o   There should be a phone and overhead lighting. There should be office controls for air conditioning and heating. These facilities, plus power outlets, should support future hardware in the office.

While these facilities may seem extravagant to some, they engender significant productivity increases as we will discuss in Section 16.3.4.

16.3.3 Office Complexes

To satisfy the requirements described earlier, an office complex or building that supports a microprocessor software development team should have additional facilities beyond the individual offices described in the previous section:

[1]Gerald M. McCue, "IBM's Santa Teresa Laboratory — Architectural Design for Program Development," IBM Systems Journal, vol. 17, no.1 (1978), pp. 4-25.

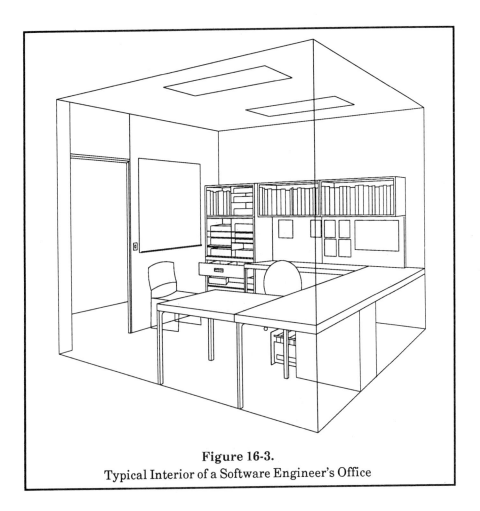

Figure 16-3.
Typical Interior of a Software Engineer's Office

o Conference and meeting rooms. To accommodate the various types of reviews there should be conference rooms to handle ten people comfortably. The rooms should have a table, chairs, a whiteboard, and an overhead projector. A good guideline is to have one conference room for every two first level management groups (typically from four to ten people per group). Larger rooms, providing seating for up to fifty people, should be available for lectures and team meetings.

o Laboratories. Separate rooms should be provided for the debug and test of the microprocessor-based system being developed. These rooms should be large enough to accommodate machines, equipment, and personnel. These rooms should provide desks and tables at which engineers and technicians may work. They should provide power and cooling facilities for substantial amounts of equipment. Laboratories should also provide connections to the network so engineers can send the software developed in their offices to the laboratory for debug and test.

o   Special services. In addition to the usual facilities described above, it is beneficial to have a

-     technical library with reference books and current periodicals to provide information to software engineers

-     training facility to educate engineers on new equipment

-     network service/support area which may house print and file servers, and provide facilities for service

Such facilities in an office complex complement the office facilities described earlier to provide a complete microprocessor software development environment.

16.3.4 Perspective on Office Facilities

The office facilities we have described contrast with those of another trend, the Japanese office style in which groups of four or more desks fill large rooms. The ideas behind this "bullpen" arrangement are that proximity promotes communication and that constant supervision gives engineers the incentives to work hard. Our experience is that much of the communication in such an environment is more disruptive than beneficial. Furthermore, we feel that incentives should be structured with the objectives of the organization to generate self-motivation, rather than forcing it unnaturally on workers.

TRW has conducted some experiments to determine the effects of the working environment on software development productivity.[2,3] One survey

---

[2]Barry W. Boehm, et al., "The TRW Productivity System" (September 1983).

[3]Geraldine Brooks, "Faced with Changing Work Force, TRW Pushes to Raise White-Collar Productivity," The Wall Street Journal, September 22, 1983.

queried people who had worked for six months in offices like we have described. The survey asked workers to estimate subjectively the change in their productivity. The average response was an estimated gain of 39 percent! Another survey queried people who had worked in the special environment but had subsequently moved into a more traditional environment. These workers reported a 47 percent average increase in productivity while they were in the specially designed environment.

The TRW study[4] made several conclusions which reflect the environment we have described:

o   Private offices improve productivity.

o   Office automation support is required for all project personnel.

o   There is a high payoff in placing all software artifacts on-line and providing tools to support easy access to them.

o   Local area networks strongly support distributed work environments.

o   The integrated approach produces a high payoff.

[4]Barry W. Boehm, et al., "The TRW Productivity System" (September 1983).

17

INTEGRATING

MICROPROCESSOR SOFTWARE

INTO EMBEDDED PRODUCTS

17.1 Motivation for Integration

In many applications for which microprocessor software is developed, the
end product is not the software itself but is instead a larger system that is
controlled by the microprocessor software. Thus the microprocessor is
embedded in a complex system consisting of hardware that may span a
variety of technologies: electromechanical (as in controlling robotic sensors
and switches), paper movement (as in printer control), optical (as in
supermarket scanning systems), and chemical (as in industrial process
control). In such systems the software development cost is a small fraction
of the total system development cost and the microprocessor cost is a small
fraction of the total system cost, yet the microprocessor software must
control the operation of the entire system and do so within demanding
tolerances. "In general, the costs of changing the other parts of this complex
are so high that their characteristics are considered essentially
unchangeable, and the software is expected both to conform to their
specifications, and to take up the slack on any unforeseen difficulties
encountered or changes required within the other parts of the complex. As a
result, the embedded-mode project does not generally have the option of

negotiating easier software changes and fixes by modifying the requirements and interface specifications. The project must therefore expend more effort in accommodating changes and fixes."[1]

The situation is further complicated by the fact that microprocessor technology is usually a young technology compared to the other technologies that constitute a complex product, which leads to organizations in which senior managers (especially product managers) have little knowledge or experience in microprocessor software technology, development, and management.

The software/system interaction and inexperienced product management constitute significant differences between the development and management of microprocessor software products and traditional software product development and management. Thus successful integration of microprocessor software with other technologies into complex embedded system products requires special technical direction and management interaction processes.

17.2 Technical Direction in Integrating Microprocessor Software into Embedded Products

17.2.1 Organizational Interfaces

The activity of integrating microprocessor software development into a total product development scenario encompasses interactions with a variety of groups. The nature of these interactions depends on the type of product and the structure of the organization developing the embedded microprocessor product. Despite the variety in product types and organization structures, there are common interfaces in types of personnel with whom microprocessor software engineers interact. These certainly include engineers developing the other subsystems which the microprocessor software controls, and are also likely to include manufacturing engineers who are responsible for building the final product to quality and cost specifications. Other personnel with whom microprocessor software engineers may interact include product management team personnel, product planners, and marketing representatives. Due to the interaction between software and the rest of the product system, microprocessor

---

[1]Barry W. Boehm, <u>Software Engineering Economics</u> (Englewood Cliffs, New Jersey: Prentice-Hall, 1981), p. 79.

software engineers should devote special attention to certain aspects of the software development process.

17.2.2 Requirements Specification

The key element in directing the development of the requirements specification for an embedded product is to form a team that includes not only product planners and other engineering personnel but software engineers as well.

In the requirements analysis activity the software engineers on such a team will address the features that will be implemented by software and the constraints within which the software will operate. Without software engineers on the team these factors are easily overlooked, usually resulting in significant problems later in the development cycle.

The investigations conducted during requirements analysis are manifested in the description of functions and performance in the customer requirements document. Here the software engineers play a critical role on the team, as these descriptions must comprehend not only customer wishes but also the capability to implement them within the design and development constraints. For example, certain functions that other engineering disciplines may enable could be impractical due to constraints such as the memory size in the microprocessor system. As another example, certain performance criteria such as the response time required to support multiple independent events may be unrealizable due to constraints in the instruction execution speed of the microprocessor. The constraints that affect the achievability of requirements which the microprocessor software engineers should comprehend are

o   The cost of the microprocessor-based control system and its implications on system capabilities.

o   The spending constraint on personnel and support systems and its implication on the amount of software that can be produced.

o   The schedule constraint and its implication on time that can be devoted to software design, coding, and testing.

In the final activities of developing the requirements specification document, i.e., writing the user manual and the software requirements specification, the roles of the software engineers and other engineers change. In these activities the software engineers play the lead role and the other engineers describe constraints, review documentation, and approve specifications.

17.2.3 Design Specification

The multidisciplinary engineering team aspect of microprocessor systems development initiated in the requirements specification phase should continue into the analysis stage of the design phase. During this analysis activity, engineers begin making design tradeoffs, and it is important to have software engineers participate to ensure that demands placed upon software and the microprocessor control system do not compromise the ability to deliver the microprocessor software within the aforementioned design constraints. Because software provides a flexibility and capability previously unachievable at similar costs in embedded systems, other engineers have incentives to design their subsystems in a manner that places huge demands on the microprocessor software and control system. This is sometimes called "sloppy" design, the connotation being not messy but rather pushing tolerances to the limit.

In the synthesis stage of the design phase the engineering teams shift their focus to their specialties. Just as members of the multidisciplinary engineering team should consider tradeoffs among the various product subsystems in design analysis, the microprocessor software and hardware engineers should consider architectural tradeoffs between microprocessor hardware and software, and between the various software components in design synthesis. These tradeoffs are discussed in Chapter 18. Even though microprocessor software engineers have the responsibility for developing software design documents, other engineers should participate in design reviews during this phase to ensure that the software design both meets their understanding of requirements and does not affect their design.

17.2.4 Coding and Debugging

Although the coding/debugging activity is traditionally software intensive, interaction with other engineering groups is often critical in embedded microprocessor systems. The development of some nonsoftware subsystems in complex products requires coding support so that other engineers can test prototypes of their design before committing them for final product build. An example of such coding support is a routine that records the time at which keys are depressed on a keyboard, so that engineers can determine the sensitivity of the technology used to implement the keys. This type of coding support is sometimes called fixture support, named after the microprocessor fixture that controls the engineering subsystem.

Another interaction between microprocessor software developers and other engineers centers around the use of a simulator. As described in Chapter 3, it is advantageous for microprocessor software engineers to work with a simulator because it provides

o   A vehicle to debug software before the system product can be manufactured

o   A stable environment to debug software that is not prone to variances typically seen among the first manufactured system products

An effective method for helping the microprocessor hardware and software engineers learn the operation of the system product is to have them design and build the simulator. In addition to the obvious advantages of having the microprocessor hardware and software engineers learn the design of the system product and producing a simulator for their use, this approach

o   Establishes communication between the microprocessor engineers and other engineering groups

o   Provides a vehicle for other engineering groups to observe the results and constraints of their design

Thus the investment in simulator development pays off handsomely.

The final role that the microprocessor software engineer often plays in debugging is in leading the debug of the first manufactured system product. It is appropriate for microprocessor software engineers to play this role because they are typically the only ones with expertise on the operation of the entire system. Being familiar with the control of the system they must isolate problems to the offending subsystems (microprocessor hardware, software, mechanical, optical, chemical, and so forth) or to the interfaces among subsystems. They must then demonstrate the cause of the problem to the responsible engineering groups, and later check that it has been resolved. Acting in this role, software engineers are essentially playing the role of the traditional system engineer.

17.2.5 Testing

Although the actual testing of software does not start until late in the development process, preparation for testing should begin early in the development process. Thus the engineers who will be involved in testing should begin developing organizational interfaces early.

Software engineers responsible for "black box" system testing will test the microprocessor software system for functional and performance characteristics. As these characteristics are specified in the requirements documents, test personnel should interface with the developers of the requirements to determine

o   The schedule for the completion of the various requirements documents. Test personnel require this information to plan their schedules and staffing activities.

o   The proper understanding of the requirements themselves. If test personnel do not understand some aspect of the requirements for a system, it is likely that customers and users will misunderstand them also. Thus test personnel should be a principal group for reviewing and requesting change in requirements documents.

o   The effect of changes in requirements when they do occur. Test personnel should work closely with other software developers to ensure that their tests reflect changes in requirements.

When the software test personnel and the requirements developers address these issues properly, effective test plans can be developed which test the functional and performance characteristics of the system. Should errors be found in the system, software testers should work with requirements developers, designers, and coders to determine and correct the errors. In this activity test personnel act as system integrators.

Software engineers responsible for "glass box" testing of modules have a different responsibility and a different organizational interface. They interface with the designers and coders who have developed modules, in order to test the input/output characteristics of modules and groups of modules. As software testers combine groups of modules to test them as subsystems they too act as system integrators. Thus the two types of testing have both differences and similarities in their responsibilities and interfaces.

The interfaces of the software testing personnel go beyond those of other software developers. An important job performed by software test personnel is the preparation of test plans. The use of test plans is important to manufacturing engineers and service engineers. Manufacturing engineers perform tests on machines as they roll off the assembly line to ensure that systems work properly before they are shipped. Service engineers perform diagnostic tests on machines in the field to determine the correctness of system operation or the cause of system malfunction. While the tests to support manufacturing and service may be somewhat different from those developed for traditional black box and glass box testing, there is usually enough similarity to warrant their development by the same group of software test personnel.

17.2.6 Maintenance

The maintenance activity may be broadly classified into two categories: customer support and software update. Software engineers who provide customer support receive information regarding problems and desired enhancements in the software system. To obtain precise information, they should help the customer with his immediate concern, correct customers' misperceptions or lack of knowledge on system use, and describe the desired changes or enhancements so that another software engineer can update the system. While such customer support work often requires interfacing with people who have little technical knowledge about software, this interaction is often refreshing to software engineers because it demonstrates the "real-world" usage and utility of a product. As such, this type of work is often good training for software engineers who will do system design, and it provides incentives to engineers to develop software that has high functionality and few errors.

Motivating software engineers who are responsible for updating existing microprocessor-based software systems is one of the most challenging responsibilities for software managers. Updating software comprises making enhancements and fixing bugs; each of these activities requires detailed knowledge of the existing software. Acquiring such knowledge requires a significant investment of a software engineer's time, and software engineers often find it distasteful, viewing the activity as being less creative and challenging than the initial design and coding activities. As a result, managers must find special incentives to motivate software engineers responsible for updating existing systems. When managers are unable to provide special incentives, software engineers frequently create special situations, such as hording knowledge and making changes that are difficult to comprehend. Software engineers thus ensure job security or even "guru status" where their specialized knowledge warrants extraordinarily high salaries or other special benefits. Assuming that software engineers responsible for updating existing software have proper incentives, it is important for them to interface with a variety of personnel:

o   Engineers involved in customer support, to understand requested
     updates

o   Marketing personnel responsible for product planning, to understand
     requests for new features and priorities of new features and updates

o   Designers of the software system, to understand the design intent so
     that the system maintains design integrity

o   Test personnel, to enable testing so that the modified system will have
     fewer errors than the original one

These interfaces are especially important in ROM based systems, where the
cost of releasing a new version of software is high as it involves at least
changing ROM chips and may involve replacing boards. In such systems
correcting a release with errors in it may cost a company millions of dollars.

17.3 Interaction with Management in Integrating Microprocessor Software into Embedded Products

17.3.1 Organizational Interfaces

The interfaces involved in integrating microprocessor software into
embedded products extend beyond the technical interactions described in
the previous section; interfaces with management with a variety of
responsibilities (program management, product planning, manufacturing,
and so forth) are a reality that must be addressed by software managers. As
described in the introductory section of this chapter, other managers
involved in product development often have little software knowledge.
Good software managers not only recognize this situation but also provide
information to other managers so as to elicit their assistance; indeed, failure
to handle these interfaces properly often results in the imposition of
additional constraints by other managers. We devote the rest of the chapter
to the critical aspects of interfaces with other managers during the product
development cycle.

17.3.2 Requirements Specification

The fundamental concept that software managers must instill in other
managers is that requirements specification is the most important phase in
the development of embedded microprocessor-based systems. Without

specific requirements, software engineers envision such a range of possible system designs that even a best guess as to the nature of the desired system often requires substantial modification later in the project when the complete specifications are made available. Of course the later the specifications are made available, the costlier is the software development.

As discussed in detail in Chapter 6, a software requirements specification describes the functions the software is to perform, the performance the software is to achieve, and the constraints of the software run-time and development environments. It is too often the case that nonsoftware managers fail to realize the effects that constraints have in the time and effort required to develop software, especially for embedded systems. A good example of such a constraint is the size of the memory in which the software is to run. Recall from the COCOMO model, discussed in Chapter 12, that memory size has a significant effect on required software development time. Indeed, a severe constraint on memory size can increase software development time by more than 50 percent! Clearly there is a cost/benefit tradeoff analysis that should be performed when considering constraints. We can generalize this statement readily: managers should perform the cost/benefit tradeoffs of all elements of a software specification – functions, performance, and constraints.

17.3.3 Design Specification

It is common for nonsoftware managers to track progress in software development by measuring the number of lines of code written. Good software managers prevent this misconception by describing to other managers the activities involved in the design specification phase of software development, and by holding frequent reviews during the design specification activity. Thus other managers can see that the design phase does produce required intermediate results even though software engineers are not producing lines of code. In addition to demonstrating progress, reviews illustrate the effect of requirements on the design of the system; thus reviews with other managers are useful forums for revisiting requirements specifications before making a substantial commitment to coding.

17.3.4 Coding and Debugging

During the coding phase of development nonsoftware managers see the first tangible result of the software activity – code that produces visible effects in the operation of an embedded system. While this is reassuring, there are misconceptions associated with it that require attention by software managers. Nonsoftware managers often track progress by computing the fraction

$$\frac{\text{lines of code written}}{\text{total lines of code expected in the system}}$$

and using this number as an indicator of completion percentage. This measure is not a good indicator of percent completion because it does not take into account software testing, software integration, and hardware/software interactions that require additional time for testing and integrating when developing embedded systems. Thus the software managers should avoid intimating that "coded" implies "completed." Software managers should establish measurable milestones for reporting progress to nonsoftware managers. The milestones typically address the debug of software modules on prototype hardware, and the modules correspond to the implementation of demonstrable features. While demonstrating modules controlling hardware indicates progress, it is important to indicate that subsequent subsystem and system integration and debug activities grow increasingly complex. These integration and debug activities on embedded systems take longer than typical software debug due to the interaction between software and immature hardware.

In this phase of development the deliveries from groups directed by nonsoftware managers become critical. If the hardware in which the microprocessor software is to be embedded is delivered late, then software managers may be asked to shorten their schedules in order to meet a product delivery date. This is usually difficult to accomplish without a reduction in the quality of the product. The result is similar, although less obvious, when the hardware fails to perform to specification and software engineers are expected to make the system as a whole perform to specification. The moral for managers responsible for developing software for embedded systems is clear: plan substantial time in schedules for system integration and debug. It is unfortunately the case that many organizations are structured so that nonsoftware managers viewing situations where hardware is late or not performing to specification have incentives to blame software managers for failure to deliver the final system on time.

17.3.5 Testing

Nonsoftware managers responsible for embedded system development may appreciate the demand for testing of the system as a whole without understanding the demand for software testing before system testing. In embedded systems development, system testing may be viewed as another level of integration testing from a software planning viewpoint. Software managers should describe to nonsoftware managers the plan for regular software testing activities, and they should support system test activities as well. It is often the case that software engineers are the only developers with specific knowledge about the operation of the entire system, and this knowledge simplifies locating problems discovered in system testing.

17.3.6 Maintenance

The specific knowledge software engineers have about the operation of embedded systems means that they can play a useful role in both aspects of maintenance. In customer support (or in training customer support personnel), software engineers' knowledge of system operation enables them to relate anomalies in system operation to offending hardware/software subsystems. In updating the system, software engineers' knowledge of system structure enables them to estimate the cost of changes and to make changes in a manner that limits costs and side effects. Software managers should make nonsoftware managers aware of these capabilities so that maintenance of the embedded system proceeds effectively.

18

DEVELOPING MICROPROCESSOR

SOFTWARE ENGINEERING

TECHNOLOGY

18.1 An Historical Viewpoint

In the foreword to The Proceedings of the First National Conference on Software Engineering (1975), Harlan Mills wrote: "The large data processing installations that have grown up in the last 25 years since the advent of electronic computers, typify the future in the complexity of operations and evolution that such systems must undergo, and what software engineering must address."[1] The examples addressed by early software engineering developments typically embraced business data processing and standard system software applications since they constituted the large majority of computer software development activities. In particular the inherent difficulties that lie in the development and management of large programs that such applications engender led to the development of techniques such as structured programming, top-down refinement, structured design, formal testing, egoless programming, and chief programmer teams.

With the emergence of microprocessors, it becomes necessary to extend the principles of classical software engineering to other application areas, especially the control of real-time systems. Mills evidently envisioned the role of software engineering extending beyond the traditional boundaries:

[1]Proceedings of the 1st National Conference on Software Engineering, IEEE, New York, 1975, p. iii.

"We can identify software engineering with the blueprints for the harmonious cooperation of people and machines in a systematic operation."[2] Following this broader interpretation, we see software engineering technology realized through:

o   Methodology

o   Architecture

o   Tools

o   People

Previous chapters have described approaches to use for these areas in developing and managing microprocessor software. In this chapter we describe techniques for developing technological capabilities in these areas.

We note that the development of methodology, architecture, tools, and people is not a one-time process. It is an ongoing process that builds on previous developments, new research results, new microprocessor hardware capabilities, and new demands for software capabilities.

18.2 Developing Microprocessor Software Methodology

18.2.1 The Fundamental Concept of the Software Life Cycle

Perhaps the most difficult concept to teach novice microprocessor software developers is the concept of a software life cycle that encompasses several phased activities. Microprocessor software development involves much more than the repeating code/debug death spiral. Unfortunately many microprocessor software developers concentrate on the code and debug phases. The reason for this behavior is that many training methods teach programming by

o   Describing statements in a particular programming language.

o   Demonstrating how statements may be combined to form programs.

o   Assigning simple problems that can be solved with small programs that require only straightforward combinations of programming language statements.

[2]Ibid.

Similarly many training methods teach microprocessor applications by

o   Describing specific microprocessor instruction sets.

o   Demonstrating how a short sequence of machine instructions solves simple problems.

o   Assigning simple problems that can be solved by short machine or assembler language programs.

Too often training methods fail to address adequately significant large activities such as problem analysis, design synthesis, and team interactions which constitute the foundation of microprocessor software development. As a result, many microprocessor software developers are not prepared to attack the sizable problems typically found in modern microprocessor applications.

It is interesting to note that the personal computer revolution has actually lowered the average skill level of software developers. While the availability of personal computers at moderate prices has certainly increased the number of "computer literate" people, many personal computer users learn coding from the language manuals supplied with the computers or from books that describe elementary coding techniques. The techniques for developing significant programs are seldom addressed. Thus a large number of people have developed capabilities for simple coding but few have developed capabilities for engineering the software for significant microprocessor applications. As a result, the average skill level of software developers has decreased.

The first step in developing microprocessor software methodology is institutionalizing the concept of the software life cycle comprising the phases described in Chapters 2 through 10:

o   Requirements specification

o   Design specification

o   Coding

o   Debugging

o   Testing

o   Maintenance

18.2.2 Creating the Demand for Knowledge of the Software Life Cycle

An effective technique for creating a demand for knowledge of the software life cycle is to present a problem to microprocessor software developers that cannot be solved by the traditional trial-and-error code/debug methods in a limited time.   One such exercise has been used for several years in a software training course within Xerox.[3]

A group of five or six people are told they must write two programs. The first is to accept data from a keyboard, until a command is received to write the data on a removable magnetic medium. The second program is to read this data, do some calculations, and print a report. The group is permitted to meet together, until they pass a design review of their work. Then they are split into two rooms, where that design is implemented. Only telephone communication is permitted between the two rooms during this phase. Typical groups spend half their time doing the design and interface specifications, before they begin implementation. All readily admit afterward that they could not have done the task in such a short time, unless they had been forced to design the solution first. Then, as most participants put it, "The code writes itself."

Another scenario presents a poorly defined problem to a small group with a specific program completion deadline.[4] The group usually devotes substantial time to the development of clever coding approaches and features but fails to complete the program on time. When told that the customer would have been happy with a simple program some time after the deadline, the software development group feels cheated but they never forget the need for requirements specification and approval.

A more advanced scenario presents a problem to a team and monitors the team's progress through requirements, design, code, debug, and test; then changes the problem statement slightly. Allowing the team to pursue the typical solution, making changes to the code just before program delivery, usually results in the program failing to perform as desired. This provides the lesson that the software life cycle is not a linear process but a cyclic process in which changes to the problem statement mandate revisiting all the previous steps and revisiting the outputs of those steps.

[3]We are indebted to Michael Nekora of Xerox Corporation for this exercise.

[4]We are indebted to Gerald Weinberg for this exercise.

18.2.3 Developing Knowledge of the Software Life Cycle

Techniques such as those described in the preceding paragraphs can readily be extended to "real-life" applications, whereby microprocessor software engineers will want to incorporate a basic understanding of the software life cycle into their daily operating activities.

The translation of this demand for knowledge of the software life cycle into the actual understanding of details of the software life cycle is actually a simpler activity than the creation of the demand in the first place. Creation of demand involves changing people's value systems, a difficult endeavor in itself; in our scenario it is exacerbated by the reluctance of engineers to internalize new processes which are often introduced and presented by outsiders. Once the demand is created, however, the open market offers numerous mechanisms to satisfy the demand: courses, seminars, books, consultants, tapes, and so forth. Many of these can provide the fundamental information described in Chapters 2 through 10 (or roughly equivalent knowledge) to a respectable level. It may take weeks, months, or even years to have a number of people learn, understand, and begin to use these techniques, however, this educational process is straightforward compared to the initial problem of creating demand.

18.2.4 Adapting the Software Life Cycle to Particular Applications

Having established fundamental concepts of software life cycle methodology in an organization, it is useful to adapt or tailor the basic life cycle concepts for more effective application to particular microprocessor-based systems. The basic thrust of this activity is to select a subset of a general life cycle methodology, such as described in Chapters 2 through 10, and extend it to the particular applications environment of interest.

Software Development Standards

A software development standards document[5] identifies those basic aspects of the software development cycle which do not change from one project to

---

[5] The discussion on software development standards and guidelines draws on work done at Xerox Corporation in the Software Systems Design Section, in the early 1980s.

another within an organization. Furthermore it describes the manner in which these aspects will be conducted or the documentation that will be produced. Software development standards must take into account the fact that many organizations develop microprocessor software that varies in

o   Application type, e.g., real-time control applications, operating systems, machine diagnostics, business applications, and language translators.

o   Size, ranging from short routines of a few lines of code to systems with hundreds of thousands of lines of code.

o   Schedule requirements, ranging from days to years.

o   Intended users, ranging from people who are unaware that a microprocessor controls a system to knowledgeable computer users.

Software development standards may thus be worded in terms of goals and content rather than specific forms in order to provide the flexibility to accommodate these variations. The software standards document should contain the following:

o   A list of the phases in the software life cycle (patterned after that described in Chapters 2-10).

o   For each phase a description of the objectives for the phase, the process for accomplishing the objective, the phase deliverables, the manner in which deliverables are approved, and the criteria for phase completion.

In some cases the descriptions may indicate differences where variations are well understood, e.g., the people who should review and approve diagnostics requirements may constitute a group distinct from those who should review the requirements for a language translator. In other cases the descriptions in the standards document may indicate that the variations among projects for some aspect of software development are so great that each project should develop its own standards. For example, the schedule for a project can be determined using the COCOMO model, however, the values of the factors in the model will vary from one project to another and should be determined on a project-by-project basis.

   To provide incentives for an organization to use a standards document, all members of the organization should contribute to the writing, review, and adoption of the standards. While we dislike overreliance on committees to accomplish group objectives, we feel that assigning one person or a small group to the task of developing standards creates the "we-they" attitude reflected by statements like "It's their standards document. Let them use it." One technique for accomplishing the task of developing a standards document is to assign the task to a small group containing key people with backgrounds in software technology and the particular applications of the organization. Each of the groups that constitute the organization should have a representative to this activity, so that each group can work on a particular part of the document and have a vehicle for injecting their opinions into the overall document preparation.

The management of the organization must support the development and use of standards. It can support standards development by

o   Giving the task priority and visibility through its recognition as a separate task.

o   Assigning specific people to the task

o   Allocating time for the assigned people to the task

o   Establishing a schedule for completion of the task

o   Reviewing task progress

Management can support the use of standards by giving employees appropriate incentives:

o   Incorporating the standards into the planning process, for scheduling and staffing

o   Incorporating employees' use of standards into the performance appraisal and review process

Management support must be a continuous process for software standards to gain and maintain effectiveness.

Software Development Guidelines

A software development guidelines document elaborates on the basic aspects of the software development cycle described in the standards document. The guidelines document suggests practices that may be applied to realize the software standards. Some practices may be useful for particular projects, while other practices may be inappropriate. Guidelines differ from standards in that guidelines offer detailed practices that may be considered for use on a project, whereas standards are rules that should be followed for all projects. Guidelines thus describe the specific form project activities may follow.

The software guidelines document should follow the outline of the standards document, and therefore should contain sections on each of the phases in the software life cycle. For each phase the guidelines document may contain the following:

o   A detailed description of the process for accomplishing the phase objectives including responsibilities of various people in the organization.

o   An outline of documentation deliverables.

o   Conventions for drawings such as hierarchy charts and data flow diagrams.

o   Conventions for assigning names to software artifacts.

o   Techniques for developing software within the organizational structure.

Assigning the task of writing the guidelines document, approving the document, and supporting the document should be handled in a manner like that for the standards document, except that the guidelines document should continually be updated as people incorporate their experiences on project development activities.

18.2.5 The Role of Documentation

Documentation plays a critical role in the software life cycle. Most of the milestones specified in the standards and guidelines are documents: the customer requirements document, user manual, software requirements document, data flow diagram, PDL design document, code package, test plans, and so forth. These documents are important because they represent accomplishments in the the software development process where progress is often difficult to quantify. Furthermore these documents can be evaluated against criteria established in the standards and guidelines. The completion and approval of a document frequently serves as the completion criterion for a phase in the product development cycle.

Documents are also important for historical reasons. They provide the opportunity for tracing features or problems in system behavior back through code documents, design documents, and requirements documents to understand the genesis of the features or problems. In addition documents provide a basis for development on products which are modified versions of earlier products. Documents also provide the opportunity for people to learn the technology of a particular application and to see the way in which technology has evolved for different products over time.

18.3 Developing Microprocessor Software Architecture

18.3.1 The Hardware/Software Classification

In many microprocessor applications, particularly embedded applications, the fundamental architectural decisions address which functions are to be performed by hardware and which functions are to be performed by software. Recall from Chapter 7:

> *The first step in the synthesis of*
> *software requirements is to classify*
> *the functionality of the hardware and*
> *the functionality of the software.*

The selection of hardware implementation or software implementation for a function depends on performance, cost, and flexibility tradeoffs.

Hardware implementation alternatives may be considered to range through the following points: custom designed hardware, semicustom designed hardware (such as programmable logic arrays), and off-the-shelf hardware (such as commercially available microprocessors which may be programmed to provide desired functions). Figure 18-1 shows tradeoffs among these implementation alternatives. From a simplistic viewpoint, the selection of the implementation medium for a function involves

(1)   Determining the values for the curves shown in Figure 18-1

(2)   Calculating the most desirable point given one's relative values for performance, cost, and flexibility

(3)   Selecting the point on the curve closest to the most desirable point calculated in step (2)

In considering the architecture for the entire system, one should iterate this procedure taking into account interactions among the implementation of various functions, and making tradeoffs to determine the best overall system solution. A system solution usually consists of a combination of types of hardware designed so that changing the implementation medium for one function will prohibit the system from achieving a particular

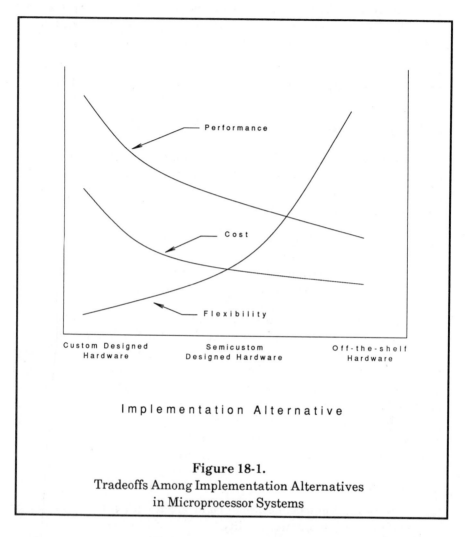

Figure 18-1.
Tradeoffs Among Implementation Alternatives
in Microprocessor Systems

performance, cost, or flexibility goal. For example, changing the implementation of a communication control function from a special purpose chip to software in an off-the-shelf microprocessor may make the system ten dollars cheaper but shortfall the requirement to respond to communication requests in less than fifty milliseconds.

The flexibility criterion requires some foresight in that it must comprehend effects of future changes to requirements. Thus a system which has no flexibility cannot handle changes, and this defeats a principal reason for using microprocessors in system design.

As microprocessor systems become more sophisticated, the performance criterion must also be considered in a new light. No longer does performance mean simply the ability of a microprocessor to perform a function, rather it means the ability of a microprocessor to perform a function in addition to all the other functions it must perform. This viewpoint emphasizes the system aspects of developing microprocessor architectures.

18.3.2 The Software Breakdown − Operating System, Diagnostics, and Applications

The software in microprocessor-based products may be classified into three components:

o   Operating system software

o   Applications software

o   Diagnostic software

This section summarizes the particular functions each type of software performs; subsequent sections describe tradeoffs among methods for developing these software components for particular projects.

An operating system can be defined as "a set of software extensions of primitive hardware, culminating in a virtual machine that serves as a high-level programming environment."[6] Thus an operating system consists of a hierarchy of levels in which each level uses the operations of the level beneath it to effect a new and more capable set of operations. The lowest two levels in the hierarchy shown in Table 18-1 actually constitute hardware capabilities of the host microprocessor.[7] In the third level in Table 18-1, microprocessor instructions implement procedures for handling simple data types, and these procedures are used in the fourth level to provide interrupt handling capabilities. Higher levels in the hierarchy add the abilities to control multiple processors, control I/O devices, and manage virtual memory by using capabilities provided by lower levels. Levels 1 through 8 of this operating system model control the resources of a single

6Robert L. Brown, Peter J. Denning, and Walter F. Tichy, "Advanced Operating Systems," Computer, vol. 17, no. 10 (October 1984), p. 174.

7Ibid., p. 175.

Table 18-1.
An Operating System Design Hierarchy © 1984 IEEE

Level	Name	Objects	Example Operations
15	Shell	User programming environment scalar data, array data	Statements in shell language
14	Directories	Directories	Create, destroy, attach, detach, search, list
13	User Processes	User Process	Fork, quit, kill, suspend, resume
12	Stream I/O	Streams	Open, close, read, write
11	Devices	External devices and peripherals such as printer, display, keyboard	Create, destroy, open, close, read, write
10	File System	Files	Create, destroy, open, close, read, write
9	Communi-cations	Pipes	Create, destroy, open, close, read, write
8	Capabilities	Capabilities	Create, validate, attenuate
7	Virtual Memory	Segments	Read, write, fetch
6	Local Secondary Store	Blocks of data, device channels	Read, write, allocate, free
5	Primitive Processes	Primitive process, semaphores, ready list	Suspend, resume, wait, signal
4	Interrupts	Fault-handler programs	Invoke, mask, unmask, retry
3	Procedures	Procedure segments, call stack, display	Mark_stack, call, return
2	Instruction Set	Evaluation stack, micro-program interpreter	Load, store, un_op, bin_op, branch, array_ref, etc.
1	Electronic Circuits	Registers, gates, buses, etc.	Clear, transfer, complement, activate, etc.

processor. Above level 8, the operating system deals with external processors and peripheral devices to provide control for a sophisticated hardware/software system. The top level, the shell, serves as the interface to the user of the operating system (i.e., the applications programmer) by interpreting a high level command language. The instructions of this language form the virtual machine seen by the user; from the viewpoint of the user the system performs a specific set of instructions (or functions) at a given performance level and the fact that the instructions are implemented by lower levels in the operating system rather than by hardware is irrelevant. The operating system design hierarchy shown in Table 18-1 serves as a generic comprehensive model of operating system structures.

The purpose of diagnostic software is to

o   Check the operation of the microprocessor and the system in which it is embedded

o   Determine if a failure has occurred

o   Isolate or assist an operator in isolating the cause of a failure

Diagnostic software may be categorized into two classes:[8]

o   Automatic diagnostics are performed by the software system without initiation by the operator of the system. Examples of automatic diagnostics are software routines that test microprocessor operation, memory, printed circuit boards, connectors, and peripherals when the system is powered on or when it is otherwise idle.

o   Semiautomatic diagnostics must be initiated by the system operator and are only valid when the system is in a special diagnostic mode. Examples of semiautomatic diagnostics are software routines that allow the operator to stimulate or sense specific system components; these are especially useful for an operator who is trying to isolate intermittent problems.

Some microprocessor software systems provide interaction between automatic and semiautomatic diagnostics. For example, an automatic diagnostic routine may record statistics about the operation of a system (such as the number of times a certain system component is used) which can

[8]We are grateful to Dennis Miazga of Xerox Corporation for discussions on diagnostics.

later be queried in the semiautomatic diagnostic mode. The design of diagnostic software depends on the architecture of the hardware system, and the richness of diagnostic software capabilities ranges considerably.

The remaining software in a microprocessor system is applications software. It is difficult to describe applications software generically due to the rich variety of functions such software performs. For the present it is sufficient to say that applications software uses the operating system software to implement the features seen by the user of the microprocessor-based system. In a subsequent section, 18.3.5, we examine general tradeoffs in application software design.

18.3.3 Tradeoffs in Operating System Design and Development

The first step in operating system design is to determine the functions that are desirable for the operating system in your application environment. While Table 18-1 presents a general framework for hierarchical operating system design, most microprocessor operating systems are much simpler. Indeed, operating systems for microprocessor-based systems are much smaller than for minicomputers and mainframes as a general rule because they generally offer fewer features in the areas of peripheral device support, memory management, and task management. Microprocessor operating systems are, however, becoming more capable with the evolution from simple embedded applications to sophisticated multiuser multidevice systems. Many embedded systems do not require all the features of a general purpose operating system, so it may be the case that only certain levels in the hierarchy of Table 18-1 are appropriate for a particular application. A typical example of this situation is the case where a system employs no intelligent or sophisticated external devices. Another simplifying situation is the case where levels in the hierarchy can be combined to provide the functions desired in an operating system.

Having determined the benefits accorded by a desired set of operating system functions, it is necessary to calculate the costs of developing and using the operating system in a particular application. The costs associated with using an operating system depend on the amount of memory and real time that operating system uses. Although a common view of memory is that memory is cheap and should not be considered in a cost formulation, one must consider the opportunity cost of using memory for operating system functions rather than for applications or diagnostics functions which might provide additional benefits. For many microprocessor system applications the utilization of real time is an important criterion; poor response time may cause system failure or dissatisfied users, thus operating system design should carefully examine tradeoffs between time and space utilization. Having calculated costs it is necessary to reexamine the functions desired for the operating system under consideration. When a new set of features is determined its costs should be calculated, and this process should be iterated until the appropriate balance between costs and benefits is determined.

The third step in operating system design and development involves the make/modify/buy decision. At one end of this spectrum, designers can buy operating systems for microprocessors. There are a number of microprocessor operating systems available on the market today, providing capabilities varying from simple file handling systems to more sophisticated systems that provide real-time support, sophisticated memory management, and device support. The benefits of buying an operating system include a short acquisition time and low cost. The disadvantages of such operating systems are the possibility of a poor match between desired functions and provided functions, and an associated possibility of poor memory utilization. At the other end of the spectrum, an organization may decide to develop its own proprietary operating system. The advantages of such a development scheme are the ability to develop exactly the features desired and implement them in a minimal amount of memory; the disadvantages of such a scheme are the time and cost required to do the development. Intermediate between these two extremes is the option of modifying an operating system that has already been acquired, either by development or by purchase. To make the economic decision as to which of these routes to consider, one must take into account factors such as the number of systems to be developed, the performance of the operating system selected, and the cost of developing and using the system. Many embedded systems do not require all the features of a general purpose operating system, so to economize on space it may be appropriate to develop a proprietary operating system or to buy a commercial operating system and modify it for a particular application. If the decision is to develop a proprietary operating system or to modify a purchased operating system, there is a flexible boundary between the operating system and the applications/diagnostics of software. In this situation one can redefine the virtual machine by making software routines part of the operating system. This may be useful in situations where certain routines are referenced frequently by the applications software. The advantage of this scheme of redefining the virtual machine is that the time required to switch to the routine in the operating system may be faster than the time required to switch to the routine if it were still in application software. The disadvantage is that the applications programmer may lose control over the software, and thus he loses flexibility.

18.3.4 Tradeoffs in Diagnostic Design

The tradeoffs in diagnostic design, like those of operating systems, are fundamentally economic in nature. Thus we examine the costs and benefits of the extent to which diagnostics are implemented in a microprocessor software system. The benefit of diagnostics is the time they save in assisting an operator or service representative in determining if a failure has occurred, in isolating an error, and in checking that a microprocessor system is working properly after it has been repaired. For a microprocessor-based system product in the market, the monetary value of diagnostics software may be estimated as follows:

Monetary savings from diagnostics

= Number of products sold

× Product life

× Average frequency of repair

× (Mean time to repair system without diagnostics
– Mean time to repair system with diagnostics)

× Wage rate of service representatives

As an example, consider a microprocessor used to control a washing machine (for sequencing through the various cycles, testing the water temperature to minimize use of hot water, detecting off balance loads, handling the user interface, and so forth) with the following parameters:

Number of products sold = 100,000

Product life = 5 years

Average frequency of repair = 1 time per year

Mean time to repair system with diagnostics = 1 hour

Mean time to repair system without diagnostics = 2 hours

Wage rate of service representative = $15/hour

Applying the previous formula, we can develop an estimate for the monetary savings:

Monetary savings from diagnostics

$$= 100,000 \times 5 \text{ years} \times 1 \text{ repair/year}$$

$$\times (2 \text{ hours/repair} - 1 \text{ hour/repair}) \times \$15/\text{hour}$$

$$= \$7,500,000$$

This example illustrates that the benefits of diagnostic software can be substantial, even though the model used is simplistic. The formula does not consider, for example, the benefits accruing from improved customer satisfaction resulting from less system downtime or the benefits accruing from improved morale of service representatives resulting from using more capable tools.

The costs of diagnostics comprehend four aspects:

o   The time and cost required to develop the diagnostic software.

o   The memory required for the diagnostic software. If the microprocessor system is memory constrained this cost may be more than the memory itself; it may be the cost of opportunities lost because applications software that implemented features which sold machines was replaced with diagnostic software.

o   The time required for the execution of the diagnostic software. As with memory constraints, execution time constraints may cause opportunity costs in the overall system.

o   The time required to train service people to use the diagnostics.

As before, we can use this information to compute the monetary cost of the diagnostics.

Monetary cost of diagnostics

$\quad$ = Cost of diagnostic software development

$\quad\quad$ + (Cost of memory required for diagnostic software
$\quad\quad\quad$ × Number of products)

$\quad\quad\quad$ + Cost of lost opportunity from memory and
$\quad\quad\quad\quad$ execution time constraints

$\quad\quad\quad\quad$ + (Cost of training one service representative
$\quad\quad\quad\quad\quad$ × Number of service representatives)

Continuing with the example of the washing machine, we consider the following parameters.

Diagnostic software development cost
$\quad$ = 10 man-years @ $100,000 /man-year

Memory cost = 8K bytes @ $16/8K byte chip

Cost of lost opportunity = $16 per machine (the cost of the memory)

Cost of training service representatives
$\quad$ = $10,000/service representative

Number of service representatives = 50 (Note that without diagnostics twice as many service people would have been required.)

Applying these parametric values in the previous equation, we find for our washing machine example:

Monetary cost of diagnostics

$\quad$ = $1,000,000 + $16/product × 100,000 products

$\quad\quad$ + $16/product × 100,000 products

$\quad\quad\quad$ + $10,000/service representative
$\quad\quad\quad$ × 50 service representatives

$\quad$ = $4,700,000

In this example the cost is substantially lower than the benefits, so it would be beneficial to implement the diagnostics.

In real situations the calculations should go beyond the simple model presented here. Other factors should be considered, such as the cost of training the trainers, and the benefits of using the diagnostics during hardware development and debug. Nevertheless, a cost/benefit analysis should be performed, taking into account the sensitivity of the risks associated with the accuracy of the data, before deciding the extent of diagnostics to be implemented in a microprocessor-based system.

18.3.5 Tradeoffs in Application Software Design

Despite the variety in applications for which microprocessor software is developed, there exist some tradeoffs in designing multiple products for a particular family of applications. The fundamental tradeoff is one between generality and specificity in the design (or architecture) of the applications software.

A general design is one which can be used for a number of products. With a general design the structure of the software system varies little from one product to another. Many software modules used in one product may be used in another product, perhaps with no changes, perhaps with changes in the values of some parameters. The benefit of such a general design is a relatively low cost for developing software systems for products after the first one. The costs include a relatively high development cost for the first system and possible sacrifices of efficiency for a particular product due to the general nature of the architecture.

Developing a specific architecture for a product reduces the extent to which it can be used as a basis for other products. Thus the costs are relatively long development times for subsequent products. The benefit is that each product may be optimized for memory utilization and real-time utilization, possibly effecting a lower product cost.

As with operating system and diagnostic software, the costs and benefits of various design approaches should be calculated for applications software before implementation begins.

18.4 Developing Microprocessor Software Tools

The acquisition of tools to assist in the development of microprocessor software is often the most controversial aspect of developing microprocessor software technology because the costs are so visible. Whether tools are purchased or developed in-house by one's organization, it is simple to compute a direct monetary cost for their acquisition.

Presented with spending decisions concerning the acquisition of tools, many managers (especially those with little software background) emphasize the short-term costs but deemphasize the long-term benefits. As a result, the tools that are acquired for a microprocessor software development project often provide a minimal set of capabilities. This is unfortunate because tools form the basics for improving other aspects of software technology: methodology, software architecture, and people.

There are basically two types of tools used to aid the development of microprocessor software:

o   Tools that assist in the development of the microprocessor software itself. Examples include compilers, editors, and simulators.

o   Tools that assist in the management of the software development process. An example we have used is the COCOMO model described in Chapter 12.

We categorize tools broadly. A tool may be a software program that runs on the target microprocessor system, such as a debugger. A tool may be a software program that runs on another perhaps much larger computer, e.g., an off-line compiler. A tool may be a combination of hardware and software such as a simulator. A tool may also be a special technique or process, e.g., the COCOMO model used for planning software projects.

The selection of tools to assist in the development of the microprocessor software itself determines not only the level of technological maturity, but it also is a determining factor in the effort required to develop a microprocessor software system as described in the COCOMO model. Table 18-2 lists a variety of tools to assist in the software development process.[9] Several of these tools were mentioned in Chapters 2 through 10. The additional tools provide capabilities that can further increase microprocessor software development productivity.

The tools available for assisting managers of microprocessor software development projects are fewer and less sophisticated than the tools for assisting developers themselves. The reason is basically historical; developers realized long ago that tools could help them with their problems which were frequently clerical in nature. The three management activities for which tools provide some support are planning, staffing, and reviewing.

[9]Adopted from Barry W. Boehm, Software Engineering Economics (Englewood Cliffs, New Jersey: Prentice-Hall, 1981), p. 460. Reprinted by permssion of Prentice-Hall, Inc.

Table 18-2.

Tools to Assist the Process of Microprocessor Software Development

Rating	Typical Tools
Very low (Basic microprocessor tools)	Assembler Basic linker Basic monitor Batch debug aids
Low (Basic mini)	Higher level language compiler Macro assembler Simple overlay linker Language independent monitor Batch source editor Basic library aids Basic data base aids
Nominal (Strong mini, Basic maxi)	Real-time or timesharing operating system Data base management system Extended overlay linker Interactive debug aids Simple programming support library Interactive source editor System simulator Real-time data collector

High (Strong maxi)	Virtual memory operating system
	Data base design aid
	Simple program design language
	Performance measurement and
	   analysis aids
	Programming support library with basic
	   configuration management aids
	Set-use analyzer
	Program flow and test case analyzer
	Basic text editor and manager

Very high (Advanced maxi)	Full programming support library with
	   configuration management aids
	Full, integrated documentation system
	Project control system
	Requirements specification language
	   and analyzer
	Extended design tools
	Automated verification system
	Special-purpose tools:
	   Crosscompilers, instruction set
	   simulators, display formatters,
	   communications processing tools,
	   data entry control tools, conversion
	   aids, etc.

As described in Chapter 12, the COCOMO model is a useful tool for predicting the effort and schedule required for a software development project. Standard management tools such as the PERT chart provide a further capability for reviewing progress in meeting milestones established for the development process. For assisting in the staffing process, a data base system is useful for tracking résumés, scheduling interviews, recording hiring recommendations, and so forth. A tool to assist in the review and evaluation process is POWER[10], a knowledge-based menu driven data base system that runs on popular personal computer systems. POWER poses a set of questions to the reviewers of a software development project, and computes metrics for major software project categories (requirements, design, implementation, test, and so on). These metrics provide information about the quality of the software development process; used over a period of time, POWER tracks trends for a project and for projects in an organization.

The process for selecting tools to develop or purchase employs the Net Present Value (NPV) method of analysis. In this process one computes the costs and benefits of each of the tools that can be used by software developers or managers. While costs are usually realized immediately (unless money is borrowed over a period of time), benefits and hence monetary savings may be realized over several years. Thus the costs and benefits should be computed in terms of present dollars, and tools should be acquired which have positive NPV, that is, for which benefits are greater than the costs. When tools are to be developed, the order of development should be in decreasing NPV order. It may be helpful to examine tradeoffs between various aspects of microprocessor development and management to ensure that all the cost and benefit factors are considered. For example, Figure 18-2 illustrates that manufacturing costs for a product depend significantly on the microprocessor selected for incorporating into the systems; manufacturing costs depend much less on the implementation language chosen (there is some effect due to efficiency of memory utilization) and very little on the software methodology and architecture. Development costs, however, exhibit just the opposite cost trends. Another example of a tradeoff is that the tools designed expressly for developers have little direct effect on managers and vice versa. NPV analysis should also consider "hidden costs" such as tool maintenance costs, the effects of tool availability (or lack thereof) on developers' morale and productivity, and synergy between tool developers and application developers.

[10]POWER™, Expertware Inc., Mountain View, California.

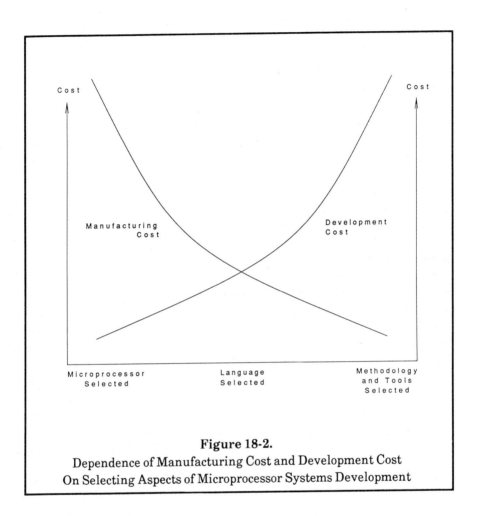

Figure 18-2.
Dependence of Manufacturing Cost and Development Cost
On Selecting Aspects of Microprocessor Systems Development

18.5 Developing Microprocessor Software Personnel

In previous sections we have addressed microprocessor software methodology, architecture, and tools, yet the technological capabilities of an organization are truly represented not by these aspects but rather by the capabilities of the people that constitute the organization. Good methodology, architecture, and tools do not provide advantages if the people in an organization cannot use them.

Organizations generally want to increase the technological capabilities of its personnel because it makes them more productive.

Conversely, people generally want to increase their technological capabilities because it makes their jobs easier and because it increases their value. Given such an environment where technological development is a mutually beneficial activity, organizations can employ a variety of techniques to develop its people.

Many organizations are faced with the situation of wanting to develop people with a wide variety of backgrounds. At one extreme are new employees with a strong recent educational background, but with little experience in industrial environments or in the particular application systems developed by the organization. At the other extreme are experienced employees who have a strong knowledge of the application but little recent technological knowledge regarding microprocessor software. Developing people with such a variety of backgrounds is a challenging task.

The first step in this task is realizing that people development is an ongoing activity. The goal of developing everyone in a microprocessor software development organization to be an expert in all aspects of technology and in the particular application being pursued is difficult to achieve because microprocessor software engineering technology (reflected in methodology, architecture, and tools) continues to evolve rapidly and because changes in customer demands causes the characteristics of the application (such as features, performance, and cost) to evolve. Thus people development activities should not be a one-shot activity but rather continue over time.

The second step in the task of people development is the selection of educational experiences to cover the range of activities from developing technological capabilities in experienced people to developing applications capabilities in inexperienced people. These educational experiences include attending live seminars, viewing videotape seminars, interacting with consultants, taking college courses, reading professional literature, attending professional meetings, and working with experienced mentors. A comprehensive educational program includes both on-the-job and off-the-job training.

The third step in the task of people development is the integration of technology into the product development activities. A useful approach is to form a technology group whose function is to develop and support tools and technology used by other microprocessor software people. The technology group pioneers the introduction of software engineering methodology and tools, it interacts with users to develop methodology and tools to support their requirements, and it provides technical support to the development of application software architectures. From a personnel development viewpoint this gives technologists an opportunity to work with applications developers and vice versa. The movement of people between technology and applications groups strengthens both groups by providing complementary expertise; in addition, it provides additional growth opportunities for people to explore. Furthermore, in a large company, a technology group provides a vehicle for improving the software development process even though normal organizational incentives resist such changes.

To conclude the discussion on personnel development, you should note that if your organization does not provide opportunities for development you can be assured that another organization will.

SOFTWARE MANAGEMENT LESSONS

OR "WHY DOES SOFTWARE COST

SO MUCH AND TAKE SO LONG?"

19.1 The Problem

Oh, how often have we heard these laments:

> "Why does software development cost so much?"
>
> "Why does software development take so long?"

Indeed, one often reads of software problems even in major electronics companies. The following quotes are typical:

> "It was a very complex program and for a number of months we held up a number of customers while we found mistakes we made."[1]
>
> "An eleven month delay ... because of software integration and testing problems."[2]

---

[1]Mini-Micro Systems, December 1979, page 26.

[2]Electronic News, December 24, 1979, page 1.

Several symptoms characterize the usual software development problems:

o Schedule overruns. The classical software schedule problem comes as a surprise to managers. The project starts well. After "n" months one-quarter of the code is written; after "n" more months, one-half of the code is written, and the metrics in lines of code per man-month are being met. After "n" more months, three quarters of the software is written and the outlook is rosy for timely project completion. When management checks on progress just before the final "n" months have passed, they are slightly dismayed to find the project only 90 percent complete. Another "n" months goes by and the software is only a little more than 90 percent complete. There are still problems, but a prerelease may be delivered soon. The late software syndrome has begun. Management may add people to the project only to make it worse. If a project reaches this mode, it may be canceled because it costs too much or it will be delivered too late to meet a marketing window.

o Cost overruns. The cost of microprocessor software development can be broken into two general categories: labor and capital. When a schedule is overrun, the labor cost naturally overruns expectations. Even worse, the most common "solution" to schedule problems — adding manpower — exacerbates the cost problem. Capital costs for microprocessor software development are manifested in facilities such as computers, terminals, microprocessor development systems, simulators, and so on. Even when a project is on schedule, the cost of additional equipment may be proffered as justification to "keep the project on schedule."

o Reliability or performance shortfalls. To keep a microprocessor-based product on schedule or within cost, its original reliability or performance objectives may be compromised. This is manifested in system symptoms such as excessive downtime, the need to reset the system frequently, slow response time, and missed transactions.

19.2 The Causes

19.2.1 The Fundamental Tenet – Management Is the Problem

Most microprocessor software projects that fail to meet their original objectives do so as a result of inadequate management; few microprocessor software projects fail due to difficult technical problems.

We have seen this maxim manifested on a number of projects, in a number of organizations. Understanding that management mistakes are the principal cause of microprocessor software development problems is a fundamental concept in learning to improve an organization's software development process. Indeed, the techniques described in the first part of this book make technical problems trivial compared to the management problems.

As it is the inadequacy of managers that causes the microprocessor software development problem of schedule overruns, cost overruns, and performance shortfalls, we consider how this happened to management and why it is so difficult to correct.

19.2.2 Managers Lack Software Knowledge

Microprocessor technology is very young when compared to other subsystems in most microprocessor-based products. Microprocessors became commercially available in the early 1970s, and became widely used in products and systems some years later. While early microprocessor products used small amounts of software (less than 4K bytes of code), the amount of software in products has grown surprisingly quickly; in recent years microprocessor software development has accounted for the largest part of the cost and time in the development of electronic subsystems. Thus microprocessor software technology has matured very rapidly, and in many organizations has been adopted only recently.

Second and third level managers frequently have little or no education or experience in microprocessor software development technology. The technology has passed them by. As a result, they do not have a technical foundation on which to base managerial decisions that affect software schedules, cost, and reliability. Their decisions often negatively impact the software development activities on a project. The observation on the inadequacy of software management is a special case of Putt's Law: "Every technical hierarchy, in time, develops a competence inversion."[3] In the case of microprocessor software technology, the time period is short compared to other technologies. Section 19.3 describes a real product in which well-intentioned but unprepared managers caused major delays in a large product development project.

If managers lack the knowledge to direct properly the development of microprocessor software, why don't they change? The answer is deceptively simple: organizations do not give managers the incentives to change. Managers who make mistakes, especially out of ignorance, attribute problems to other areas in which they have some experience, and thus see no requirement for software education. Furthermore, upper management, which has even less software knowledge, fails to realize the cause of the problem, takes no remedial actions, and effectively encourages continued failure in the future.

19.2.3 Managers Do Not Develop Viable Plans

One of the authors attended a lecture given by a staff member of a respected minicomputer manufacturer a few years ago.[4] He listed fourteen reasons why software projects fail. Eight of them were "POOR PLANNING." How right he was! How right he is! There are several aspects of the failure to plan software projects adequately. The following paragraphs discuss some of the more common ones.

Managers do not develop overall plans for software projects. Recall from Chapter 12 that an overall plan must be consistent, complete, and reasonable. It should cover all the phases of software development: requirements specification, design specification, code and debug, testing, and maintenance. It should use a constructive model such as the COCOMO model developed by Boehm. The overall plan should comprehend such diverse aspects as productivity, the activities involved in releasing a microprocessor software package that may be embedded in a larger

---

[3]Archibald Putt, Putt's Law and the Successful Technocrat (Smithtown, New York: Exposition Press, 1981).

[4]Mike Olasin, "Software Management," presentation to Rochester IEEE, March 20, 1980.

hardware package, and time to develop detailed plans for each of the phases of project development. Documentation is a large part of such a plan. The attitude of too many managers and engineers is "We don't document, we write code." Such an attitude will guarantee problems in microprocessor-based systems development. Furthermore, a plan should describe and prioritize objectives such as real-time response, project schedule, and ease of using the end product.

Managers do not develop detailed plans for each phase, but concentrate on a plan based only on the coding activity. Too often project plans are based on estimates of a few individuals whose attitude is "Design is unnecessary; let's just code it." Project schedules based on estimates given from this viewpoint will specify much less than the time required to do a project properly. In addition to the coding activity all the other phases of software development must be planned in detail to the individual module level. This refinement of the overall plan may proceed as the project matures, nevertheless, the development of a detailed plan is as necessary a part in good project development as is development of an overall plan.

The development plans do not have crisp measurable milestones. One of the most perplexing aspects of software development is the "90 percent complete" syndrome described in the typical software development problem scenario presented in Section 19.1. Detailed plans must have specific measurable milestones that can be reviewed before they are considered to be complete. A milestone such as "90 percent done with coding" is not measurable. An example of a measurable milestone is "module Start Process coded, debugged on simulator, and reviewed and signed off by project manager."

*Managers do not realize the computer corollaries of Parkinson's Law: "Work expands so as to fill the time available for its completion."*5 These corollaries are

(1)   The functions to be implemented in a microprocessor software system expand so as to require more memory than is allocated to implement them.

5C. Northcote Parkinson, <u>Parkinson's Law</u> (New York: Ballantine Books, 1957).

(2) The functions to be implemented in a microprocessor software system expand so as to require more real time than is allocated to implement them.

As illustrated in Figure 2-1 the development time required when these laws manifest themselves increases not linearly but exponentially. The reason for this phenomenon is that as physical limits are approached developers spend more time optimizing functions already implemented and less time implementing new functions. Thus it is easy to fall into the situation where 80 percent of the functions have been implemented, but only 20 percent of the total time required to accomplish the project has elapsed.

Managers do not plan for changes. During the development of a modern microprocessor-based product, changes to requirements will undoubtedly occur. This phenomenon has been commonly observed; Putt summarizes it as the first law of innovation management: "Change is the status quo."[6] When developing a plan one must anticipate some level of changes. This does not mean that you add a lot of slack to a project plan. It does mean that in making plans you should be aggressive and success oriented, but not to the point of creating risk beyond the level intended for the project.

19.2.4 Managers Do Not Staff Projects Properly

The appropriate staffing of a microprocessor software development project is probably the most critical aspect of a manager's job, yet it is often the activity to which managers devote the least attention. This is most unfortunate because the staffing activity plays such a determining role in other project activities; indeed, people are the most important resource in software development projects. There are several aspects to managers' improper staffing of projects.

Managers do not have realistic expectations about recruiting. A typical opinion of a software manager is that his project is the most important one, and therefore deserves special attention when staffing considerations are addressed. We have heard many managers express the feeling that "this is a **really** important project." As a result of this expectation, managers feel that they have a right to the best people in the organization to work on their

6Putt, op. cit.

projects. Of course this is unrealistic; if every group could get the best people it would violate Rauscher's second law of organizations: "Half the people in any organization are below average."[7] Of course this is a trivial statement, however, it does not mean that managers should not try to recruit the best people they can. In most cases it will be in the company's best interest to recruit a mix of people with a variety of backgrounds, experiences, and education for each project.

Managers do not devote enough time to recruiting activities. They expect the personnel department to do it, or they expect their management to do it. Such opinions are far removed from reality. In microprocessor software development projects, it is often necessary to recruit personnel from outside one's organization, and to develop a group as the software functionality in a class of projects grows. Managers must therefore devote a significant part of their time to recruiting activities. At the front end of a project, this should be on the order of 20 to 25 percent of a manager's time. Staffing is not just a burst activity; over long periods managers should develop long-term working relationships with schools, recruiters, and other people who will be interested in helping them staff future projects.

Managers do not consider long-term requirements when recruiting. The result can be an inappropriate mix of software development people for a company, especially on subsequent projects. For example, if a company hires many experienced product development people as contractors, it will devote significant time to their training and education on their products and applications. This investment will be lost in future projects after these contract people leave. On the other hand, staffing a project entirely with new college graduates can lead to a situation where a company serves as a kind of graduate school; after a few years when people have learned their industrial lessons they may leave to find other work, thus leaving the original hiring company with a void.

Managers do not consider a variety of sources for people when they are recruiting. The results can be an inappropriate mix of people for projects. When staffing a project it is appropriate to consider several dimensions in the background of personnel:

[7]To be more precise statistically, the correct work is "median" not "average;" however, in normally distributed groups there is no difference.

o   Accomplished veterans versus developing novices

o   Applications software experience versus system software experience

o   Hardware expertise versus software expertise

o   Experience on similar projects versus insights from dissimilar projects

When selecting people a manager must consider the backgrounds of the individuals in light of these and other criteria. A good staff is one that has complementing capabilities among the people selected.

19.2.5 Managers Do Not Organize Projects Properly

As a project is staffed, it should be organized so that the accomplishments of individuals and groups within the organization are synergistic; the organizational structure should reduce the communication costs that arise from the time expended when individuals and groups interact.

Managers do not delegate authority. This problem is especially characteristic of new first level managers who have been appointed to their management positions due to their technical capabilities. Managers in such positions must avoid trying to do all the detailed technical work themselves; they must concentrate on planning, assigning tasks, scheduling activities, and monitoring and reviewing progress. Even in a chief programmer team organization, the chief programmer must delegate many activities to other personnel in the group.

Managers do not recognize costs inherent in an organization. Any organizational structure has inherent costs caused by the requirement to interface among individuals. Often organizations are established looking at the benefits that will accrue, but without investigating the costs that are involved in the organization. Some very common examples of these costs are

o   A project organization in which there are no incentives to improve the technological capabilities of the people and hence of future products

o   A functional organization in which people have few incentives to commit to product development schedules

Managers do not address all of the phases of software development activities. This is especially true of managers who do not have software management training. They are looking for immediate results in terms of produced code and do not recognize the required activities of requirements development, design specification, testing, documentation, and proper use of tools.

19.2.6 Managers Do Not Provide Facilities That Optimize Productivity

In addition to project planning, staffing with a balance of people, and organizing to achieve objectives, managers must provide facilities which permit software engineers to work effectively. The two aspects of facilities which we consider are the office environment in which engineers work, and the computer systems with which engineers work. Our intention is not to assert that engineers must be given elaborate facilities or excessive computing capabilities; rather, we describe facilities which provide outstanding benefits at reasonable costs.

Managers do not provide an office environment that is productive in the effective accomplishment of tasks. We see many instances of this in companies we have visited: "bullpen" office arrangements or overcrowded cubicles, office furniture that was not designed to support the use of computer equipment or printed computer output, and desks and chairs that were poorly designed for engineers' use. Productivity is greatly improved when each software engineer has a private personal office. It need not be large, but it should contain room for a work area, computer equipment, filing computer output, and books and manuals. Experiments[8] have demonstrated significant productivity increases in this arrangement over the more typical two or three persons per cubicle office environment. Offices should be private so that an engineer may close his door and work without interruption; the room should also have a guest chair so two-person discussions can be readily effected. In addition to personal offices, there should be several meeting rooms that will comfortably accommodate several people. These rooms are for technical meetings such as the reviews at various stages of development, for administrative meetings, and for informal gatherings.

Managers do not provide adequate computer systems facilities for engineers. There are not enough terminals or computers for people to use. The system response time is poor or there is a long queue of batch jobs awaiting

---

[8]Barry W. Boehm, et al., "The TRW Software Productivity System," September 1983.

processing. The tools available on a computer system are weak and require substantial personal time on the part of engineers to perform common software systems development operations. For the development of microprocessor software, there should be one computer terminal (or personal computer system) for each software engineer plus enough systems to support the debug activities of the projects that are in the debug and testing stages. Such systems are usually found in laboratories separate from individual offices. At one IBM facility we visited, the guideline is three terminals or computers per person: one in the office, one in the laboratory, and one at home. If you are using microprocessor development systems rather than terminals, there should be enough systems so people can schedule their time effectively. A centralized computer system that accommodates a large batch or time sharing operation should be large enough so response to simple commands is less than one second, and so turnaround times for small jobs are only a few minutes. If the times are longer than these then the organization is ineffectively using its most valuable resource, the time of its software engineers. In addition to these physical facilities, computer systems must be supported by an adequate staff, consisting of computer operators, systems programmers, user interface people, data entry clerks, and software librarians. Such personnel can effectively reduce the time required by engineers to perform many tasks. Since the procurement of computer facilities is a process that often takes weeks or months, an organization should monitor the use of facilities and plan to improve them before the facilities they have become saturated.

19.2.7 Managers Do Not Monitor Projects Properly

After planning, staffing, organizing, and providing facilities, the software engineers working on a microprocessor-based product begin the process of software development. At this point a software manager's job has only just begun. Although a foundation for the project work being undertaken may be in place, it is necessary to ensure that the group meets its milestones and deliverables.

Managers do not plan enough time for reviews. The review process, described in Chapter 15, is a fundamental part of microprocessor software development, yet it is frequently overlooked. Following the data collection phase of requirements definition approximately 20 to 25 percent of a software engineer's time should be spent in reviews. This includes reviews of the requirements specification, design specifications, code, test plans, and test results.

Managers do not schedule frequent semiformal reviews. On a week-to-week basis managers should be scheduling subsystem design reviews, code walkthroughs, module test plans, and other activities.

Managers do not schedule formal reviews on a month-by-month basis. A project should have major milestones at which deliverables are approved only as a result of a formal design review. These include such deliverables as the requirements specification, the design documents, and the code package. It is too often the case that managers pass by such milestones just saying, "we're effectively done."

Managers do not give engineers incentives to participate in reviews. Even though software engineers should devote 20 to 25 percent of their time in reviews, they frequently avoid such activities because it detracts from accomplishing individual objectives such as designing and coding individual modules. It is important to recognize that software development is a team project that can only be effectively accomplished when people work together. Thus managers should give incentives to people to participate in reviews, for example, by having their contributions to reviews affect a significant part of their performance appraisal and salary increase.

19.2.8 Managers Do Not Select the Proper Technology

Technology selection is a tradeoff between costs and benefits. It may be easy for managers to grasp the costs involved in improving the technology used in product development; however, because managers of microprocessor software development projects often have little knowledge of software technology, it is difficult for them to evaluate the benefits provided by improved technology.

The costs involved in improving the technology used in microprocessor software development can be classified into two categories: the acquisition of tools and the acquisition of techniques. Tools can also be divided into two classes — software and hardware. Software tools include such programs as compilers, linkers, editors, debuggers, data collection programs, and so on. Hardware tools include computers, terminals, microprocessor development systems, and simulators. The costs involved in acquiring techniques (expertise, such as the techniques described in the first part of this book), are the costs for training and the lost opportunity cost of the time that software engineers use during training and learning to use new techniques effectively. While the cost of technique acquisition may not be as obvious as the cost of tools acquisition, it is nevertheless real and should be considered in computing total costs of technology acquisition.

The benefits of improved technology are seldom visible to upper management, and the quantification of monetary savings is even more difficult to determine. The fundamental benefits of improved technology are in the higher productivity of the engineers involved in software development. This higher productivity is seldom visible to upper management because the increases in requirements and complexity of projects over time may grow faster than productivity improvements. There are two aspects to these benefits of improved technology. The first aspect is in the production of more reliable software at lower cost. The second benefit is the less quantifiable psychological aspects of improved morale and lower personnel turnover which result from engineers having more sophisticated tools and techniques that simplify their job.

One must exercise extreme caution when measuring productivity. Productivity should not be measured by simply computing the bytes of code delivered per man-year. The amount of software developed depends on a number of factors such as the complexity of the software, real-time utilization of the microprocessor, memory size constraints, and so on. A more appropriate measure is delivered source instructions per man year weighted by such factors. This is the approach used in the COCOMO model described earlier in the book.

19.3 Project Z – A Project That Cost Too Much and Took Too Long

Some time ago, we participated in the review of a project we will call Project Z. Project Z is now a commercial product; it uses a microprocessor for controlling an electromechanical system, typical of microprocessor applications. The software system for Project Z is a real-time embedded microprocessor software system of the kind we have been discussing in this book. While the product is now considered a successful commercial product, we found several inadequacies in the software development process; these inadequacies contributed to unnecessary costs and delays.

At the time the review took place, the project had been underway for about eighteen months and was six months from scheduled delivery. It was eventually completed six months late and cost much more than had been planned. If the project had been managed properly, it could have been completed on time and within cost. Project Z cost too much and took too long for several reasons.

Poor planning. The review team quickly found that some major milestones for Project Z had not been identified. The design of the operating system was still changing when system level debugging and testing should have been occurring. While the operating system was changing, application software that depended on operating system stability was being optimized. This situation necessitated further rework in the applications software. Not only was poor planning in evidence, assignments were not optimally balanced. Software developers were still requesting changes in the tools they were using, at a time when the tools should have been completed.

Improper staffing. Staffing for Project Z had been done hurriedly. The third level manager had little background in fundamentals of software technology and the requirements for software in a product. Although the second level manager had experience in software development, he had no previous experience as a second level manager and had just been promoted to his position. Two of the three first level managers had just been promoted to their positions. To summarize, the management team was very inexperienced. Shortly after the review was completed, the project managers committed the cardinal sin of breaking Brooks's Law[9]; they added engineers to a late project late in the project schedule. As you might expect, that action made the project later.

Misguided organization. The electronic subsystem development group for Project Z, of which the software development team was a part, was organizationally separate from the rest of the product development team. Although one would expect that this organizational separation would cause communication and interface problems that would impede progress, in fact, the third level manager had incentives from his management to support the decisions of the product development team regardless of their effectiveness. In many cases his support of these decisions, while politically appropriate, hurt the overall project and actually slowed it down. This organizational structure combined with a lack of knowledge by the third level manager and the lack of experience by the second level manager led to major problems.

Inadequate monitoring/reviews. Monitoring and reviews were given little attention on Project Z. Product managers made many changes, and the

---

[9]Frederick P. Brooks, Jr., The Mythical Man-Month — Essays on Software Engineering (Reading, Massachusetts: Addison-Wesley, 1975), p. 25.

organization provided no incentives to restrict this progress-impeding activity. The constant level of change meant continued redevelopment and made reviews almost worthless.

Poor facilities. At the initiation of Project Z, the product management team requested that the software team be located in the same building as the rest of the product developers. In many circumstances, locating the software team with the other engineering teams would be advantageous as it would facilitate better communications. Due to organizational incentives, the third level manager agreed to such a move. Unfortunately the facilities impacts were not considered. This led to major problems since the building to which the software team moved had poor computer facilities. It took time to install the computer facilities, and it took time to make them work reliably. After the reliability was improved the demand for computer resources was so high that jobs often remained in queues for over four hours. But there were more than just computer problems. In an effort to speed up the schedule, the product management team developed a plan for having other engineering groups:

(1) upgrade prototype machines with their revised subsystems, and

(2) use the upgraded prototypes for testing to obtain information on the performance of their subsystems

This reduced machine availability for software testing. When machines were available, they were configured differently from one another, thus software people often had to generate a special software configuration to support the debug and test activities on a specific machine. The decision of the product management team to upgrade prototypes continuously thus slowed down the project considerably.

Old technology. The review team felt that there were some technological techniques which the Project Z software team should have been utilizing. The first has already been mentioned: reviews. The second technological shortcoming was lack of specifications for the software being developed. This problem was compounded by the frequent changes requested by the product management team. Another aspect of the project development activity was the use of a macroassembler language, when a higher level language could have been available for a small investment.

There were so many things wrong with Project Z that we were surprised management could not understand why they were having problems. We predicted a two- to three-month slip in the delivery schedule. Our prediction was only half right; the project took six months longer than originally planned.

Especially noteworthy was the fact that the software managers and engineers had good intentions and worked very hard. Project Z stands as an example that good software management requires much more than good intentions. To paraphrase an old saying: The road to cost overruns and schedule slips is paved with good intentions.

19.4 Improving Software Management

There are two fundamental and complementary approaches to improving software management. The first approach is education for managers at all levels in the organization. Education should not be oriented toward teaching programming. Education should improve the abilities of managers in controlling and monitoring software activities, help managers understand the similarities and differences between software engineering and other engineering disciplines, and dispel myths about software development. The second approach is to provide incentives to managers to perform in certain ways. These incentives must be reflected in the performance appraisal system and the reward and punishment system in the operation of the organization.

Regarding planning activities, software expertise must be included as an integral part of the product planning team. Managers must learn that software planning should be based on a constructive model such as COCOMO. Planning should follow these rules.[10]

o   Planning is different from regurgitating. Suppose that your manager gives you this request: "Give me your plan for how long it will take for your group to add feature X to product Y between now and this time next year." If your response is one year your manager will be pleased with your planning capabilities, but you have not planned anything; you have only regurgitated.

o   Planning is different from negotiating. In response to the above request, you may say, "It can't be done by this time next year. I need fifteen months." You may still not be planning. You may be negotiating.

_____

[10]Adapted from Tom DeMarco, <u>Structured Analysis and System Specification</u> (Englewood Cliffs, New Jersey: Prentice-Hall, 1979).

o   Plans are not subject to bargaining. If you say it will take fifteen months, and your boss counters with thirteen, you should hold to your plan of fifteen. If your manager insists, then the plan is his, and the responsibility is his.

o   Planning is not subject to alterations based on risk. When you develop a plan, the level of risk which you assumed should be in line with that of the rest of the project. Accepting more risk to make the plan shorter is irresponsible, and it is irresponsible for your manager to suggest that one part of the project assume more risk than another.

o   Planning is different from dividing a fixed duration into component parts. If your manager asks for a schedule for your group to complete a project in one year and you respond by applying 35 percent to requirements, 40 percent to design, 10 percent to coding, and 15 percent to testing, you are not planning, you are dividing.

For staffing, we reiterate that a balanced mixture of people is appropriate for most projects. The balance should be between experienced people and new graduates, software systems people and hardware systems people. Upper level management should be included in decisions about recruiting, and the actual recruiting should be delegated to a knowledgeable, responsible manager.

A microprocessor development team must be an integral part of the product development organization. This is especially true for embedded microprocessor applications. A second fundamental aspect of organizational structure is to assign decision rights where the specialized knowledge exists. Too often the decision maker for software is a product manager who does not know the costs or consequences of his decisions. When educating managers about software, a common mistake is to provide only a simple introduction to programming. That barely scratches the surface of what a manager should know about software. It is too easy for a manager with a minimum amount of education to fall into the "all you have to do is" syndrome. It is easy to think that to fix a software problem all you have to do is change a few lines of code or a few bits of memory, when problems can be more deeply rooted in a design or requirements specification.

Managers must learn the importance of reviews and monitoring. Each phase of software development must be checked to ensure that measurable milestones were actually completed. Managers have to give incentives to engineers to achieve these milestones.

Managers must provide facilities that do not discourage or inhibit work; they must provide facilities that support the desired level of productivity. Managers should provide individual workstations, computers, or terminals to support software development.

Technology development is especially difficult for new software managers. It is easy for a manager who is experienced in product development but not in software development to say that some aspect of design worked in a product ten years ago and that it should work now. If that is the attitude of the managers, an organization will produce ten-year old products. In using the software life cycle methodology managers must learn that the coding phase is the least important and that the requirements specification phase is the most important. Managers must develop productivity measures that give engineers the right incentives to produce; managers must monitor variables that can affect software development productivity.

Our experiences demonstrate that investment in manager education, software staff, and facilities can more than <u>double</u> the effectiveness of organizations developing microprocessor software.

ANNOTATED BIBLIOGRAPHY

Requirements and Design

Tom DeMarco, *Structured Analysis and System Specification,* Englewood Cliffs, New Jersey, Prentice-Hall, Inc., 1979.

Noting that "Analysis is the study of a problem, prior to taking some action," DeMarco explores in some detail three important analysis tools: the data flow diagram, the data dictionary, and structured English. These tools form the basis for "structured analysis" in producing a structured specification document. DeMarco describes the methods for using these tools and illustrates them with several examples.

Peter Freeman and Anthony I. Wasserman, *Tutorial on Software Design Techniques (Second Edition),* Long Beach, California, IEEE Computer Society, 1977.

Freeman and Wasserman have assembled an excellent collection of 23 papers that address the fundamental issues of software design. The papers have been organized into six sections: Introduction, Framework of Design, Elements of Design Techniques, Design Tools, Design Methodologies, and Examples. These papers represent a foundation for many of the methodologies that are in wide use today. The editors complement their tutorial with an annotated bibliography on software design.

Chris Gane and Trish Sarson, *Structured Systems Analysis: Tools and Techniques,* Englewood Cliffs, New Jersey, Prentice-Hall, Inc., 1979.

Viewing the problems that analysts face in playing the role of the middle man between the user community and the programming community and the inadequacy of previous tools, Gane and Sarson describe a methodology for doing design analysis. First, draw a logical data flow diagram. Next, put the detail in a data dictionary. Then, define the logic of the processes using decision trees or structured English. The authors conclude their book with a discussion of introducing structured systems analysis into your organization.

David A. Higgins, *Program Design and Construction*, Englewood Cliffs, New Jersey, Prentice-Hall, Inc., 1979.
    Higgins divides his book into two parts. The first part addresses tools and techniques to analyze a problem and then synthesize a process that will solve it, i.e., design analysis and synthesis. The second part of the book addresses the techniques for transforming the design into implemented code. Noting that flow charts are a poor tool for design, Higgins describes in some detail the Warnier-Orr diagram and its applications in software design activities.

Glenford J. Myers, *Composite/Structured Design*, New York, Van Nostrand Reinhold, 1978.
    Myers's book "is about some solutions to the problems of global or structural complexity (understanding it, dealing with it, and minimizing it)." Three ways to reduce complexity in developing a software system are partitioning the system into parts, representing the system as a hierarchy, and maximizing the independence among the subsystems. Myers describes in great detail the process of developing hierarchy charts and the characteristics of good designs. He describes the relation of structured design to other methodologies and includes several exercises for the reader.

Meilir Page-Jones, *The Practical Guide to Structured Systems Design*, New York, Yourdon, 1980.
    "Structured design is a disciplined approach to computer system design, an activity that in the past has been notoriously haphazard and fraught with problems." After introducing the ideas behind structured design and the basics of design, Page-Jones describes the tools of structured design: the structure chart, the structured specification, and module specification methods. The structured specification includes the data flow diagram, the data dictionary, and structured English. The qualities of a good design include coupling and cohesion. Page-Jones describes the design strategies of transform analysis and transaction analysis in some detail and illustrates his book with numerous examples and exercises.

Edward Yourdon and Larry L. Constantine, *Structured Design: Fundamentals of a Discipline of Computer Program and Systems Design*, Englewood Cliffs, New Jersey, Prentice-Hall, Inc., 1979.

Yourdon and Constantine have written an extensive book on the subject of software design. The book comprises six sections. The first section consists of fundamental concepts, and the second describes coupling and cohesion as part of the foundation for structured design techniques. The third section describes the technique of structured design in some detail, including design heuristics, transform analysis, transaction analysis, and alternative design strategies. Section IV describes the pragmatics of communication in modular systems, packaging, and optimization of modular systems. The fifth section describes advanced topics, and the sixth section discusses management and implementation issues. Each chapter contains a summary, and the book contains useful appendices that describe the notation and symbology of structure charts.

Coding and Debugging

William E. Howden, "Contemporary Software Development Environments," *Communications of the ACM,* Vol. 25, No. 5, New York, Association for Computing Machinery, May 1982.

Howden describes four classes of development environments for supporting medium and large software projects. Successive environments contain more sophisticated tools; however, each environment provides some support for all the phases of the software development life cycle. The environments comprise both tools and techniques. Howden gives a cost associated with acquiring each environment and notes that each of the four environments can be built using state of the art technology. Howden makes the important observation that "an environment is more likely to be used if the interface between the user and the environment tools and data base is human factor engineered."

Brian W. Kernighan and P. J. Plauger, *The Elements of Programming Style (Second Edition)*, New York, McGraw-Hill, 1978.

Using the form and approach of Strunk and White's classic *The Elements of Style*, Kernighan and Plauger provide several guidelines on how to program well. The book has chapters that deal with expression, control structure, program structure, input and output, common blunders, efficiency and instrumentation, and documentation. Their first rule "write clearly — don't be too clever" sets the tone for the book. They illustrate their rules with numerous examples and summarize their list of rules at the end of the book.

Imsong Lee (Editor), *Tutorial: Microcomputer Programming and Software Support*, Long Beach, California, IEEE Computer Society, 1978.

Lee collected an interesting set of papers for what, at the time, was a controversial subject. In Part I of the collection, Lee provides an overview of the subject of microcomputer programming and support systems. Part II contains nine papers on choosing programming languages for microcomputers. Languages discussed include BASIC, PLZ, FORTH, and Pascal. Part III contains nine papers on microcomputer software development. The capabilities described include in-circuit emulation, operating systems, and program instrumentation. The final part of this collection includes examples of microcomputer software development systems from Intel, Zilog, and Tektronix.

Anthony I. Wasserman (Guest Editor), *Computer*, Vol. 14, No. 4, Los Alamitos, California, IEEE Computer Society, April 1981.

Wasserman was editor for this issue of *Computer*, whose theme was automated development environments. Wasserman notes that a good software development methodology must exhibit a number of characteristics: complete cycle coverage, ease of transition between phases, repeatability, teachability, and automated support. Several of the papers in this issue address present and future automated development support systems. Two important characteristics for future programming environments are user friendliness and a tight integration of capabilities.

Testing

W. Richards Adrion, Martha A. Branstad, and John C. Cherniavsky, "Validation, Verification, and Testing of Computer Software," *Computing Surveys*, Vol. 14, No. 2, New York, Association for Computing Machinery, June 1982, pp. 159-192.

Noting that "software quality is achieved through the application of development techniques in the use of verification procedures throughout the development process," the authors survey current approaches to verification, validation, and testing and discuss their strengths and weaknesses. The paper includes a glossary and an extensive reference list.

Robert L. Glass, *Software Reliability Guidebook*, Englewood Cliffs, New Jersey, Prentice-Hall, Inc., 1979.

Glass begins the guidebook with definitions of terms in software reliability. He then discusses the role of reliability in the phases of the software development life cycle. The main portion of the book is a survey of technological and management tools and techniques, written as a menu. For the items on the menu, Glass provides an evaluation, examples, and references for further study. Examples of menu items include peer code review, environment simulator, interactive debug, and test procedures. The book concludes with software reliability case histories and an annotated bibliography.

William E. Howden, "Validation of Scientific Programs," *Computing Surveys*, Vol. 14, No. 2, New York, Association for Computing Machinery, June 1982, pp. 193-227.

Howden's paper describes a comprehensive approach to validating computer software. He notes that validation is a part of each phase of the software development cycle. Concentrating on the use of informal validation methods, Howden addresses document analysis techniques, source code analysis, program testing, and management and planning. Howden illustrates his discussion with numerous figures and includes a list of over 50 references.

Edward Miller (Guest Editor), *Computer*, Vol. 12, No. 8, Long Beach, California, IEEE Computer Society, August 1979.

The six papers that constitute this issue address a variety of topics in the area of software quality assurance. In particular, the papers address program testing techniques for nuclear reactor protection systems, certification testing, path testing and static analysis, automated testing experience, and standards for software quality testing and software quality assurance plans.

Edward Miller and William E. Howden, *Tutorial: Software Testing and Validation Techniques*, Long Beach, California, IEEE Computer Society, 1978.

Miller and Howden have collected a set of 32 papers that address the topics of software testing and validation. The papers are grouped into seven major sections: Introduction, Theoretical Foundations, Static Analysis: Tools and Techniques, Dynamic Analysis: Tools and Techniques, Effectiveness Assessment, Management and Planning, and Research and Development. The editors introduce each section by summarizing the papers reprinted in the section. The book concludes with a substantial bibliography of 16 pages and a glossary, making this tome a principal reference in this subject area.

General Software Engineering

Frederick P. Brooks, Jr., *The Mythical Man-Month — Essays on Software Engineering*, Reading , Massachusetts, Addison-Wesley, 1975.

Brooks's book of 15 short essays is one of the classic and most profound books on the subject of software engineering. Observing that large systems programming is a tar pit in which many have thrashed violently, Brooks illustrates fundamental principles of software engineering with true gems of literature. The most famous is Brooks's law: "Adding manpower to a late software project makes it later." Other insights include "conceptual integrity is *the* most important consideration in system design," "architecture must be carefully distinguished from implementation," "representation is the essence of programming," "plan the organization for change," and "how does a project get to be a year late? . . . one day at a time." One of the authors had the great opportunity to study software engineering under Brooks and found it one of the greatest educational experiences of his life.

Peter Naur, Brian Randell, and J.N. Buxton (Editors), *Software Engineering — Concepts and Techniques*, New York, Petrocelli/Charter, 1976.

In 1968 and 1969, the NATO Science Committee sponsored two conferences on software engineering. This book is an edited version of the reports of these conferences. The book includes papers from a variety of authors that probe the fundamental concepts of what was then an emerging new technology. The book contains a number of discussions that were recorded at the conference to reflect the opinions of the participants. The list of participants at each conference reads like an early *Who's Who* of software engineering; many of the participants went on to be early contributors to the field of software engineering.

Randall W. Jensen and Charles C. Tonies, *Software Engineering*, Englewood Cliffs, New Jersey, Prentice-Hall, Inc., 1979.

Jensen and Tonies have prepared a book of seven chapters, written by them and others, that addresses many of the aspects of software engineering. The chapters address software design, structured programming, verification and validation, security and privacy, and legal aspects of software development. Their chapter on project management fundamentals provides a useful overview of all the steps in a software project.

Peter Wegner (Editor), *Research Directions in Software Technology*, Cambridge, Massachusetts, The MIT Press, 1979.

Wegner notes in his introduction that "the primary purpose of this book is to provide an understandable but nontrivial description by active research workers of concepts and research issues in principal subareas of software technology." The active research workers include over 90 individuals who have written papers and contributed to the discussions presented in the book. The first part of the book contains four papers on software problems; and the second part of the book addresses research directions, which are divided into three categories: software methodology, computer systems methodology, and application methodology. Sixteen papers and numerous discussions constitute this second part of the book, making the entire book of well over 800 pages a noteworthy contribution to the field.

Marvin V. Zelkowitz, Allen C. Shaw, and John D. Gannon, *Principles of Software Engineering and Design*, Englewood Cliffs, New Jersey, Prentice-Hall, Inc., 1979.

The first part of this book, Chapters 1 and 2, presents a summary of the software engineering field and describes several programming techniques. The second part of the book, Chapters 3 through 5, present six small and two large examples of program design. The examples not only present designs, but also discuss why certain design decisions were made.

Management

Barry W. Boehm, *Software Engineering Economics*, Englewood Cliffs, New Jersey, Prentice-Hall, Inc., 1981.

Boehm's book of over 750 pages is indeed a masterpiece. Just as knowledge of economics is fundamental to sound management, so software engineering economics is fundamental to sound software management. Boehm's book comprises four parts. In the introduction, he presents two case studies and the goals of software engineering. In Part II, Boehm presents the software life cycle and the basic and intermediate COCOMO model, for COnstructive COst MOdel. Basic COCOMO estimates software development effort and cost as a function of the size of the software product in source instructions. The intermediate COCOMO model estimates software development effort as a function of the most significant cost drivers besides size. Part III addresses the fundamentals of software engineering economics and is broken into three parts: Cost-Effectiveness Analysis; Multiple-Goal Decision Analysis; and Dealing with Uncertainties, Risk, and the Values of Information. Part IV describes the art of software cost estimation and is broken into three sections: Software Cost Estimation Methods and Procedures, The Detailed COCOMO Model, and Software Cost Estimation and Life-Cycle Management. The detailed COCOMO model presents phase by phase effort multipliers for each factor that affects software productivity. Sixty-three completed projects were used to calibrate and evaluate the COCOMO model. Using the insights provided by COCOMO and software cost estimation technology, the final chapter presents a fine discussion on improving software productivity. Our experience has demonstrated that knowledge of the material in this book is fundamental to sound software management.

Michael W. Evans, *Productive Software Test Management*, New York, John Wiley and Sons, 1984.

In his introduction, Evans states that "testing, the backend of the project, must be planned for from the beginning of the development effort in parallel with the design and implementation tasks, and it must be the focus of all project activities." Evans addresses several topics on the subject of testing: Test Requirements Identification; The Software Test Environment; Early Test Planning; Motivating the Work Force; Test Specification; and Test Development, Tooling, and Execution. He concludes the book with a testing example, a summary, and a bibliography.

Michael W. Evans, Pamela H. Piazza, and James B. Dolkas, *Principles of Productive Software Management*, New York, John Wiley and Sons, 1983.

Based to a large extent on the authors' combined experiences, this book presents a practical perspective on the subject of software management. The authors cover a broad array of topics and include chapters on configuration management, documentation development and production, project data flow, and planning the project.

Robert L. Patrick, *Application Design Handbook for Distributed Systems*, Boston, CBI Publishing Company, 1980.

This handbook is a manual that addresses "distributed data processing applications which allow some of the processing to be performed and some of the data to be stored immediately adjacent to the originating source, with the remainder of the data stored and the remainder of the processing performed elsewhere." It is organized according the the phases in the systems development life cycle. The standard five phases of software development are divided into 15 life cycle activities for distributed systems development and operation. These are in turn broken into 186 detailed activities. Examining these in a step-by-step presentation, Patrick provides a thorough discussion of development and management activities.

Donald J. Reifer (Editor), *Tutorial: Software Management*, Long Beach, California, IEEE Computer Society, 1979.

Reifer has collected a number of articles on software management and arranged them carefully in this volume. The introductory section discusses the nature of software management and why projects fail. Sections II - VI address the principal management activities we have discussed in this book: Planning, Organizing, Staffing, Directing, and Controlling. (In the current book, we use the slightly different categorization − Planning, Organizing, Actuating, and Controlling.) Part VII of Reifer's collection addresses the interaction between management and software technology. Part VIII presents five case studies treating both commercial and military systems. Reifer introduces each section with an overview of the articles which represent a broad cross-section of the literature.

Gerald M. Weinberg, *The Psychology of Computer Programming*, New York, Van Nostrand Reinhold, 1971.

"This book has only one main purpose − to trigger the beginning of a new field of study: computer programming as a human activity, or, in short, the psychology of computer programming." Weinberg has indeed accomplished his goal. The first three parts of his book − Programming as Human Performance, Programming as a Social Activity, and Programming as an Individual Activity − provide a useful insight into the values of programmers, both as individuals and groups. With this knowledge, managers can better understand the incentives required to make programming a successful and rewarding activity.

Gerald M. Weinberg and Daniel P. Freedman, "Reviews, Walkthroughs, and Inspections," *IEEE Transactions on Software Engineering*, Vol. SE-10 No. 1, New York, IEEE Computer Society, January 1984, pp. 68-72.

This article, which appears in a special section on software engineering project management, addresses formal technical reviews, which supply the quality measurement information in software project management. Weinberg and Freedman differentiate management reviews from technical reviews, describe types of technical review reports, and review principal varieties of review disciplines. The authors provide an interesting perspective by discussing how reviews evolved. The authors note that reviewing procedures continue to evolve and that the best evidence for the effectiveness of reviews is that their use continues to spread.

INDEX